In the Name of Apartheid

ALSO BY MARTIN MEREDITH

The First Dance of Freedom:
Black Africa in the Postwar Era

In the Name of Apartheid

★

SOUTH AFRICA IN THE POSTWAR PERIOD

★

MARTIN MEREDITH

1817

HARPER & ROW, PUBLISHERS, New York
Cambridge, Philadelphia, San Francisco
London, Mexico City, São Paulo, Singapore, Sydney

FIRST U.S. EDITION

LIBRARY OF CONGRESS CATALOG CARD NUMBER: 88-45044

ISBN: 0-06-43 5659-0

88 89 90 91 92 HC 10 9 8 7 6 5 4 3 2 1

For H

Contents

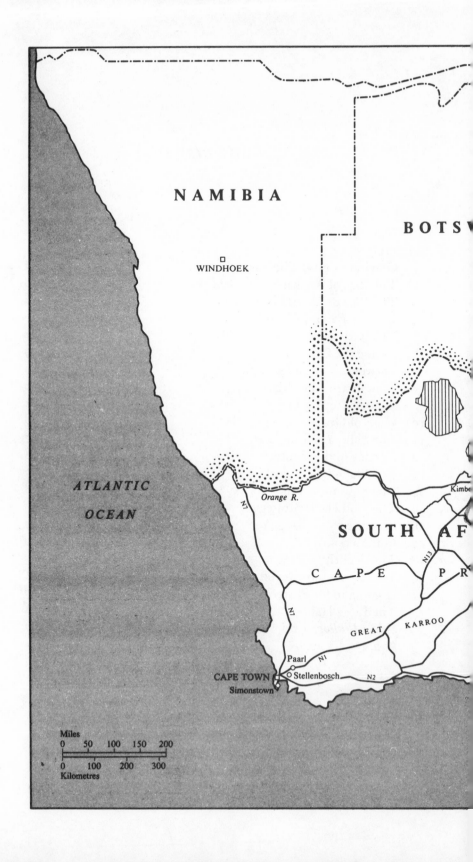

NAMIBIA

BOTSW

□
WINDHOEK

BOTSW

ATLANTIC

OCEAN

Orange R.

SOUTH   AF

C A P E   P R

GREAT   KARROO

N13

N7

N7

N1

Paarl
Stellenbosch

CAPE TOWN
Simonstown

N2

Kimbe

Miles
0   50   100   150   200

0   100   200   300
Kilometres

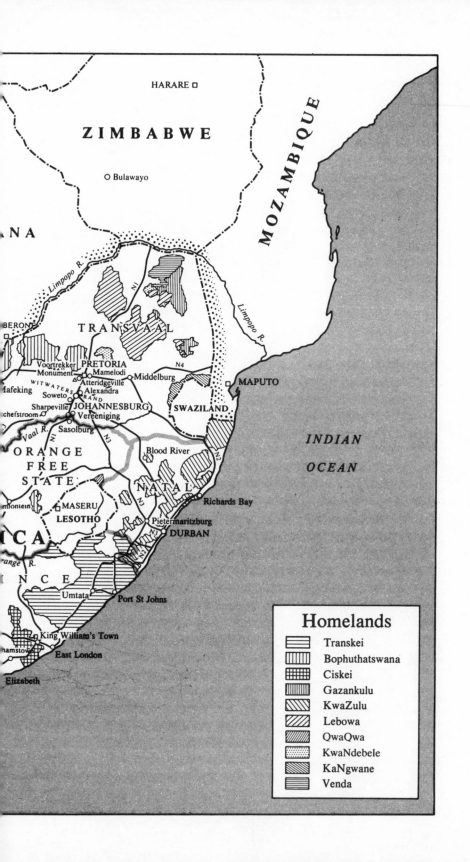

HARARE □

ZIMBABWE

O Bulawayo

MOZAMBIQUE

Limpopo R.

BERON

TRANSVAAL

Limpopo R.

N1

N4

Voortrekker
Monument   **PRETORIA**
            Mamelodi   Middelburg
Atteridgeville
WITWATERS Alexandra
Mafeking   Soweto   RAND
Sharpeville   **JOHANNESBURG**
chefstroom   Vereeniging

□ **MAPUTO**

SWAZILAND

Vaal R.   Sasolburg

N1   N3

**ORANGE
FREE
STATE**

Blood River

N2

INDIAN

OCEAN

mfontein   □ **MASERU**
            LESOTHO   **NATAL**

N3

Richards Bay

Pietermaritzburg

ICA   N3   **DURBAN**

range R.   N2

NCE

Umtata   Port St Johns

King William's Town

hamstown   East London

Elizabeth

Homelands

▦	Transkei
▥	Bophuthatswana
▦	Ciskei
▦	Gazankulu
▧	KwaZulu
▨	Lebowa
▨	QwaQwa
░	KwaNdebele
▤	KaNgwane
▤	Venda

In the Name of Apartheid

Preface

South Africa is a country constantly watched for signs of revolution. Under the control of white politicians determined to keep political power, wealth and land largely in the hands of the white minority, it has evolved a system of government which confines the black majority to a subordinate role and severely restricts their opportunities for advancement. At the end of the Second World War, South Africa's racial practices differed in detail rather than in essence from the discriminatory policies employed elsewhere in Africa under European rule. But while Europe's colonial powers became increasingly committed to ideas of racial equality and colonial freedom, South Africa moved in the opposite direction. In 1948, Afrikaner Nationalists came to power bearing their own version of racial rule known as apartheid and proceeded to construct the most elaborate racial edifice the world has ever seen. In the name of apartheid, millions of people were uprooted from their homes; millions more were denied basic rights. In their attempts to resist apartheid, black nationalists tried public protest, petitions, passive resistance, boycotts, sabotage, guerrilla warfare and urban insurrection. At each stage, the confrontation has become more widespread and more violent. At times of crisis, many black activists believed that victory was within their grasp. Yet after forty years of Nationalist government, white rule remains as firmly entrenched as ever. The country's white rulers, moreover, show no sign of willingness to lessen their hold on power. Hence, South Africa seems condemned to live in the shadow of conflict and revolution.

This book sets out to chart the course that South Africa has taken in the postwar era. It is an overview of the period, not a history of it. It seeks to portray the collision between Afrikaner nationalism and the African nationalist movement as each asserted itself in postwar years. It traces the origins of apartheid and examines the way in which it was implemented. It describes the attempts by anti-apartheid activists to oppose the system and relates the government's methods of dealing with them. It also looks at the pressures which forced government policies to change and assesses the changes that have occurred. In the past forty years, apartheid has undergone many modifications, growing from a crude formula for white domination into an elaborate and complex system of racial rule. It has taken on new appearances and acquired new terminology. It has shed much of its ideological and religious coating. But the heart of apartheid beats as firmly as before. White control remains the government's overriding objective.

On my visits to South Africa over a twenty year period, I have encountered much generosity and goodwill. Many people on many occasions have given me valued help and assistance and shown great hospitality. In normal circumstances, I would have liked to record my thanks and appreciation to them individually. In present conditions, however, it is prudent only to express my gratitude for all the acts of kindness and help I have received there to friends, colleagues and acquaintances in general. My thanks also go to colleagues at St Antony's College, Oxford, for their steadfast encouragement.

M.M.
Oxford
February 1988

CHAPTER ONE

General Smuts: The Twilight Years

The Big House, as it was known throughout South Africa, stood in a peaceful valley surrounded by rocky ridges on the highveld south of Pretoria. It was not a comfortable place. The building was an old wood and corrugated iron structure. In winter, cold draughts cut through cracks in the weatherboard walls. In summer, beneath the tin roof, it grew hot, and wild bees nesting in the partitions between wood and iron would become irritable. The furniture was simple; there were few carpets, the linoleum was worn. Everywhere shelves were laden with books. Decorating the walls was an odd assortment of objects ranging from flywhisks to signed photographs of royalty, usually left hanging askew. Visitors to the Big House often noted how untidy it was.

Doornkloof had served as Jan Smuts' retreat for forty years. As prime minister he much preferred to return there at the end of the day than to stay at Libertas, the imposing official residence in Pretoria. Indifferent to luxury, he found in the old house and the surrounding bush a profound sense of tranquility. As old age began to overtake him and the burdens of office became more wearisome, he looked to Doornkloof more and more to provide him with a refuge from the outside world.

The house had been built originally as a recreation hut for British officers of the Anglo-Boer war stationed at Lord Kitchener's headquarters at Middelburg in the Transvaal. Smuts, a Boer General in that war, had bought it from the British, transported it by ox wagon to his farm at Doornkloof and there turned it into a family home. The large billiards room had become his study, its walls lined with books, old photographs and political cartoons. The range of books was remarkable. In all there were some 6000 volumes, with whole sections devoted to philosophy, law, religion, botany, ethics and evolution, all subjects in which Smuts maintained an intense interest. The range of languages was equally diverse: Afrikaans, Dutch, English, French, German, Hebrew, Latin and Greek.

Standing at one end of the house, the study was Smuts' personal sanctum. No one was allowed to disturb it, and rarely were the large contingent of grandchildren to be found at Doornkloof permitted entry; it was a place of solitude.

As a politician, Smuts was held in high esteem in some quarters but reviled in others. Abroad, he was hailed as an international statesman. Powerful men around the world sought his views. Honours had been showered upon him. He had earned the admiration of Lloyd George and Woodrow Wilson, of Churchill and Roosevelt. To the British public he had become a legendary figure; the Boer general who had fought courageously against Britain during the Anglo-Boer war, but who in peacetime had urged reconciliation between the Boers and the British and who subsequently had stood as a fervent champion of the British Commonwealth. Twice he had used his influence to ensure that South Africa enlisted as Britain's ally in wartime. The British were duly appreciative. During the First World War, Smuts had been appointed a member of Lloyd George's Imperial War Cabinet. During the Second World War he had been awarded the rank of field marshal and invited to participate in Churchill's war cabinet whenever he visited London. He had represented South Africa at the Paris Peace Conference in 1919 and played a leading role in establishing the League of Nations. More recently, at San Francisco in 1945, he had been entrusted with the task of drafting the Preamble to the United Nations Charter, earning widespread applause for the emphasis he placed on fundamental human rights. Indeed, it was only on the international stage that Smuts believed that his full talents could be properly exercised. The parish pump politics of South Africa, as he described them, held little interest for him. He was never at ease with the humdrum routine of local issues and constantly sought an escape from them.

In South Africa, Smuts' allegiance to Britain and its Common-wealth had won him the confidence of the English-speaking com-munity. But the view of many Afrikaners was that he was a traitor to his own people. The grievances held against him were often repeated. He was remembered as the man who at the bitter end of the Anglo-Boer war in 1902 had advocated surrender to the British rather than fight to the last; who, only twelve years later, despite the hatred many Afrikaners still felt for Britain, had joined Britain's side in its quarrel with Germany, even though Germany had supported the Boers against Britain, and who had not hesitated to crush his former Boer comrades when they rose in rebellion soon after. The grievances multiplied in 1939 when Smuts, against the vehement opposition of other Afrikaner leaders, enrolled South Africa in another of 'England's wars'. Their abiding ambition was to be rid of ties with Britain, its crown, its flag and its anthem for ever.

Smuts was unperturbed by criticism from men he regarded as extremists. 'The dogs may bark,' he was fond of saying, 'but the caravan moves on.' As the principal architect of the Union of South Africa which in 1910 had joined together the two British territories of Cape Colony and Natal to the two old Boer Republics of the Transvaal and the Orange Free State, Smuts considered his primary task was to build a bridge of trust between the British and the Boers, to weld them into a united nation which could take its rightful place as a leading member of the British Commonwealth. The Commonwealth, for Smuts, had become a 'great cause'. By playing an active role in its councils, both in war and in peace, South Africa, he believed, would enhance its prestige, its security and its influence in the world. These were aims which in his mind far outweighed the narrow purpose of Afrikaner nationalists.

Smuts had known that his determination to take South Africa into the Second World War would create deep rifts within Afrikanerdom. He himself referred at the time to South Africa's 'divided soul'. Some Afrikaner politicians spoke of the possibility of civil war. The government split over the issue, but Smuts had seemingly been vindicated. When he called for volunteers, about one in three Afrikaners of military age joined up. By the end of 1940, Smuts had 137,000 men under arms. A general election in 1943 gave him strong endorsement. His United Party gained a clear majority over all other parties, making advances not only in the cities but in country districts – the *platteland* – where his Afrikaner opponents had hitherto seemed impregnable. With the Allied victory in 1945, Smuts' prestige reached new heights. On his return home from the United Nations conference in San Francisco, he was given a tumultuous reception. He now confidently expected to be able to dedicate himself to the task of building a new world order from the ruins of war. South Africa too was at the pinnacle of its prestige, a valued partner in the Western alliance, the most advanced economic state in Africa, a regional power whose vast mineral wealth and control of the Cape shipping routes gave it high strategic importance.

The postwar years, however, were full of difficulty. Smuts found his attention diverted to issues at home for which there seemed no easy solution. Among the African population a new mood of militancy was taking hold. Thousands of Africans, hoping to escape from poverty and hunger in the reserves and drawn by the prospects of opportunities in booming wartime industries, were flooding into urban areas, creating tension. Despite attempts by the authorities to restrict African entry, teeming shantytowns proliferated on the fringes of cities like Johannesburg and Durban. On the outskirts of Johannesburg a militant squatters' movement had organized settlements into which white officials could not enter except under squatter escort. African trade unions were also becoming more aggressive. A rash of strikes had broken out during the war even though the government had introduced emergency measures to prevent them. In 1946, some 70,000 mineworkers went on strike in the biggest labour protest in South Africa's history. Even moderate African spokesmen were becoming more critical of the government, demanding not just improvements in African conditions but political and social rights.

Smuts was perplexed by this African ferment. He had never paid much attention to 'the Native problem', preferring to leave it in the hands of the Native Affairs Department. While he acknowledged that Africans possessed genuine grievances, when told that they wanted rights, as well as improvements, he was disbelieving. His reaction to the mineworkers' strike was severe. Though African wages in the mines had fallen to less than half the minimum amount advocated by a government commission a few years earlier, Smuts chose to attribute the strike to the influence of agitators. Police were called in to crush the miners' resistance. At the heart of Smuts' philosophy was a deep conviction about the virtues of European civilization and government. As he wrote to a friend after the war: 'I am a South African European proud of our heritage and proud of the clean European society we have built up in South Africa, and which I am determined not to see lost in the black pool of Africa.'

His views about the importance of European rule were common enough at the time, not only in South Africa but throughout the African continent and in the capitals of Europe from where most of Africa was then ruled. It was the same with South Africa's racial practices; they tended to differ in detail rather than in essence from the discriminatory policies employed elsewhere in Africa under colonial rule. In the Colonial Office in Britain, the most enlightened European colonial power at the time, the conventional view was that because of the backward nature of most of the African population, European rule was essential for many more generations, in some cases for far longer.

Yet to Smuts' dismay, he was suddenly caught up in a racial controversy that was to lead to his most humiliating setback. What made matters worse was that the setback occurred on the international stage at the United Nations where Smuts had only recently been accorded such high acclaim for his part in drawing up the United Nations Charter.

The controversy involved South Africa's minority Indian population, descendants of indentured workers in the sugar plantations of Natal in the nineteenth century. Indians at the time possessed no vote, but they were entitled to buy land. What Smuts was faced with simultaneously was an increasingly vociferous white protest against Indian 'penetration' of white areas in Natal and the Transvaal together with Indian demands for political and social rights. Smuts' answer was a piece of parliamentary legislation – the Asiatic Land Tenure and Indian Representation Bill of 1946 – which offered Indians limited parliamentary representation while restricting their rights to land purchase and residence. The measure succeeded in provoking a storm of protest amongst whites and Indians. White opposition politicians attacked any notion of Indian representation. Indians rejected the franchise offer as inadequate, denounced the legislation as a Ghetto Act and started a campaign of passive resistance which resulted in hundreds being sent to jail. Their case was taken up by Pandit Nehru's Provisional Government in Delhi which proposed that South Africa's treatment of its Indian population should be placed on the agenda of the United Nations General Assembly.

When Smuts arrived in New York in October 1946 to attend the General Assembly, the reception he was given was far less cordial than he had previously known. Of the fifty-one original members of the United Nations Organization, twenty-seven were former colonial territories eager to take a stand on issues like the plight of South Africa's Indian population. Smuts' attempt to prevent a debate on the Indian issue on the grounds that it was an internal matter was swiftly rejected. One delegation after another rose to condemn South Africa's Indian policy. Time and again Smuts found the Preamble to the United Nations Charter to which he had devoted so much attention quoted against him. His efforts to defend South Africa's record were to no avail. The General Assembly passed a resolution critical of South Africa's treatment of Indians. It also adopted another resolution rejecting a South African proposal that neighbouring South West Africa, administered by South Africa since the First World War as a trust territory, should be officially incorporated into South Africa, a scheme on which Smuts had pinned great hopes.

It was a disheartening experience for Smuts. His prestige no longer counted for much at world gatherings. A large majority voted against him on the Indian resolution. Not a single nation voted in support of his claim to sovereignty over South West Africa. He wrote to a friend in England at the time,

> Colour queers my pitch everywhere. I quite understand and look at it philosophically. But South Africans cannot understand. Colour bars are to them part of the divine order of things. But I sometimes wonder what our position in years to come will be when the whole world will be against us.
>
> And yet [he added] there is much to be said for the South African point of view who fear getting submerged in black Africa.

There were, of course, still many compensations. Smuts' standing among the older nations of the world remained high. In the New Year's honours list in 1947 he was awarded the Order of Merit. The following year he was elected Chancellor of Cambridge University where he had studied law more than fifty years before. He took particular delight in escorting King George VI, the queen and the two royal princesses when they toured South Africa in 1947, including in their itinerary an afternoon visit to Doornkloof. Smuts was fascinated by royalty and made a special journey to London in 1947 to attend the wedding of Prince Philip and Princess Elizabeth. Seated next to Winston Churchill in Westminster Abbey, and overcome by the splendour and pageantry of the wedding ceremony, he whispered to Churchill: 'Winston, this is wonderful, this is the Middle Ages.'

That the modern world seemed so full of uncertainty to Smuts was hardly surprising. He had been born in the middle of Queen Victoria's reign in an age accustomed to change at a gradual pace. His entrance into public life – as State Attorney of President Kruger's ill-fated Transvaal Republic – had occurred fifty years before. At the end of a long and distinguished career he found many pressures in the postwar world bewildering. When his old friend Churchill was defeated in the 1945 election in Britain he sent a letter congratulating him on his discharge from the British electorate, adding that he saw no such chance of release for himself: 'No mercy for this sinner, this old sinner, who will have to continue to carry his burden – for the present at any rate.'

By the fateful year of 1948, Smuts was nearing the age of seventy-eight. Though he often wearied of the business of politics, he remained confident enough about his own future. Yet there were powerful forces at work within South Africa, among his own Afrikaner people and among the African population, of which he was barely aware. Two rival nationalisms had developed which were approaching the stage of mortal combat. Their roots went deep. Both had been born out of hardship and turmoil; both were adamant about their right to possession of the country. Their struggle was to cast South Africa into perpetual conflict.

CHAPTER TWO

The Rise of Afrikaner Nationalism

The Anglo-Boer war lasting from 1899 to 1902 had been fought by Britain to establish British supremacy throughout southern Africa, and by the Boers to preserve the independence of their republics. It left a legacy of bitterness among the Boers that endured for generations. Faced with guerrilla warfare for which they were ill-prepared, British military chiefs devised a scorched earth policy designed to erase all possible resistance by Boer commandos. Boer villages were razed to the ground; some 30,000 farmsteads were destroyed; cattle and sheep were slaughtered or carried away on such a scale that by the end of the war the Boers of the Orange Free State had lost half their herds, those in the Transvaal three-quarters. Reporting back to London in a despatch in 1901, the British High Commissioner, Lord Milner, described the Orange Free State as 'virtually a desert'. To make sure that captured burghers would not fight again, the British deported thousands to prison camps in St Helena, Bermuda, Ceylon and India. Women and children were rounded up and placed in what the British called concentration camps where conditions were so appalling that some 26,000 died there from disease and malnutrition, most of them children under the age of sixteen. In London, the Liberal leader, Sir Henry Campbell-Bannerman, accused Britain in its conduct of the war of employing 'methods of barbarism'.

After the Peace of Vereeniging, which formally marked the demise of the two Boer republics, the British authorities made every endeavour to reestablish Boer farmers on the land and to resuscitate the shattered economy of the new colonies. But their principal objective still remained to establish British dominance in the region. Lord Milner, who had played a major role in provoking the war in the first place, was now left in charge of executing British policy in South Africa. A man who described himself as 'an Imperialist out and out', he believed that Britain had a special mission to perform throughout the world, and the methods he employed were as deliberate and determined as those used during the Anglo-Boer war. Milner was convinced of the need to anglicize the Boer population and to expose it to modern Western influences. English was made the official language, at Milner's insistence, even though Boers outnumbered British. In the Transvaal and the Orange Free State the whole educational system was swept away. English teachers and English inspectors were appointed. English became the sole medium of instruction, except for a few hours a week allowed for teaching in Dutch. Milner also tried to encourage immigration from Britain in the hope of establishing a permanent British majority among the whites in South Africa. 'If, ten years hence, there are three men of British race to two of Dutch, the country will be safe and prosperous,' he said. 'If there are three of Dutch to two of British, we shall have perpetual difficulty.'

Facing such relentless onslaught from an imperial power at the peak of its fortunes, the Boer communities of South Africa seemed destined for decline and oblivion. The war had reduced them to an impoverished rural people. Many had been uprooted from the land altogether. Some ten thousand stayed on for months in concentration camps because they had nowhere else to go. The plight of the Boers was made even worse in 1903 by a record drought; that same year marked the beginning of an agricultural depression lasting six years. A growing number drifted to the towns hoping to find work, but the towns offered no refuge. They were the citadels of British commerce and culture where Boers from the *platteland*, possessing no skills or education, found themselves scorned and despised for their poverty, their country ways and their language.

The war, moreover, had left Boer communities deeply divided. Some Boers had collaborated with British forces, serving as members of the National Scouts; others, known as *hensoppers* –'hands-uppers' – passively accepted British rule; many thousand more – *bittereinders* – had fought on to the end, ill-equipped, weary, malnourished – 'starving, ragged men, clad in skins or sacking, their bodies covered with sores' was how the young Deneys Reitz described the Transvaal commandos. Even the eventual surrender of the Boer armies in the face of overwhelming odds caused bitter dispute with those who wanted to continue fighting. When General Smuts explained the peace terms to his own commando, a voice cried, 'Jan Smuts, you have betrayed us.'

But far from being absorbed into the Empire, as Milner intended, the Boers – or the Afrikaners, as they were becoming more commonly known – responded to Milner's strategy by organizing new forms of resistance. Rather than submit to Milner's new school system and to his insistence on the use of the English language, Afrikaner leaders in the Transvaal and the Orange River Colony (Free State) founded their own private schools for what was called Christian National Education which used Dutch as well as English as a medium of instruction, adhered strictly to Calvinist traditions and promoted a sense of Afrikaner national consciousness among students. At the forefront of the schools campaign were the Dutch Reformed Churches, the most powerful Afrikaner institutions to survive the war, determined to preserve Afrikaner culture and religion as much for their own interests as for wider nationalist motives. Afrikaner writers joined the language campaign, debating the rival merits of Dutch, the language of the Church and school textbooks, and Afrikaans, a vernacular with no standard written form as yet and virtually no literature. Afrikaans, at the time of the Anglo-Boer war, was regarded as inappropriate for educated discourse. At Stellenbosch in the Cape, the main centre of higher education for Afrikaners, the language used by students in debates, journalism and private letters was generally English. As a student in the 1890s, Jan Smuts wrote to his betrothed in English because High Dutch was considered too stiff and Afrikaans then too much of a 'kitchen language'. Now the need for their own language and their own literature was seen to be of paramount importance for Afrikaner survival. In 1908, a *predikant* of the Dutch Reformed Church at Graaf-Reinet, Dr Daniel Malan, who was destined to become a prominent Afrikaner leader, urged: 'Raise the Afrikaans language to a written language, let it become the vehicle for our culture, our history, our national ideals, and you will also raise the people who speak it.'

Milner left South Africa in 1905 with little to show for his attempts to anglicize the Afrikaner population other than a few thousand British immigrants who had been established on the land and a depth of hostility among Afrikaners greater than anything that had existed before the war. His ambitious plans for South Africa soon foundered. Later that year a new Liberal government in London, under Sir Henry Campbell-Bannerman, came to office, inclined to grant the new colonies self-government. Smuts travelled to London to meet the new prime minister. 'I put a simple case before him that night in 10 Downing Street,' Smuts wrote. 'It was in substance: Do you want friends or enemies?' By 1907, only five years after Britain had conquered the Boer republics at a cost in British lives of 22,000 men, the Transvaal and the Orange Free State were again self-governing under the control of defeated Boer generals who had signed the terms of surrender. To Milner's supporters it was a 'great betrayal'. To Smuts, it was 'a miracle of trust and magnanimity' for which he held Campbell-Bannerman in high regard. A portrait of Campbell-Bannerman hung on the wall behind his desk in the study at Doornkloof, and when King George VI saw it there in 1947, Smuts remarked that South Africa owed more to Campbell-Bannerman than to anybody else in Britain.

The Union of South Africa was launched in 1910 with much goodwill and with the hope that the Boers and the British might now find a way of resolving their differences and merge into a single South African nation. The prime minister, Louis Botha, was a former Boer general well respected by both sides. His cabinet contained two other Boer generals, Jan Smuts and Barry Hertzog, as well as a large contingent of English-speaking South Africans. Dutch was recognized as an official language of the Union equal to English. The 1910 election result showed that an overwhelming number of Afrikaners supported the government's policy of reconciliation. Outwardly there seemed a reasonable prospect that it could be achieved.

Yet fear and resentment of British domination ran deep. Many Afrikaners never accepted the idea of being part of the British Empire and mourned the loss of their own republics. Everywhere they were reminded of the presence of British authority. 'God Save The King' became the official anthem. The national flag was a British Red Ensign, with the Union Coat of Arms in a lower corner. The Privy Council in London, rather than the Supreme Court, was the final arbiter in the administration of justice. Moreover, on questions of war and peace, South Africa, under the 1910 constitution, was not a sovereign independent state, but bound by decisions of the British government. Most civil servants were English-speaking; even on the *platteland* English civil servants and teachers played a prominent role. The towns too were British. The British dominated industry, commerce and the mines and controlled the banks and finance houses. They also held an almost complete monopoly of industrial skills and training.

Believing that the sheer weight of British influence would eventually engulf the Afrikaner people and turn South Africa into a mere appendage of the British Empire, a group of Afrikaner leaders began openly to repudiate the policies of reconciliation which Botha and Smuts propounded. Among them was General Hertzog, the Minister of Justice, a former commando leader from the Orange Free State. Hertzog at heart was a republican. He had accepted the imperial connection only because it served to allay the fears of the English-speaking minority and thereby promote good relations between the two groups. But he was determined that South Africa should develop a separate and independent identity within the Empire, embracing both English and Afrikaners on a basis of complete equality. 'I am not one of those who always have their mouths full of conciliation and loyalty,' he said in 1912, 'for those are vain words which deceive no one.' And in a clear reference to a recent meeting of the Imperial Conference in London that General Botha had attended, he added: 'I would rather live with my own people on a dunghill than stay in the palaces of the British Empire.'

Hertzog swiftly became the acknowledged champion of Afrikaner interests. His plan for a 'two-stream' policy for South Africa, by which Afrikaners and English would develop separately their own culture and traditions until the Afrikaner stream attained an equal status with the English, met with a ready response. Dropped from the cabinet in 1913, Hertzog travelled from village to village in the Orange Free State, promoting the Afrikaner cause and leaving in his wake a host of Afrikaner vigilance committees. The following year, with a handful of parliamentary colleagues, he formed a new National Party. Its manifesto dwelt on three main points: South African interests first; mother-tongue education; and compulsory bilingualism in the public service.

By taking South Africa into the 1914 war, Botha and Smuts outraged Hertzog's Nationalists and provoked serious conflict among Afrikaners. Urging support for Britain, Botha reminded his people of the noble action of Campbell-Bannerman in awarding self-government to the Transvaal and the Orange Free State. But for Hertzog a different issue was at stake. 'This is a war between England and Germany,' he said. 'It is not a South African war.' Several of his old Boer war colleagues thought the time was ripe for rebellion and issued a call to arms. In sporadic encounters lasting three months, government troops fought Afrikaner rebels. It was an episode which again left bitter memories and a new list of folk heroes. When a young Afrikaner officer, Jopie Fourie, was court-martialled for treason, prominent Afrikaners like the *predikant* Dr Daniel Malan pleaded with the government for leniency. But Smuts, then Minister of Defence, refused to commute the sentence of death. Fourie was executed, without a blindfold, on a Sunday, singing a psalm, his name enshrined with other martyrs to the Nationalist cause. To many Afrikaners, it was Smuts who was the traitor.

The National Party benefited considerably from these events. In the 1915 general election, it made impressive gains, capturing nearly 30 per cent of the vote. In the 1924 general election, it won 33 per cent of the vote, obtaining more seats in the House of Assembly than any other party. By making a temporary alliance with the English-speaking Labour Party, Hertzog became the first Nationalist prime minister at the head of coalition government.

Over the next eight years, Hertzog achieved many of the original goals of the National Party. At the Imperial Conference in 1926 he obtained recognition from Britain of South Africa's claim to sovereign independence, and in 1931 the Statute of Westminster, conferring Dominion status on South Africa, freed it from any formal control by Britain. Hertzog also settled the issue of a national flag. After a year of intensely emotional debate, parliament approved a new flag to fly alongside the Union Jack; it consisted of red, white and blue colours with small replicas of the flags of the Orange Free State, the Transvaal and the Union Jack arranged along the centre. The language dispute was also resolved; in 1925, Afrikaans became an official language for the first time. Hertzog's outlook too began to change. He no longer feared that Afrikaner culture was in danger of being submerged by the weight of English tradition; there was no longer any reason, he said in 1930, why South Africans belonging to the two cultures should not feel and act together in the spirit of a consolidated South African nation. He was satisfied too, now that South Africa had gained Dominion status, that the aspirations of Afrikaners for independence had been properly met.

To a small core of Afrikaner nationalists, however, Hertzog's willingness to abandon republicanism meant betrayal. In secret, they began to organize a network of opposition to Hertzog, taking advantage of immense social upheaval afflicting the Afrikaner community.

*

The 'poor white problem', as it was called, had cast a shadow over South Africa since the turn of the century. It grew out of the difficulties facing a rural people ill-prepared to cope with profound economic change which, by the 1930s, had pitched hundreds of thousands of Afrikaners into an abyss of poverty and degradation. This spectacle of destitution provided further humiliation for the Afrikaners, aroused anew their fears of survival and spurred on nationalist ambitions.

The problem of white impoverishment in rural areas began with the closing of South Africa's frontiers in the late nineteenth century; land was no longer readily available and the white rural population continued to grow. As a people almost entirely tied to rural areas, the Boers were most directly affected. Their difficulties were made worse by poor farming methods, by drought and disease like the rinderpest epidemic of 1896–7 and by inheritance laws which meant the continual subdivision of land into small, uneconomic holdings. The growth of commercial agriculture forced many *bywoners* – landless white tenants – off the land. Britain's policy during the Anglo-Boer war of laying waste vast areas of the Transvaal and the Orange Free State compounded the process by destroying much that reconstruction could never replace.

The result was a steady exodus from rural areas to the towns – *die trek na die stad* – particularly to the goldfields of the Witwatersrand which by the turn of the century were producing one third of the world's gold supplies. In 1900 there were less than 10,000 Afrikaners living in towns; by 1904 the number had grown to 40,000 out of a total of 630,000 Afrikaners; by 1914 it amounted to nearly one third of the Afrikaner population. Yet, as the Afrikaners found them, the towns were an alien and often hostile world. The language of industry, commerce and the civil service was overwhelmingly English; their own language, derided as a 'kitchen language', was treated with contempt. Lacking skills, education and capital, many were forced to seek work in competition with cheap black labour and to live cheek by jowl in slums on the ragged edges of towns. Urban poverty became as common as rural poverty. 'I have observed instances in which the children of Afrikaner families were running around naked as kaffirs in Congoland,' Dr Daniel Malan told a conference on urban poverty in 1916. 'We have knowledge today of Afrikaner girls so poor they work for coolies and Chinese. We know of white men and women who live married and unmarried with Coloureds.'

The degradation of poor Afrikaners in the towns alarmed many Afrikaner leaders. The rough mining communities which had sprung up along the Witwatersrand after the discovery of gold there in 1886 were already notorious as places of drunkenness, immorality and crime. Johannesburg, in the words of a visiting Australian journalist, Ambrose Pratt, in 1910, had become 'a city of unbridled squander and unfathomable squalor'. Now it was feared that poor whites would sink to the level of African life, breaking barriers of blood and race, debasing the entire Afrikaner stock.

The plight of poor Afrikaners, both in rural and urban areas, was frequently blamed on the evil designs of 'British Imperialism' and 'Anglo-Jewish Capitalism'. Many of their troubles were attributed to the arrival of British and Jewish magnates – the Randlords – bringing with them thousands of foreigners – *uitlanders* – to work in the goldmines, throwing into disarray traditional Afrikaner society and then, in collaboration with Lord Milner and British politicians in London, exploiting the presence of the *uitlander* community on the Witwatersrand to provoke a war of conquest. British capital was also accused of preferring to employ cheap black labour in the mines rather than Afrikaner workers so as to enlarge its profits. The figure which symbolized all these machinations for Afrikaners was a cartoon character in the Afrikaans press called Hoggenheimer; he was a vulgar and opulent tycoon, waxing fat on Witwatersrand gold at the expense of honest South Africans.

The animosity between white workers and mining magnates flared into open conflict in 1922. Alarmed by a sharp drop in the gold price, the Chamber of Mines resolved to cut costs by replacing semi-skilled white workers, many of them Afrikaners, with cheaper black labour. The miners went on strike, declaring they were fighting 'to protect the White race'. Afrikaner commandos arrived from rural areas to give help. A huge demonstration of miners took to the streets of Johannesburg in February, led by a brass band blaring the 'Red Flag' and followed by a banner which proclaimed: 'Workers of the World, Fight and Unite for a White South Africa.' By March the strike had developed into an armed insurrection. As disorder spread along the Witwatersrand, Smuts, then prime minister, was forced to call out the army and the air force to suppress it. In four days of fighting, during which artillery and aircraft were used to shell and strafe working-class districts of Johannesburg, where the revolt had its centre, the strikers suffered 153 dead and more than 500 wounded.

Smuts, once again, was cast as the villain, an ally of 'big finance', said Hertzog, 'whose footsteps dripped with the blood of his own people.' Though white miners lost the battle with the mining companies, they won the political campaign that followed. At the next election the Nationalists and the English-speaking Labour Party joined forces to throw Smuts out of office. Never again, after the 1922 revolt, was any attempt made to replace white labour by black labour at a lower wage.

In an attempt to deal with the problems of poor white unemployment, Hertzog's coalition government, soon after it came to power in 1924, devised what was known as a 'civilized labour' policy. An official circular defined 'civilized' labour as 'the labour rendered by persons whose standard of living conforms to the standard of living generally recognized as tolerable from the usual European standpoint'. It went on: 'Uncivilized labour is to be regarded as the labour rendered by persons whose aim is restricted to the bare requirements of the necessities of life as understood among barbarous and undeveloped people.' In practice the policy meant that wherever feasible whites replaced black workers in the public service. The greatest effect occurred on the state-owned railways: between 1924 and 1933 the number of white employees increased by 13,000; some 15,000 Africans and Coloureds lost their jobs. Other government agencies and departments were similarly affected. The aim, said Hertzog, was to protect white living standards and to prevent the white man from becoming 'a white kaffir'.

Such measures, however, were not sufficient to keep pace with the flood of rural immigrants seeking work in towns. By 1926, the proportion of Afrikaners living in towns and villages increased to 41 per cent. The number of poor whites also rose, from an estimated 106,000 in 1916 to 160,000 by 1923. Periodic droughts (in 1919 and 1924–7) and depressions (in 1920–23) drove more and more whites off the land. On average, each year brought a further 12,000 whites to the towns. In the depression years of 1928–32 the scale of misery affecting poor whites was immense. A Carnegie Commission report estimated that in 1930 about 300,000 whites, representing 17.5 per cent of white families, were 'very poor', so poor that they depended on charity for support, or subsisted in 'dire poverty' on farms. A further 31 per cent of whites were classified simply as 'poor', so poor that they could not adequately feed and clothe their children. At least nine out of ten of these families were said to be Afrikaans-speaking.

In rural areas, the Commission reported, many families were living in hovels woven from reeds or in mud huts with thatched roofs similar to those used by Africans. One third of these dwellings were said to be 'unsuitable for civilized life'. Many white families lived a narrow and backward existence. More than half of the children did not complete primary education. 'Education was largely looked upon, among the rural population, as something foreign, as a thing that had no bearing on their daily life and needs.'

Facing social upheaval across the land and finding themselves in the towns at the mercy of British commerce and culture, Afrikaners responded by establishing their own organizations to try to hold the *volk* together and to preserve their own traditions. A host of welfare and cultural associations sprang up. In Cape Town, a group of wealthy Cape farmers and professional men established a publishing house and the first nationalist newspaper, *De Burger*. Schools and churches took root in urban areas. Among the organizations that were founded during this period was the *Afrikaner Broederbond*. It began as a small select society, interested principally in the promotion of Afrikaner culture and language. But it was to grow into the most formidable organization in South African history and to become a major factor in determining its fate.

For the first ten years of its existence, the Afrikaner Broederbond made little impact on Afrikaner society. Formed in 1918 in Johannesburg by a small band of ardent Afrikaners – railway clerks, policemen and clergymen – it set out to defend Afrikaner heritage at a time when, as one of its founders recalled, 'the Afrikaner soul was sounding the depths of the abyss of despair'. By promoting the cause of separate Afrikaans schools, it attracted a large number of teachers. It also began to interest a group of academics from the Calvinist University of Potchefstroom. But it was frequently wracked by internal dissension and purges. By 1925, four years after changing itself into a secret organization in an attempt to enforce discipline, the Broederbond consisted of no more than eight cells in the Transvaal, with 162 members.

Its prospects were transformed after Prime Minister Hertzog returned from the Imperial Conference in 1926 and announced that, as he considered the constitutional aims of the National Party had been largely satisfied by the Balfour Declaration granting South Africa Dominion status, he would henceforth abandon republican demands. Outraged by this decision, hardcore nationalists within the Broederbond decided to expand their activities beyond the cultural field and to infiltrate every facet of the Afrikaner community. From the late 1920s, the Broederbond developed into a tightly disciplined, highly secretive group which gradually extended its range of influence and contacts throughout the country. The guiding force behind the Broederbond now became Afrikaner academics from Potchefstroom University, able to provide a new coherence to the aims of Afrikaner nationalism. Those aims were no longer confined merely to defending Afrikaner traditions. Their essential theme was to establish Afrikaner domination. In a private circular issued in 1934, Professor J. C. van Rooy, the chairman of the Broederbond, wrote: 'Let us keep constantly in view the fact that our chief concern is whether Afrikanerdom will reach its eventual goal of mastery [*baasskap*] in South Africa. Brothers, our solution for South Africa's troubles is . . . that the Afrikaner Broederbond shall rule South Africa.'

One by one, new institutions were established to promote Afrikaner interests. Behind each one, acting in strict secrecy, lay the Broederbond. Its first major success was the formation in December 1929 of the *Federasie van Afrikaanse Kultuurverenigings* (Federation of Afrikaans Cultural Associations, or FAK), an umbrella organization designed to coordinate a multiplicity of Afrikaner cultural groups. In reality, as the Broederbond's official history makes clear, it was also used as the Broederbond's 'public front', providing a cover for most of its activities. With the help of the FAK network, the Afrikaans language was given new stimulus. New words, new terms and concepts were added in an attempt to transform it from the language of the veld to the language of the city. Afrikaans literature also gained greater prominence, bringing to a wider audience new versions of Afrikaner history, with its tales of suffering and heroism. The FAK was also instrumental in fostering the formation of separate Afrikaans organizations: the *Voortrekkers* replaced the Boy Scouts; the *Noodhulpliga* replaced St John's Ambulance Brigade; Afrikaner students formed their own *Afrikaanse Nasionale Studentebond*.

By 1932, the Broederbond felt confident that its cultural work had taken firm root. It was ready to move on to new spheres, to the economy and to politics. In a secret message to members that year, Professor van Rooy wrote:

After the cultural and economic needs, the Afrikaner Broederbond will have to devote its attention to the political needs of our
people. And here the aim must be a completely independent,
genuine Afrikaner government for South Africa. A government
which, by its own embodiment of our own personal Head of State,
bone of our bone and flesh of our flesh, will inspire us and bind us
together in irresistible unity and strength.

While the Broederbond was nurturing these ideas, Afrikaner
nationalists were plunged into a new crisis, even more traumatic than
that caused by Hertzog's decision to abandon the cause of republicanism. In 1932, as South Africa struggled to cope with the
consequences of the great depression, Hertzog agreed to take the
Nationalists into a coalition with Smuts' opposition South Africa
Party in what became known as Fusion government. The following
year, the two leaders went a stage further in their search for unity,
deciding to merge their two parties as the United Party.

The split that occurred over fusion represented a fundamental
turning point for the Afrikaner people. Hertzog's purpose, now that
he no longer feared the threat of British imperialism, was to establish
Suid Afrikaanse volkseenheid – a unity between all South Africa's
whites. Smuts, his new ally, was fully in agreement with this
objective; but to Afrikaner nationalists, fusion threatened both their
republican aspirations and their hopes for eventual Afrikaner
control. Distrusting any link with Smuts and his connections with
big business, they believed that Afrikaner interests would inevitably
be dominated by the superior strength and organization of their
English-speaking rivals, consigning Afrikaners permanently to the
ranks of second-class citizens. Instead of Hertzog's *Suid Afrikaanse
volkseenheid*, they wanted Afrikaner *volkseenheid*. Hertzog, they
feared, no longer stood for their interests and thereby had forfeited
any claim to the leadership of Afrikanerdom.

The nationalist mantle now passed to Dr Daniel Malan, the Dutch
Reformed Church *predikant*, who had forsaken the pulpit for
politics in 1915 to become the first editor of *De Burger* and
subsequently leader of the National Party in Cape Province. Malan
represented a new breed of political intellectual emerging from the
ranks of urban middle-class Afrikaners and destined to play a
decisive role in the development of Afrikaner nationalism. Repudiating Hertzog's 'betrayal' over fusion he launched the *Gesuiwerde*

National Party (GNP) – a 'purified' National Party claiming to stand for the aims and objectives of 'true' Afrikaners. *Gesuiwerde* nationalism differed markedly from any of its predecessors. It was not simply a return to the 'pure' nationalism of the past, of the kind once espoused by Hertzog. It was a new nationalism brought forth from the depths of deprivation, hardened by new ideology and driven by a ruthless determination to dominate.

The GNP made little impact when it was launched in 1933. The Fusion government remained strong and showed no sign of splitting. The mood of the country's white population was clearly in favour of union. When the split occurred, only eighteen members of parliament followed Malan into the GNP, most of them from the Cape province, only one from the Transvaal, an insignificant minority in a parliament of 150 members. For the next few years Malan's Nationalists remained in the wilderness. Hertzog dismissed them as a group of fanatics merely intent on stirring up discord and hatred. Yet during that time the foundations were laid for a dramatic revival of Nationalist fortunes.

At the centre of this revival, directing events from behind its screen of secrecy, lay the Broederbond. By the mid-1930s its influence extended to every level of Afrikaner society and to every area of the country. Its elite membership, carefully selected and bound together by oath, had risen to 1400 in eighty separate cells, mostly professional men, teachers, academics, clergymen and civil servants, many of them based in urban areas in the Transvaal. Through the FAK, the Broederbond possessed a tight grip over Afrikaner cultural activities. It had penetrated the civil service and the teaching profession; and its efforts were now directed to infiltrating members into 'key positions' in all leading institutions. With the formation of the GNP, it had also gained what was effectively a political wing. Malan and other Nationalist MPs were swiftly recruited to its ranks.

It was also under the Broederbond's auspices that a coherent ideology for the new nationalism began to take shape. At Afrikaans universities like Potchefstroom, Pretoria and Stellenbosch and at favourite meeting places like the Koffiehuis in Cape Town, nationalist intellectuals gathered for intense and often abstruse discussion on the finer points of nationalist doctrine. Their theories were aired in obscure journals and pamphlets, often provoking fierce dispute. New ideas were imported by young Afrikaners returning to South

Africa from study in Europe, where they had been strongly influenced by the rise of European fascism. The audience that this intellectual ferment reached was limited. The vast majority of Afrikaners showed no interest either in nationalist theory or in the people promoting it. Yet, through their discussions, the intellectuals accomplished a transformation of Afrikaner nationalism and eventually succeeded in gaining a mass following for it by embellishing Afrikaner history with powerful myths that endured for generations.

The new nationalism – Christian-Nationalism, as it was called – was essentially a blend of the Old Testament and modern politics. At its core was the notion that the Afrikaners were members of an exclusive *volk* created by the hand of God to fulfill a special mission in South Africa. Their history, their language, their culture, being divinely ordained, were unique. They were an organic unity from which 'foreign elements' like English speakers were excluded. This vision of the Afrikaners as a chosen people, based on Calvinist ideas, had first been expounded systematically by Paul Kruger, president of the South African Republic (the Transvaal) from 1881 to the British conquest in 1902, and a firm believer in the scriptures of the Old Testament. Now it became an integral part of nationalist mythology. As Professor van Rooy, chairman of the Broederbond, explained in 1944: 'In every People in the world is embodied a Divine Idea and the task of each People is to build upon that Idea and to perfect it. So God created the Afrikaner People with a unique language, a unique philosophy of life, and their own history and tradition in order that they might fulfill a particular calling and destiny here in the southern corner of Africa.' In explaining the purpose of the Broederbond itself, van Rooy used much the same language: 'The Afrikaner Broederbond is born from a deep conviction that the Afrikaner *volk* has been planted in this country by God's hand and is destined to remain here as a separate *volk* with its own calling.'

Another integral part of the new nationalism was the emphasis placed on past triumphs and sufferings of the Afrikaner people. Their history was portrayed as an epic struggle against two powerful enemies, the British and the blacks, both intent on their annihilation and only prevented from succeeding by divine intervention. 'The last hundred years,' Malan asserted, 'have witnessed a miracle behind which must lie a divine plan.' In the context of the 1930s, the greatest threat to Afrikanerdom was seen to come not from the blacks, as it was at a later stage, but from British imperialism and its allies in the English-speaking population. Every effort was made to explain the present plight of the Afrikaner people by attributing it to the evil designs of British policy. This explanation of Afrikaner history had been gathering momentum since the late nineteenth century, prior to the Anglo-Boer war. It had been used with telling effect in a propaganda pamphlet, *A Century of Wrong*, written by Jan Smuts and others and published in 1899 soon after the outbreak of war to attract foreign support for the republican cause. Now it became part of Afrikaner faith.

One episode after another from the past was cited as evidence of British oppression, starting from the moment the British took possession of the Cape in 1806 and imposed their rule over its Boer inhabitants. Afrikaner history related how Boer pioneers, desperate to escape from the injustices of British rule in the Cape, embarked on a Great Trek into the unknown interior of Africa in the 1830s only to find the British in relentless pursuit. In their thrust for supremacy, the British had annexed the first Boer state, the Republic of *Natalia*; they had seized the diamond fields of the Orange Free State, the richest in the world, annexed the Transvaal in 1877 and then provoked a war to destroy the independent Boer republics, killing 26,000 women and children and driving the Boer people into penury. In postwar years, they had set out to impose their own language and education on the country and flood it with British immigrants; they had dragged South Africa into an imperial war; finally, they had used their financial strength to ensure control of the economy and to perpetuate the poverty of the Afrikaner *volk*. The troubles that Afrikaners faced could thus be summed up in one word – imperialism. This version of Afrikaner history was fortified by the work of popular Afrikaans writers like Totius, Langenhoven and Malherbe who dwelt on the heroic deeds of nineteenth-century figures and linked them to the present struggles of the Afrikaner people.

The purpose behind this history was to establish a mythical unity binding the Boer people together through their trials and torments. In a time of great social upheaval, when *platteland* communities were disintegrating and simple rural people were being flung headlong by economic pressure into the maelstrom of industrial society, when old values and traditions were being destroyed and 'foreign' interests prevailed, the need for unity – *volkseenheid* – was seen to be paramount. Through unity, the Afrikaner *volk* could overcome all the oppression and exploitation that 'imperialism' had inflicted upon them.

The Afrikaner intellectuals who developed this nationalist doctrine were not only concerned with theory. Appalled by the poverty and degradation they witnessed among Afrikaners, they sought practical ways to implement it. The solution, they believed, lay in developing Afrikaner economic strength to counter the weight of 'foreign' banks, mining house and trading interests. In answer to 'Anglo-Jewish' capitalism, they proposed *'volkskapitalisme'*. The basis for their economic recovery was to be the savings of Afrikaner workers and farmers and self-help schemes – *helpmekaar*. In much the same way as the network of Afrikaner cultural institutions had succeeded in promoting Afrikaner culture, now a network of Afrikaner business interests would be used to break through to the economic heights. An early landmark in this economic movement was the establishment of an Afrikaans commercial bank, *Volkskas*, set up by the Broederbond in 1934 to provide financial backing for Afrikaans business undertakings.

In the rise to power of Afrikaner nationalists, there was no single event more important than the celebrations in 1938 commemorating the centenary of the Great Trek of the *voortrekkers*. The reality of the Great Trek was markedly different from what was celebrated a century later. It had begun in 1836 when a group of Boer farmers on the eastern frontier of the Cape Colony, angered by the British authorities' refusal to allow further expansion eastwards into territory well-populated by Xhosa tribesmen, embittered by the failure of the authorities to provide security against Xhosa raids, and chafing under other changes imposed, including the abolition of slavery, decided to move northwards out of the range of British rule. By 1838 some 4000 men, women and children had trekked northwards in their wagons, along with their Coloured servants, cattle, sheep and moveable property. Over a decade the exodus amounted to 14,000 people. Their departure received no acclaim at the time from the rest of the Boer population. The Dutch church opposed the trek and refused to appoint a pastor. For the next half century, they were usually referred to as 'emigrants'.

But during the 1880s, as British pressure intensified against the Boer republics they had founded, Boer leaders began to interpret their history in a new, more valiant light. The 'emigrants' now became known as *voortrekkers* and were endowed with heroic qualities, men who were steadfast in their determination to protect Afrikaner freedom and solidarity, guided by a deeply religious sense of purpose. The exodus they had started from the Cape became known as 'the Great Trek', a defiant gesture against imperial Britain on behalf of the Boer nation. And the Great Trek itself became evidence that God had summoned the Boers to the same mission as the Israelites of the Old Testament who had trekked from Egypt to escape the Pharaoh's yoke and to establish a promised land. This version of Afrikaner history was propagated by a new generation of twentieth-century Afrikaner writers and politicians and used to portray the Afrikaners as a unique and godly people embarked on a special destiny.

But it was not until the Great Trek celebrations in 1938 that such beliefs caught the popular imagination. Like many other events affecting the Afrikaner people at the time, the centenary celebrations had been conceived by members of the Broederbond and coordinated by them through a front organization, in this case by the *Afrikaanse Taal en Kultuurvereniging* – the Afrikaans Language and Cultural Organization. The original plan had been to send a single ox wagon along a commemorative route from Cape Town to Pretoria, but because of the popular response to the idea a second wagon was added and given a different itinerary. On 8 August, two wagons, named '*Piet Retief*' and '*Andries Pretorius*' after famous *voortrekkers*, started out on the long journey from Cape Town. Thousands gathered at the foot of the statue of the Dutchman Jan van Riebeeck, founder of the first white community at the Cape of Good Hope three centuries before, to witness their departure. In an emotional speech to the crowd, Hendrik Klopper, a leading member of the Broederbond and one of the principal planners of the centenary celebrations, declared: 'May this simple trek bind together in love those Afrikaner hearts which do not yet beat together.' As enthusiasm for the idea spread across the country, other treks were organized: in all twelve wagons joined the *Ossewatrek*. Along the way they stopped at noted Afrikaner shrines: at Slagtersnek, the site where Afrikaner rebels had been executed by the British in 1816; at the memorial to voortrekkers killed by Zulu warriors in 1838; at the grave of Jopie Fourie, shot by Smuts' firing squad in 1914. In every town and village through which they passed, ever larger crowds turned out to greet them. Men grew beards and wore broad hats, women donned long *voortrekker* dresses and traditional bonnets; babies, brought to the side of the wagons, were baptized, and couples stood there to be married; old men and women wept at the touch of the wooden frames and wheels; countless streets were renamed after *voortrekker* heroes. In speech after speech, Afrikaners were exhorted to remember their heroic past and their chosen destiny. Together they sang *'Die Stem van Suid-Afrika'* – The Voice of South Africa – an Afrikaans anthem based on a poem by Langenhoven, which now became familiar to thousands of Afrikaners. At every meeting the theme was *volkseenheid*, the need for unity, for a new national effort.

The wagons travelled on to two destinations, one a high ridge outside Pretoria, the other the banks of the Ncome river among the hills of Natal. The climax came in two separate ceremonies on 16 December, a day then known as Dingaan's Day commemorating a famous Boer victory over the armies of the Zulu king one hundred years before. On a *koppie* outside Pretoria, amid scenes of great nationalist fervour, a crowd of 100,000 Afrikaners – perhaps one-tenth of the entire Afrikaner community – gathered to witness the arrival of the wagons and to attend the ceremonial laying of the foundation stone of a monument to the *voortrekkers*. Everywhere the colours of the old republics were on display. The occasion was carefully organized for the benefit of 'true' Afrikaners. Afrikaner supporters of Hertzog's ruling United Party were deliberately excluded from playing a leading role in the festivities. Hertzog himself, though he had done so much to restore Afrikaner fortunes, stayed on his farm. Smuts was present but only as a spectator.

The other ceremony took place at the site of the battle of Blood River in 1838 at which a Boer commando, totalling 468 men, together with their Coloured and African servants and about sixty African auxiliaries, formed their wagons into a defensive circle – a *laager* – and repulsed a Zulu army, perhaps ten thousand strong. The Zulus retreated leaving about three thousand dead; the commando lost not a single member. The occasion was held to be of the utmost significance to the Afrikaner people, not just because it marked a famous military victory, but because the events of that time were taken as proof that God had selected the Afrikaners as His Chosen People. What was especially important was a pledge said to have been made by members of the commando a few days before the battle occurred that if God granted them a victory, they would build a memorial church in His honour and commemorate the anniversary

as a day of thanksgiving for ever more. Thus the victory at Blood
River, following the covenant that had been made, and won in the
face of overwhelming numbers, was held to be a sign of God's
commitment to the Afrikaner people.

Like the stories subsequently told about the Great Trek, the
covenant made at Blood River came to mean far more to later
generations than to the participants themselves. The commando
leader, Andries Pretorius, referred to the covenant in his report of
the battle and, three years later, together with local people, he
erected a church building at the Boer encampment at Pietermaritzburg. From 1861, however, the building was no longer used as a
place of worship, but for commercial purposes. It became in turn a
wagonmaker's shop, a mineral water factory, a tea room, a black-
smith's workshop, a school and eventually a woolshed, until in 1908
the Dutch Reformed Church converted it into a *voortrekker*
museum. Nor apparently did most members of the commando take
the covenant seriously. Indeed, as Leonard Thompson has shown in
his masterly study of Afrikaner mythology, the covenant fell rapidly
into oblivion. It was not until the 1880s, when Afrikaner politicians,
writers and churchmen were facing the menace of British imperialism, that the tale was revived to fortify Afrikaner morale. It soon
became embedded in nationalist historiography.

The organizers of the *Ossewatrek* in 1938 made the fullest use of
the myth, proclaiming at every opportunity how the covenant had
linked their fate to God's leadership. But at the Blood River
ceremony, a more modern theme was added by Dr Malan, the
Nationalist leader. Afrikaners, said Malan, were now embarked on a
Second Trek, this time to the city and there they faced a new Blood
River.

> In that new Blood River black and white meet together in much
> closer contact and in a much more binding struggle than when one
> hundred years ago the circle of white-tented wagons protected the
> *laager* and the shotgun clashed with assegai . . . the Afrikaner of
> the new Great Trek meets the non-white at his Blood River, half-
> armed, or even completely unarmed, without a barricade, without
> a river between them, defenceless on the open plains of economic
> competition.

This theme was to assume increasing importance.

*

The torrent of emotion generated by the *Ossewatrek* inspired new movements and new ideas. Standing in front of the wagons in Bloemfontein, a legendary minister in the Dutch Reformed Church, 'Vader' Kestell, who had once served as chaplain to Boer commandos during the Anglo-Boer war, made an impassioned plea for a great 'act of salvation' – *reddingsdaad* – to rescue Afrikaners from poverty. A year later, an *Ekonomiese Volkskongres*, held under the auspices of the Broederbond, approved the formation of the *Reddings-daadbond*, a society whose purpose was to raise funds not merely for poor whites, as Kestell had proposed, but for the economic advance of Afrikaner business. In 1939, Afrikaner enterprises controlled no more than 5 per cent of the turnover of all trade, industry, finance and mining. By collecting subscriptions – 'loose money' – from Afrikaners across the country and investing them in Afrikaner enterprises, it was hoped their prospects would be transformed. The idea proved popular. Within a few years the *Reddingsdaadbond* attracted more than 50,000 members. In 1942, the *Reddingsdaadbond* launched the *Afrikaanse Handelsinstituut* – a counterpart to the English-dominated Chamber of Commerce. Members of the Broederbond, as directors of new enterprises, exerted considerable influence over this economic movement. Their major achievement was to harness the Afrikaner middle class to the nationalist cause. They also attempted to make Afrikaner workers 'part and parcel' of the movement. In 1944, the *Reddingsdaadbond* set up the *Blankewerkersbeskermingsbad* – the White Workers Protection League. It was open to all Afrikaners willing to help in 'the great struggle to preserve white civilization'. But its real purpose was to isolate Afrikaner workers from other unions led by English-speaking officials and to bind them to the cause of Afrikaner nationalism.

Other Afrikaner organizations sponsored by the Broederbond developed more sinister characteristics. The *Ossewa Brandwag*, or Ox-wagon Fire Guard, was founded in February 1939 ostensibly as a cultural organization to keep alive the sense of idealism aroused by the *Voortrekker* celebrations. But the OB, as it was commonly known, was run on a paramilitary basis, under the command of a *kommandant-generaal*. Its members formed commandos, paraded in uniform, took part in military drill and torchlight rallies and expressed open admiration for Hitler. Its objective was to establish an Afrikaner republic.

Many Nationalists at the time were influenced by Hitler's rise to power in Germany. Hitler's ideas of a master race bending others into submission coincided largely with their own ambitions. His attacks on Jews were also emulated. Jews, as well as the English, were blamed for many Afrikaner ills. An influx of Jewish refugees from Europe during the late 1930s led to increasing anti-Jewish agitation. Malan's Nationalists were at the forefront of the anti-Semitic campaign, demanding a ban on Jewish immigration.

The outbreak of the Second World War led to bitter strife among white South Africans. The Fusion government headed by Hertzog split apart. At a cabinet meeting on 2 September 1939, six ministers including Hertzog wanted South Africa to remain neutral; seven others, led by Smuts, argued for an immediate declaration of war against Germany. The issue went to parliament two days later. Hertzog insisted that the war was of no concern to South Africa. Smuts urged that South Africa, as a member of the Commonwealth, stand side by side with Britain. By a vote of eighty to sixty-seven Smuts took South Africa into the war. Hertzog resigned, his hopes of achieving a bridge between South Africa's whites in ruins, his career effectively at an end. A large majority of Afrikaners were outraged that South Africa once again had been dragged into another of 'England's wars'. A contemporary assessment suggested that if an election had been held on the war issue at that time, it might well have produced an anti-war majority.

Overnight, Afrikaner republicanism became a potent political force, attracting a mass following. As Hitler's armies advanced across Europe, the tide of pro-German sentiment grew stronger. National-ist newspapers like *Die Transvaler* and *Die Vaderland* cheered each Allied setback. New political alignments emerged. Support for the *Ossewa Brandwag* soared. By August 1940 it claimed a membership of 200,000, far more than the army Smuts had managed to raise. By February 1941, according to Malan, the OB's membership had risen to between 300,000 and 400,000, making it the largest popular movement in Afrikaner history. A new *kommandant-generaal*, Hans van Rensburg, infused the OB with Nazi ideas and organiza-tion. A fervent admirer of Hitler, van Rensburg derided democracy, parliamentary institutions and party politics and pinned his hopes on an imminent German victory. An elite paramilitary corps – *Storm-jaers* – was formed to sabotage the war effort. Numerous attacks were made on railways, power lines and public buildings. The government retaliated by interning thousands of OB members, among them several Nationalist figures who were later to achieve high prominence.

Van Rensburg's growing political ambitions provoked an intense struggle for power within the Nationalist movement. By 1941 Malan had come to regard the OB as a threat to his own National Party and he set out to destroy it. For much of the war, rival Nationalist factions were locked in internecine disputes and squabbles. Yet the disarray and confusion into which the Nationalist movement fell during the war years obscured a more profound development. With the end of the Hertzog era, Malan's National Party became the main focal point for Afrikaner aspirations. Once the tide of war turned against Germany, the heady atmosphere created by German successes at the start of the war soon dissipated, leaving the OB with a diminishing following.

A clear indication of Malan's potential strength was given in the 1943 election result. Outwardly it represented a decisive victory for Smuts. The ruling United Party increased its strength from seventy to eighty-five seats and, together with its allies, could count on 110 votes in the Assembly. The parliamentary opposition, meanwhile, was reduced to forty-three members compared with the sixty-seven who had voted against war in 1939. But the election also established the National Party as the sole representative of most Afrikaners: two-thirds of the Afrikaner vote went to Malan. The Nationalists gained more votes than in any previous election, raising their representation from twenty-seven to forty-three. Moreover, in twenty-eight constituencies, the United Party held majorities of less than a thousand. In the press of wartime events, Smuts was not unduly concerned.

It was during the war years that Nationalist intellectuals began to pay increasing attention to 'the Native problem'. A wartime economic boom was drawing massive numbers of Africans into urban areas. The black threat, to which Malan had referred so graphically at the Blood River celebrations in 1938, now seemed all the greater. As the problem of Afrikaner poverty receded, so the Nationalists turned to face this new challenge. It was to become their abiding obsession.

CHAPTER THREE

The Rise of African Nationalism

By the turn of the twentieth century, after a series of wars and clashes against the British and the Boers lasting more than one hundred years, the African chiefdoms lying within South Africa had all succumbed to white rule. Most of their land had been acquired through conquest and settlement. Whole tribes had become resident on white-owned land where they worked as sharecroppers or labour tenants in exchange for a place to live, raise crops and pasture their cattle. Others were confined to areas designated as Native reserves, patches of territory scattered throughout South Africa, numbering nearly three hundred at the time, which had survived intact the era of white occupation. The reserves varied in size from a few square miles to large districts. In the Boer republics of the Transvaal and the Orange Free State only a tiny fraction of land had officially been set aside for Native reserves, while in the Cape Colony and Natal, because of the military strength of Nguni chiefdoms like the Xhosa and Zulu, extensive areas remained under African control. The vast majority of Africans still lived as peasants, some securing a prosperous existence as independent farmers. But a growing number were finding their way to towns, seeking employment. The demand for black labour for mining, for the construction of buildings, railways and roads, for transport, commerce and domestic service, was rising all the time. By 1899, the gold mines on the Witwatersrand employed some 97,000 Africans. For the most part, however, the African population, like the Boers, tended to fear and dislike the corrupting influence of the towns and mining camps, the drunkenness, crime and squalor that was commonplace there, preferring to hold fast to a rural existence. White employers continually complained of the shortage of black labour to meet their needs. The Labour Commission of 1902 reported a shortage of 129,000 native labourers and warned that by the end of 1908 it was likely to reach 250,000. As South Africa's industrial revolution gathered momentum, the black population came to be regarded as what the writer Olive Schreiner, in a pamphlet in 1909, described as 'a vast engine of labour'. It was the purpose of successive governments to harness and to control it to that end.

The first attempt to achieve a uniform Native policy for South Africa was made under British auspices by Lord Milner shortly after the end of the Anglo-Boer war. Milner's administration had inherited four territories each of which maintained different traditions and different laws affecting the African population. In the Cape Colony, a relatively liberal policy had been pursued since parliament was first established there in 1854. African and Coloured men were entitled to the vote provided they attained certain income and educational standards. In practice whites dominated the polit-ical system. No Coloured or African man ever sat in the Cape parliament. Only about 10 per cent of registered voters were Coloured, and fewer than 5 per cent were African. Nevertheless, the African electorate managed to exert some influence. In 1903, according to an official report, the 8117 African voters on the register affected the results in seven of the forty-six Cape constituencies, enough to decide the fate of the election.

The three northern territories followed a harsher doctrine. In the Transvaal and the Orange Free State only whites had political rights. The only relationship tolerated between white and black was that of master and servant. So insistent were the Transvaal Boers on this matter that they had written into their constitution a clause specifically stating that no equality between white and coloured inhabitants would be permitted, either in church or state. Resolu-tions were passed from time to time to emphasize the point. As recently as 1899, a *Volksraad* resolution had prohibited Africans from walking on the sidewalks of the streets. Natal, though a British colony, adopted similar customs. In theory, franchise qualifications there contained no colour bar. In practice, the Natal parliament legislated to make it virtually impossible for all but a handful of Africans to become voters: in 1907, the voters' roll included 23,480 whites, 150 Indians, 50 Coloureds and six Africans.

Lord Milner had strong views of his own. 'A political equality of white and black is impossible,' he said. 'The white man must rule because he is elevated by many, many steps above the black man.' His main objective, now that he had won control over southern Africa, was to establish common ground between the four territories on native policy to facilitate their integration at some future date into a single country. In 1903, he appointed a South African Native Affairs Commission to investigate the matter. Its chairman, Sir Godfrey Lagden, the Commissioner for Native Affairs, and almost all its other members were English-speaking. Most were regarded as representing progressive opinion on native matters. In the South African parliament they were described as 'pro-Native men'. The report they issued in 1905 was to have a profound effect on South African thinking on race relations.

The main recommendation of the report was that whites and blacks should be kept separate in politics and in land occupation and ownership on a permanent basis. In order to avoid the 'intolerable situation' in future whereby white voters might be outnumbered by black voters, a system of separate representation should be established for the black population, though political power, of course, would always remain in white hands. Land should also be demarcated into white and black areas, as the report said, 'with a view to finality'. In urban areas, separate 'locations' should be created for African townsmen. These ideas on the need for segregation between white and black were widely shared at the time, by friends of the black population as well as by adversaries. The Rev. Charles Bourguin, a well-known missionary, produced a paper in Pretoria in 1902 giving support to the policy of keeping races apart. Alluding to increasing tension between white and black, he said: 'If we will avoid disaster I think, as many others, that the best thing for Black and White would be for the Natives to live as much as possible their own life, manage their own affairs, and have their independent institutions under the guidance of sympathetic White administrators.' The significance of the Lagden Commission was that it elevated practices of segregation commonly employed throughout South Africa during the nineteenth century to the level of a political doctrine. Segregation was used by every leading white politician as a respectable slogan and found its way in one law after another on to the statute book.

The constitution of the Union of South Africa, which came into effect in 1910, offered blacks little prospect of advancement. No Africans, Coloureds or Asians were present at the deliberations of the National Convention which drew it up. No attention was paid to black protests and petitions complaining about their lack of rights. The objective of the three northern territories was to deny blacks any political role. Only the Cape was prepared to defend their interests.

The outcome was a compromise which secured voting rights for Coloureds and Africans in the Cape but rejected them elsewhere and attached one significant condition. Under the Union constitution, African voters in the Cape could be removed from the franchise through a two-thirds majority vote of both houses of parliament sitting in joint session. From the outset of the Union, Afrikaner politicians from the north set out to get rid of the African vote.

The African population was soon subjected to a barrage of legislation designed to relegate it to a strictly subordinate role and to exploit its labour potential. The most far-reaching measure came in 1913 with the introduction of the Natives' Land Act which laid down the principle of territorial segregation along lines similar to those advocated by the Lagden Commission and shaped land policies for generations to come. The Natives' Land Act prohibited Africans from purchasing or leasing land in white areas; henceforth the only areas where Africans could lawfully acquire land was in the Native reserves which then amounted to about 8 per cent of the country. The Cape was excluded from the legislation since African land rights there affected voting rights.

The effect of the Act was to uproot thousands of black tenants renting white-owned land – 'squatters' as they were commonly known. Some sought refuge in the reserves, though overcrowding there was already becoming a noticeable feature. Others were forced, after selling their livestock and implements, to work as labourers for white farmers. A whole class of prosperous peasant farmers was eventually destroyed. The impact was particularly severe in the Orange Free State where many white farmers lost no time in evicting squatters in compliance with the law. The plight of these destitute families driven off the land was described by the African writer, Sol Plaatje, in his account of *Native Life in South Africa*. 'Awakening on Friday morning, 20 June 1913,' he wrote, 'the South African Native found himself not actually a slave, but a pariah in the land of his birth.' Plaatje recorded how, travelling through the Orange Free State in the winter of 1913, he found bands of African peasants trudging from one place to the next in search of a farmer who might give them shelter, their women and children shivering with cold in the winter nights, their livestock emaciated and starving. 'It looks as if these people were so many fugitives escaping from a war.'

The effect on conditions in the reserves in time was also

considerable. Some African areas by the turn of the century were already congested, without sufficient grazing or arable land. By the 1920s, the pressure on land had become intense. One district after another failed to produce enough food to meet local needs. Official reports continuously warned of land degradation, soil erosion, poor farming practices, disease and malnutrition on a massive scale. The Native Economic Commission report of 1932 described how the reserves were descending 'at a rapid pace' towards 'desert conditions' and said that the 'process of ruination' threatened 'an appalling problem of Native poverty'. Unable to support their families in the reserves, needing money to pay for taxes, more and more men headed for towns in search of work. In 1925, it was reported that at any given moment nearly half the able-bodied men of the Transkei, one of the more prosperous African areas in the country, were absent from home because the reserve could no longer support its inhabitants. Between 1921 and 1936 the urban African population grew by 95 per cent. In 1936 the total amount of land reserved for Africans was increased from 8 per cent to some 13 per cent of the total area of the country. But it did little to alleviate the problem.

The same process of segregation was applied to towns. With ever larger numbers of Africans moving there, white officials became increasingly preoccupied with the need for urban controls. The prevailing view since the nineteenth century had been that the towns were white preserves; Africans living there were treated as 'temporary sojourners', a convenient reservoir of labour for use when required, but whose real homes were in the reserves. This practice now became the basis of official policy. In 1921 the Native Affairs Commission, asked to consider an appropriate urban policy for Africans, reported: 'It should be understood that the town is a European area in which there is no place for the redundant Native, who neither works nor serves his or her people but forms the class from which the professional agitators, the slum landlords, the liquor sellers, the prostitutes and other undesirable classes spring.' The following year, the Transvaal Local Government Commission, headed by Colonel Stallard, recommended: 'It should be a recognized principle of government that natives – men, women and children – should only be permitted within municipal areas in so far and for so long as their presence is demanded by the wants of the white population' and 'should depart therefrom when they cease to minister to the needs of the white man.' It spoke of the 'peril' of a redundant black population. 'The masterless native in urban areas is a source of danger and a cause of degradation of both black and white.'

The Natives Urban Areas Act of 1923 embodied these ideas in legislation, providing the foundation for all future government policy. The Act established the principle that the towns were white areas in which natives were permitted to reside only as long as they served white needs. As far as possible, they were to be kept in segregated 'locations' administered and financed by a separate system of local government. To ensure this policy worked, the Act provided for 'influx controls' regulating the entry of Africans into urban areas through greater use of the pass system. Pass laws had been commonly employed since the nineteenth century for a variety of purposes. Now they became an integral part of Native policy. African men were required to carry passes recording permission to work and live in a particular white area. They needed passes for travel, for taxes, for curfews, always liable for inspection by police. Africans who were habitually unemployed or 'idle, dissolute or disorderly' were likely to be expelled. The scope of the Act was periodically extended. An amendment in 1930 enabled local authorities to exclude African women from towns. Another amendment in 1937 restricted African work seekers from the reserves to fourteen days in towns in which to find work and gave the authorities power to remove Africans 'surplus' to labour requirements. Mass police raids in the townships were regularly organized to ensure that the pass laws and liquor regulations were maintained and, as a police commission of inquiry noted in 1937, the methods used were often violent.

The migrant labour system that developed in South Africa served white interests well. White employers considered that African labourers who left their families behind in the reserves while they worked on short contracts for white enterprises could justifiably be paid less on the grounds that their families were already making a living off the land. Another advantage was that migrant labour could be housed in compounds or hostels which were cheap to run and which gave blacks no opportunity to put down roots in the white man's city. This pattern of migrant labour had already been well established by mining companies on the Witwatersrand which relied on labourers working on average for periods of nine to twelve months, then returning home to their peasant life in between spells of work. The companies thus avoided responsibility for providing family housing or services such as schools because the bulk of the population was considered to be living permanently elsewhere. The essential function of the reserves in the view of mining and industrial interests was to serve as reservoirs of migrant labour for the towns.

African workers also faced discrimination in the labour market. The common tendency had always been to confine Africans to 'unskilled' work in mines, on farms and in domestic service. But in 1911, largely in response to the demands of white miners determined to protect their own position against black competition, the government introduced an industrial colour bar. The Mines and Works Act that year relegated Africans to the lowest occupations on the mines. An amendment passed in 1926 specifically barred Africans and Indians from jobs as mine managers, mine overseers, mine survey-ors, mechanical engineers, engine drivers and miners entitled to blast. Another law, the Native Labour Regulation Act of 1911, made strike action by blacks under contract a criminal offence. In 1924 the Industrial Conciliation Act excluded them from new collective bargaining procedures. The Apprenticeship Act of 1922 prevented Africans, and to a lesser extent Coloureds and Indians, from obtaining apprenticeships by stipulating minimum educational qualifications – eight years' schooling. This measure, when coupled with Hertzog's 'civilized labour' policies, giving preference to white workers, placed severe restrictions on black employment opportuni-ties. By the 1920s, therefore, South Africa had developed an economic system allocating skills and high wages to whites and heavy labour and menial tasks to blacks on meagre pay.

The government's policies on segregation were considered respect-able enough at the time, abroad as well as in South Africa. General Smuts' views on the matter, given to a London audience in 1917, were readily accepted there. He spoke of South Africa's civilizing mission and drew attention to two fundamental axioms of South African policy: first, he said, 'there must be no intermixture of blood between the two colours'; second, the conduct of whites in dealing with blacks must be in accordance with the Christian moral code. The way forward, he suggested, might be to develop black and white communities separately. 'I am talking of the idea of creating all over South Africa, wherever there is a considerable Native community, independent self-governing institutions for the Native population. Instead of mixing up black and white in the old haphazard way, which instead of lifting up the black degraded the white, we are now trying to lay down a policy of keeping them apart as much as possible in our institutions. In land ownership, settlement and forms of government, we are trying to keep them apart.'

A major step in this direction was taken in 1936 when African voters were struck from the common roll in the Cape Province, losing a right they had held for more than eighty years. The abolition of the Cape Native franchise had been a long-standing ambition of Afrikaner politicians. General Hertzog, who led the campaign, claimed that the Cape African vote would lead eventually to demands for the African vote in northern territories. Political equality, he maintained, meant social equality which meant miscegenation. The African franchise 'was not only a canker that was eating into the souls of the white population; it was also like a disease which inevitably had to penetrate into the minds of the Natives'. In exchange for the loss of their franchise, Hertzog conceded African voters a separate roll which allowed them to vote for three white representatives to speak on their behalf in the House of Assembly and four white members of the Senate. They were also entitled to elect twelve members to a new Native Representative Council set up to serve as an advisory body to the government. The practical effect of the legislation, the Representation of Natives Act, was limited. By 1935, African voters in the Cape numbered some 10,000, amounting to only 2.5 per cent of the provincial electorate, and only 1.1 per cent of the Union's electorate. But the political significance was crucial. As the historian Cornelis de Kiewiet noted: 'To destroy the Cape native franchise was to destroy the most important bridge between the worlds of two races.'

African attempts to withstand the onslaught of segregation had little effect. For more than thirty years, African leaders organized deputations, petitions and protest meetings. In January 1912, at a gathering in Bloemfontein, several hundred prominent Africans formed the South African Native National Congress – later renamed the African National Congress – to oppose discriminatory legislation. The early African nationalists were mostly conservative men, the products of missionary schools, influenced by Christian tradition and concerned largely with their own position in society. But more radical activities were sometimes attempted. During the 1920s a union movement, the Industrial and Commercial Workers' Union, flourished in urban and rural areas, focusing attention on a wide range of grievances. By the 1930s, however, both the African National Congress and the Industrial and Commercial Workers' Union had fallen into disarray.

Then in the early 1940s a militant mood began to affect the African population. Massive numbers of Africans moved to industrial centres on the Witwatersrand, driven there by poverty and hunger in the reserves and by harsh conditions on white farms, hoping to find work in booming wartime industries, but often meeting little else but hardship and deprivation. Between 1936 and 1946, despite hindrances imposed by the authorities, the African population in towns grew by some 650,000, an increase of nearly 60 per cent. Whole families, not just single men looking for work, made the move. By 1946 almost one in four Africans were living in urban areas. Indeed, there were now almost as many Africans in urban areas as whites. The housing problem was already acute. Municipal authorities had allocated few funds for housing or other services. The main source of revenue for African services in urban areas came from nothing more than taxes on the supply of traditional sorghum beer to township residents. Few other sources were made available. Before the war the municipalities' main preoccupation had been to try to clear existing slums and to enforce health regulations.

The level of crime in African locations on the Witwatersrand was notorious. An African journalist writing of Western Native Townships in Johannesburg in 1942 complained that as long as the authorities were more concerned with enforcing municipal bylaws than in dealing with gangs of hooligans haunting the streets no decent life there was possible. An official committee appointed in 1942 to investigate crime on the Witwatersrand and in Pretoria blamed government policy for producing 'a native population of industrial serfs, called upon to perform the unskilled labour of civilization under exacting conditions and at wages which keeps it chronically on the verge of destitution'.

In 1944 the overcrowded slums of Johannesburg broke their bonds. Several hundred African families set up their own squatter camp on open land southwest of the city, building shacks from hessian sacking, cardboard boxes, scrap metal and corrugated iron sheeting. Within three years, more than 90,000 Africans were estimated to be living in squatter camps on the outskirts of Johannesburg, defying municipal authority and organized under the control of powerful squatter bosses. No whites entered the camps except under squatter escort. Other townships were no different. The Native Laws Commission reported after the war: 'The majority of locations are a menace to the health of the inhabitants . . . quite unfit for human habitation . . . mere shanties, often nothing more than hovels . . . dark and dirty . . . encumbered with unclean and useless rubbish . . . one could hardly imagine more suitable conditions for the spread of tuberculosis.'

The African labour force also showed signs of unrest. A huge expansion of industry during the war years brought thousands of Africans into industrial employment and led African trade unions to adopt a more aggressive stance towards employers. By 1945, more than 40 per cent of Africans employed in commerce and private industry had joined unions. The unions fought for minimum wages, statutory recognition under the Industrial Conciliation Act and an end to the migrant labour system. Conditions for skilled black workers improved considerably, but unskilled workers rarely earned enough to cover the costs of family subsistence. In 1942 there was a sudden rash of strikes in support of union demands for a minimum weekly wage. The government responded by passing War Measure 145 which made it illegal for black workers to strike for better conditions and imposed severe penalties if they did. But the strikes continued. A Department of Labour report for 1945 complained that 'Natives seem to be ignoring War Measure 145'. There were also notable protests in Johannesburg against bus fare increases. In 1943 a column of more than 10,000 people, including women and children, marched from the African enclave of Alexandra, twelve miles north of Johannesburg, to the city centre in support of a bus boycott. Another bus boycott organized in Alexandra the following year caused sufficient concern to merit the cabinet's attention.

All this activity prompted African politicians to sharpen their own efforts. They found grounds for encouragement in the Atlantic Charter drawn up by Churchill and Roosevelt in 1941, supporting the right of all peoples to choose their own government. In 1943, at the behest of the African National Congress, a committee of leading Africans drew up a document called 'African Claims' and presented it to the government. The document contained a bill of rights demanding the 'freedom of the African people from all discriminatory laws whatsoever', as well as greater equality in voting, education, employment and state assistance. It was formally adopted as an ANC policy statement in 1945. Members of the Native Representative Council, for the most part cautious and conservative men, also showed greater determination to press for African advancement. In 1943 an NRC committee called for an increase in African representation in parliament and asked for its own powers and functions to be enlarged. In 1944 NRC councillors carried resolutions calling for the repeal of the pass laws and the scrapping of the segregation policy. A campaign against the pass laws organized that year by the ANC and the small, but influential Communist Party, won wide support.

An even more radical approach was advocated by a group of young professional men impatient with the conservative methods hitherto adopted by ANC leaders. Based in Johannesburg, they met night after night in each other's homes in Orlando township or in the offices of an African lawyer in the city centre determined to infuse new ideas into the nationalist movement. They mocked the ANC for 'regarding itself as a body of gentlemen with clean hands' and demanded more forceful leadership. On Easter Sunday 1944, at the Bantu Men's Social Centre in Johannesburg, the Congress Youth League was formally launched as an ANC pressure group, a 'brains trust', to give 'force, direction and vigour to the struggle for African National Freedom'. Its guiding personality was Anton Lembede, a thirty-year-old former school teacher and articled clerk, the son of a Zulu farm labourer, who exerted a profound influence on nationalist thinking with his ideas on the need for black assertiveness. Lembede died in 1947 but other members of the group were destined to achieve a more lasting impact. They included Nelson Mandela, Oliver Tambo, Walter Sisulu and Robert Sobukwe.

The government itself was well aware of the need for changes in the system. Numerous commissions and reports had provided the evidence. As far back as 1925 the Economic and Wage Commission report had pointed out:

> The contact of Native and European has lasted too long and their economic cooperation is too intimate and well-established for the Native to be excluded from European areas and European industries. The provision of adequate Native reserves has been delayed too long for it to be possible now to provide reserves

within which it would be possible for the present Native population of the Union to live without dependence on outside employment; and it was for too long the policy of the Union to drive the Native by taxation and other devices to work for Europeans for it to be possible now to exclude him from the field of employment he is occupying.

In 1941, the van Eck Commission warned that further population shifts from black rural areas to the towns were an economic necessity. In 1942 the Smit committee pointed out that a Native policy based essentially on the development of the reserves was an illusion; a large and permanent African urban population was an unavoidable part of South Africa's future. It recommended recognition of trade union rights and the abolition of the pass laws which by then involved the arrest and imprisonment of tens of thousands of Africans each year. 'The harassing and constant interference with the freedom of movement of Natives gives rise to a burning sense of grievance and injustice which has an unsettling effect on the Native population as a whole.' A report by the Social and Economic Planning Council in 1946 emphasized: 'The past half-century has witnessed a decline in the stability of Native family life which constitutes a danger to the whole nation – black and white alike – in the spheres of health, of morality, and of general social structure, peace, order, reasonable contentment, goodwill and a sense of national solidarity.'

General Smuts himself spoke eloquently on the matter. Addressing a meeting of the Institute of Race Relations in Cape Town in 1942, he remarked:

A revolutionary change is taking place among the Native peoples of Africa through the movement from the country to the towns – the movement from the old Reserves in the Native areas to the big European centres of population. Segregation tried to stop it. It has, however, not stopped it in the least. The process has been accelerated. You might as well try to sweep the ocean back with a broom.

During the war years, to help maintain a quiescent African population, his government conceded some reforms. In 1942 enforcement of the pass laws was relaxed temporarily. Improvements were introduced in the field of African education, pensions and social welfare, reflecting Smuts' concern for the material conditions of African workers. But otherwise Smuts' views about the required role of Africans had hardly changed, as he made clear in the 1942 speech: 'If he [the native] is not much more, he is the beast of burden; he is the worker and you need him. He is carrying the country on his back.' Smuts showed no patience with other African demands and summarily rejected 'African Claims' when it was presented to him in 1944. Nor did his views about the need for segregation change. At a United Party congress in 1944, he pointedly reaffirmed 'our well-known standpoint of separateness in social intercourse, housing and field of employment between the colours'.

Smuts' failure to take African grievances seriously eventually led him into direct confrontation with African politicians. The sense of frustration with government policies in postwar years became so strong that even moderate leaders joined in the attack on the government. Writing in 1945 about his vision of postwar South Africa, the ANC leader Dr Alfred Xuma expressed his deep disappointment with the government, but added that it was at least a hopeful sign that Africans now realized 'that the entire South African native policy [was] for his exploitation, oppression and retardation'. In 1946 the headmaster at Adams College in Natal, D. G. S. Mtimkulu, warned that racial bitterness and distrust had increased to such an extent that moderate leaders were now preoccupied with trying to check a tendency towards hate and African prejudice and to keep some sense of balance. To signs of increasing African restlessness Smuts paid no heed. When crisis erupted, therefore, he was caught unprepared.

In August 1946 African mineworkers launched the largest strike in South Africa's history. More than 70,000 men stopped work in protest against pay and conditions. Their grievances were long-established. Mine employers continued to keep wages low on the grounds that migrant miners supplemented their income with agricultural production in the reserves and that the industry's life, given a fixed gold price, would be shortened if costs increased too steeply. A government commission in 1943 largely disproved the contention about reserve production and recommended substantial improvements. But three years later wages on the mines were less than half the minimum amount advocated by the commission, and employers ignored further demands from mineworkers. Smuts' view was that the strike was due not to legitimate grievances but to the work of agitators and he ordered appropriate action. Armed police were used to break it up. Miners staging sitdown strikes were driven to the surface 'stope by stope, level by level', according to one description; others marching from East Rand mines to the Chief Native Commissioner's office in Johannesburg were brutally repulsed. The strike ended after a week, at a cost of twelve men dead and 1200 wounded.

Two days after the start of the miners' strike, members of the Native Representative Council, who included some of the most able and respected Africans in the country, assembled in Pretoria for their annual sitting in an angry and defiant mood, appalled by the government's treatment of the mineworkers. Their temper was not improved when they discovered that, on the instructions of the National Party majority on the City Council, they had been barred from premises they normally used in the Pretoria City Hall and instead given cramped quarters in the Department of Labour, where the lavatories were for whites only. They also found, much to their irritation, that the Council's chairman, the Secretary of the Native Affairs Department, had been called away to Johannesburg on strike business and that his place had been taken by a deputy. When the deputy made no mention in his opening address about the miners' strike or police action, the councillors reacted with vigour. Paul Mosaka, a successful Johannesburg businessman, referred to the 'wanton shooting' of miners and went on to attack the government's attitude towards the Native Representative Council. The minister seldom visited the Council, he said; the prime minister had never been near the Council in nine years; resolutions were continually ignored. 'We have been fooled,' he said. 'We have been asked to cooperate with a toy telephone.' The following day, the Council unanimously passed a resolution which condemned government policy, called for the abolition of all discriminatory legislation and announced that the session would be adjourned. Even government-appointed chiefs voted in favour of the motion. At the end of the debate, a veteran nationalist figure, Selope Thema, turned to the Council chairman and warned: 'It may not happen in your day, but it may come about that the Black people will stand together against the White people.'

CHAPTER FOUR

1948: A Fateful Election

The 'black peril' issue – *swaart gevaar* – came to dominate political debate in South Africa in postwar years. Not only were there signs of growing truculence among the black population, but whites were reminded anew of the numbers that threatened to swamp them. The 1946 census figures showed that whites were a declining proportion of the population. Since 1910 the white population had increased by little more than a million to 2.4 million, whereas the non-white population had expanded by nearly 4.5 million to 9 million. About 60 per cent of Africans were now living in European-designated areas, while only 40 per cent were based in the reserves. In urban areas, blacks outnumbered whites. Smuts himself believed that for the foreseeable future the Native question was insoluble. He merely hoped, though without much confidence, that in time there might be an improvement in race relations. The impression he gave to an increasingly worried white electorate was that his government was beginning to lose control of the black population and, what was worse, lacked the will to restore control. His political opponents, meanwhile, put forward a plan which they claimed provided a permanent solution to the problem.

The word *'apartheid'* had come into common use in the mid-1930s among a group of Afrikaner intellectuals searching for more decisive methods of dealing with the Native question. By 1943, the Nationalist leader Dr Malan was beginning to mention the term in speeches in public. But it remained a vague concept. Then in 1945 a professor of sociology at the University of Pretoria, Dr Geoff Cronjé, published a book attempting to put the concept into a wider perspective. The book was called *'n Tuiste vir die Nageslag* – A Home for Posterity; its subtitle was *Die Blywende Oplossing van Suid-Afrika se Rassevraagstukke* – The permanent solution of South Africa's racial questions. Cronjé explained:

The racial policy which we as Afrikaners should promote must be directed to the preservation of racial and cultural variety. This is because it is according to the Will of God, and also because with the knowledge at our disposal it can be justified on practical grounds. . . . The more consistently the policy of apartheid could be applied, the greater would be the security for the purity of our blood and the surer our unadulterated European racial survival. . . . Total racial separation . . . is the most consistent application of the Afrikaner idea of racial apartheid.

He went on to outline many of the ideas that were later incorporated into the policy of apartheid: population registration according to race; separate residential areas; ethnic councils; ethnic homelands; a total ban on sexual relations across the colour line. The purpose of apartheid, said Cronjé, was to ensure the survival of the white race. It would also allow the blacks to preserve their own culture and identity and to develop in their own areas. Its implementation would be costly. But there was no other final and permanent solution.

Cronjé's second book on the subject, *Regverdige Rasse-apartheid* – A Just Racial Separation – was published in 1947 with similar themes; but it was given greater significance by including chapters contributed by two eminent theologians of the Dutch Reformed Church, Professor Groenewald and Dr William Nicol. The traditional Afrikaner view of blacks, justified by texts taken from the Old Testament and held to be in accordance with Calvinist notions of the elect and the damned, was that they were an inferior race, destined by the will of God to be hewers of wood and drawers of water. Now biblical justification was used to support the idea of separate development. God, according to Professor Groenewald, had ordained the division of nations and wished them to be kept separate. The evidence for this, he claimed, was contained in the Scriptures.

There was, for example, Deuteronomy 32.8:

When the Most High gave the nations their inheritance, when he divided the sons of man, he fixed their bounds according to the numbers of the sons of God. . . .

Then there was Acts 17.26:

From one single stock he not only created the whole human race so that they could occupy the entire earth, but he decreed how long each nation should flourish and what the boundaries of its territory should be.

Furthermore there was Genesis 11. When men decided to build the Tower of Babel to preserve the homogeneity of the human race, God intervened and ordained the division and distribution of nations over all the earth. . . .

Cronjé's proposals were the subject of intense discussion within the Broederbond and the National Party and gained widespread support. A National Party commission under Paul Sauer used many of his ideas to form the basis of a political manifesto which was issued in 1948, a few months before the general election. The reserves, said the Sauer report, were the proper homelands of the African population. There they would be allowed to develop to their full capacities. Urban Africans, meanwhile, would be treated as 'visitors' and strictly controlled:

> Natives in the urban areas should be regarded as migratory citizens not entitled to political and social rights equal to those of whites. The process of detribalization should be arrested. The entire migration of Natives into and from the cities should be controlled by the state which will enlist the cooperation of municipal bodies. Migration into and from the Reserves shall likewise be strictly controlled. Surplus Natives in the urban areas should be returned to their original habitat in the country areas [white farms] or the Reserves. Natives from the country areas shall be admitted to the urban areas or towns only as temporary employees obliged to return to their homes after the expiry of their employment.

Every facet of life – residence, amenities, transport, education and politics – would be kept separate wherever possible. This policy would apply to Coloured and Indian people as well as to the African population. By such means no race group would then threaten any longer the future of any other. All this, said the Sauer Report, was in accordance with Christian principles of right and justice.

A different view of the future was offered in 1948 by the Smuts government. A report by the Native Laws Commission (the Fagan Report), which Smuts subsequently endorsed, argued that the urbanization of the African population could not be reversed. Henceforth, it said, blacks should be accepted as a permanent part of the urban population. Some controls over the movement of blacks to the cities were still needed. But the system of migrant labour had become obsolete and wasteful and the idea of territorial separation of the races was 'utterly impractical'.

A multiplicity of issues affected the general election in May 1948. There were grievances over unemployment, housing, inflation and food shortages. Smuts' plan to promote large-scale immigration from Britain also provoked strong criticism. But the issue which gripped the public's attention above all was *swart gevaar*. Malan's National Party used every opportunity to play on the electorate's racial anxieties. The choice for whites, the Nationalists said, was between 'integration and national suicide' on the one hand and 'apartheid' and protection of a 'pure white race' on the other. The approaching election, declared Malan, would be the most decisive in South Africa's history. One question overshadowed all others: 'Will the European race in the future be able to maintain its rule, its purity, its civilization; or will it float until it vanishes for ever, without honour, in the black sea of South Africa's Non-European population?' A Nationalist government, he said, would provide an effective answer. It would outlaw interracial marriages, abolish the Native Representative Council and African representation in the House of Assembly, treat the reserves as the true African homelands, control African influx into the cities, protect white workers from African competition, prohibit African trade unions and generally segregate whites and blacks to the maximum extent possible. Apartheid was the best way to achieve the happiness of all South Africa.

Smuts was thought to be in no particular danger from the Nationalist challenge. Not even the Nationalists believed that victory at this election was within their grasp. The ruling United Party, together with its Labour Party and Dominion Party allies, went into the elections with a parliamentary majority of more than fifty seats. For the Nationalists to win would require a swing of opinion among the electorate unprecedented in the Union's history.

Yet the Nationalists had been working assiduously in postwar years to prepare for an eventual victory. With the help of the Broederbond, the churches, the *Reddingsdaadbond* and a host of cultural organizations, the old wartime divisions among Afrikaner nationalists were beginning to heal. A concerted effort was made by the National Party to present a more moderate image. Nationalist leaders now disclaimed their past enthusiasm for Nazi Germany, promised generous treatment for returned soldiers, tempered their demands for a republic and banished all talk of making Afrikaans the sole official language. They paid particular attention to the interests of working-class Afrikaners facing competition from cheap African labour. By 1948 about half of the Afrikaans-speaking population lived in urban areas. A large proportion were miners, railwaymen, transport, factory and steel workers for whom the Nationalist slogan of apartheid, promising protection of white jobs, had a potent appeal. The Nationalist programme also attracted Afrikaner farmers who wanted tighter controls imposed on African movement to overcome acute shortages of African labour. Throughout the campaign, Malan harped on the need for unity among Afrikaners. In total, they now constituted nearly 60 per cent of the white population. 'Bring together all who, from inner conviction, belong together' was his constant rally cry. An election pact with the small Afrikaner Party enabled him to gain the support of former Hertzog supporters and members of the *Ossewa Brandwag* who had joined it.

Smuts' campaign by comparison was lacklustre. His party was poorly organized and beset by internal differences. Smuts himself was as much in favour of white supremacy as Malan, but he was vulnerable to criticism that he had been indifferent and impotent in the face of the mounting black menace. Nationalist politicians fastened attention on the racial issue, claiming that the inevitable result of government policies would be that Africans would 'very soon cease to be barbarians' and would thus obtain the vote. They pointed to Smuts' deputy Jan Hofmeyr, and his likely successor, as a man of radical intentions, a 'Kaffirboetie' who would 'make South Africa a black man's country'. A National Party pamphlet declared: 'The road he is following leads to equality, and the downfall of white South Africa.' The Nationalists also made much with accusations that the government had dealt leniently with communists in South Africa who favoured racial equality. 'A vote for Jan Smuts is a vote for Joe Stalin,' proclaimed the National Party's official organ, *Die Kruithoring*. Day after day, the propaganda continued relentlessly.

The election on 26 May 1948 was won by the National Party coalition with a tenuous five-seat majority. For the first time ever, the Nationalists captured eight constituencies in the mining and industrial centres of the Witwatersrand and a further five seats in Pretoria. White farmers in the Transvaal and the Western Cape deserted the United Party in droves. The United Party won an overall majority of votes – 51 per cent against 41 per cent taken by the Nationalist alliance – but the favourable loading of rural seats had given the Nationalists a decisive advantage. The voters had split along familiar lines. Most predominantly Afrikaans constituencies voted for the National Party. Every predominantly English constituency voted for the United Party or its allies. The United Party received about 20 per cent of the Afrikaans vote, but from now on it was primarily an English urban party.

Smuts himself lost his seat at Standerton in the Eastern Transvaal to a Nationalist candidate known to be a member of the Broederbond. 'To think,' he exclaimed, 'that I have been beaten by the Broederbond.' He complained to a friend that his old comrades of the Boer War days in the high veld around Standerton had now turned against him. 'Oom Jannie,' replied the friend. 'They couldn't have turned against you. Because almost all of these men are dead.' Smuts died at his beloved Doornkloof home two years later at the age of eighty.

CHAPTER FIVE

The Early Years of Apartheid

In his election victory speech, Dr Malan declared, 'Today South Africa belongs to us once more. For the first time since Union, South Africa is our own, and may God grant that it will always remain our own.'

The Nationalists' determination to put their stamp upon South Africa swiftly became evident. Malan's government was the first in the history of the Union to consist exclusively of Afrikaners. All but two ministers were members of the Broederbond. The new cabinet used its powers of patronage on a scale hitherto unknown in South Africa. Claiming that under Smuts' regime Afrikaners had been unfairly treated, it began to 'right the wrongs' of the past, ordering the release of Afrikaners serving prison sentences for wartime offences, including treason, lifting the ban on Broederbond membership for government employees imposed during the war, and giving Afrikaners precedence in promotions and appointments to public bodies. The upper echelons of the civil service, the armed forces and parastatal organizations like the railways were soon filled by carefully selected Afrikaners, usually members of the Broederbond. Smuts' men were steadily removed from office. Protesting against 'unconstitutional and unwarranted interference' with the command structure of the armed forces, the chief of general staff resigned in 1949. 'The Minister sought to change the strategic dispositions of units and to appoint, promote and transfer both officers and other ranks . . . without reference to the General Staff,' he said. 'Without reference to me, he created posts for the absorption of persons in whom, irrespective of their unsuitability or otherwise, he personally reposed political confidence.' Similar purges were conducted in the police and the civil service. The state sector became virtually an Afrikaner preserve, with few appointments ever awarded to English speakers. The legal profession eventually faced the same treatment: senior English-speaking members of the Bar were systematically overlooked in the appointment of judges. The government also favoured Afrikaner business interests. A number of government and local authority accounts were switched to Afrikaner financial institutions. Important government contracts were awarded to Afrikaner companies. The state-owned Industrial Development Corporation was used to promote Afrikaner participation in industry, against its English rivals. The overall effect, as the Broederbond had intended, was to place Afrikaners in commanding positions in every sphere in which the Nationalist government had power or influence.

The English-speaking community found itself on the defensive at every turn. Smuts' plan to recruit British immigrants was immediately suspended. Nationalist spokesmen declared that if there was to be white immigration to South Africa, they preferred immigrants from Holland or Germany to those from Britain. A citizenship bill placed before parliament in 1949 made it harder for British immigrants to acquire South African citizenship and the vote. The period of residence required for British subjects was extended from two years to five years. Citizenship was no longer automatic but held at the discretion of the Minister of the Interior. In an acrimonious debate in parliament, English-speaking members found themselves accused of dual allegiance and questioned on their right to be considered full South Africans. The English would be given equal treatment, said one Nationalist speaker, but 'the country belongs, in the first instance, to those people who opened it up'. To make sure that their own slender majority in parliament presented them with no difficulties in implementing their legislative plans, the Nationalists increased their numbers there by creating six new seats for South-West Africa which they duly proceeded to win. 'This means,' said Malan, 'that we can stay in power for another fifteen or twenty years.'

As well as consolidating Afrikaner interests and putting the English in their place, the Nationalists turned their attention to the Native problem. Malan, in his mid-seventies when he came to office, had never shown much interest in Native policy. His preoccupation had always been to achieve Afrikaner unity. He possessed no grand design for the African population of the kind advocated by Professor Cronjé and other intellectuals. The measures his government embarked upon were designed primarily to reverse the trend towards inter-racial integration rather than to devise some final solution to the Native problem. Nevertheless it was during Malan's administration that Afrikaner Nationalists began to construct an apparatus of laws,

regulations and bureaucracies which successive Nationalist governments developed until they had built the most elaborate racial edifice
the world had ever witnessed.

An early target for the Nationalists was marriage and sex. In 1949
parliament passed the Prohibition of Mixed Marriages Act outlawing
marriages between Europeans and non-Europeans. Few such marriages ever took place; in 1946, there had been seventy-five mixed
marriages out of a total of 28,000 white marriages, but for the
Nationalists it was a blurring of racial lines they were not willing to
tolerate. The following year parliament passed an amendment to the
Immorality Act extending a ban on sexual intercourse between
Europeans and Natives, in force since 1927, to Europeans and
Coloureds. The aim, as one minister explained it, was 'to try to
preserve some sort of apartheid in what one may call prostitution'.
Next came the Population Registration Act designed eventually to
allocate every person to one of three racial groups: White, Coloured
or African. Malan declared, 'A national register is the whole basis of
apartheid.'

The government also lost no time in breaking political links that
tied Africans, Indians and Coloureds tenuously to the white system.
The token enfranchisement of Indians that Smuts had proposed in
1946 was scrapped. The Native Representative Council was abolished. A new electoral law made it harder for Coloured voters in the
Cape to register for their qualified franchise on the common roll.
Then plans were devised to eliminate Coloured voters from the
common roll altogether.

Major parts of the apartheid system were set in place. In 1950
parliament passed the Group Areas Act, a law developed from
previous segregation measures, which Malan described as 'the
essence of apartheid'. It established machinery for demarcating
separate residential areas for each racial group. Over a period of years
every town and village in South Africa would be divided into racial
zones. The ultimate objective was complete segregation, even
though this would involve uprooting whole communities. The
Minister of the Interior explained:

We believe that if we remove the points of contact that cause
friction, then we will remove the possibility of that friction and we
will be able to prevent the conflagration which might one day
break out. This is what the Bill stands for. . . . Its object is to

ensure racial peace. . . . It has been introduced because we do not believe that the future of South Africa will be that of a mixed population, and this is one measure . . . designed to preserve White South Africa while at the same time giving justice and fair play to the Non-Europeans in this country.

An immediate target for government action was African freehold areas lying within white urban districts, 'black spots' as they were known, in particular three African townships within the boundaries of Johannesburg – Sophiatown and its neighbours, Martindale and Newclare. Sophiatown was one of the oldest black settlements in Johannesburg. First established in 1905 next to a municipal refuse dump on the bare veld four miles west of the city centre, it had become a vibrant, densely packed community of 60,000 people where Africans could possess land and live largely free from administrative control. Much of Sophiatown was a slum, but it could nevertheless boast of twenty churches, seventeen schools, cinemas, shops, shebeens and jazz clubs. The street gangs there, bearing names like the Gestapo, the Berliners, the Americans and the Vultures, were among the most renowned in the country. 'Whatever else Sophiatown was, it was home,' wrote Bloke Modisane, 'we made the desert bloom; made alterations; converted half-verandas into kitchens, decorated the houses and filled them with music. We were house-proud. We took the ugliness of life in a slum and wove a kind of beauty.'

With the growth of Johannesburg, however, Sophiatown became encircled by white suburbs. Bowing to white agitation, the Johannesburg municipality in 1944 approved a scheme for its removal. But no action was taken until the Nationalists came to power. In 1951 the government insisted that black spots in Johannesburg had to be removed as part of a slum clearance programme. When the municipality prevaricated, the government passed legislation in 1954, the Natives Resettlement Act, empowering it to carry out the move itself. Sophiatown was destroyed, its inhabitants transferred to a government settlement at Meadowlands, eleven miles south-west of Johannesburg. In its place, a new white suburb arose from the rubble. It was given the name, Triomf.

The separation of races continued apace at every level. Under the Reservation of Separate Amenities Act, passed in 1953, different race groups were compelled to use separate facilities in all spheres of public life, buses, trains, post offices, stations, restaurants and theatres. In many places what had previously been accepted as custom now became law. Everywhere signs proclaiming *Slegs vir Blankes* and *Nie Blankes* abounded. There were separate doors and separate counters in public buildings, separate benches in public parks, separate seats in public buses.

New controls were imposed on the African population. The Natives Abolition of Passes and Coordination of Documents Act of 1952, despite its title, replaced passes with new 'reference books', recording details of birth, employment, taxation, movement and fingerprints, and made it compulsory for all African men to carry them at all times. The same system was extended to African women. An amendment to the Natives Urban Areas Act in 1952 – the infamous 'Section Ten' provisions – decreed that no African could remain in an urban area for longer than seventy-two hours without a permit unless he or she had lived there continuously for fifteen years or served under the same employer for ten years. An African's right to remain there was to be stamped in his pass for any policemen to inspect at any time of day or night. Anyone who could not prove his right to remain there was likely to be 'endorsed out' – expelled to an African rural area. As enforced, the law split families apart, separating husbands from wives, parents from children.

Labour regulations were also tightened. A government circular in 1949 reaffirmed the 'civilized labour' policy of 1924 and instructed government departments to substitute white employees for Africans. African building workers were barred from competing in white areas. An extensive network of labour bureaux was set up in towns to control the flow of workers from rural to urban areas. Any African wanting to move from a rural area to an urban area first required permission from a labour bureau. Officials there had awesome powers over work seekers, able to decide where they worked, for how long they worked and even what kind of work they could do. At first only rural work seekers were directed through labour bureaux. Later the range of their powers was extended to cover the employment of all African workers in urban areas, whether residents there or migrants. New restrictions were placed on black trade-union activities. The Native Labour (Settlement of Disputes) Act of 1953 outlawed all strikes by Africans and refused African trade unions legal recognition. The Minister of Labour explained that Africans working in industry and commerce – now numbering nearly one million – were 'primitive and illiterate natives who have not the faintest conception of the responsibilities of trade unionism'. If the government gave unions official recognition it would hand them a political weapon with which they would create chaos. Once the new legislation was in force, he hoped that African unions would 'die a natural death'. A new Industrial Conciliation Act introduced in 1956 gave the government power to enforce racial separation in trade unions and to order job reservations for whites in specified industries.

It was soon evident to what lengths the Nationalists would go to satisfy their ambitions. In 1951 the government put forward legislation to remove the Coloureds of the Cape from the common roll on which they had been entitled to vote since 1853. They were to be given instead a separate roll allowing them to elect four white representatives to parliament. The move was of considerable benefit to the Nationalists since the Coloured vote affected the outcome of elections in about half of the Cape's fifty-five constituencies; in seven it was decisive. There was a nagging fear that at some stage Coloureds might vote with the English to overturn the narrow Afrikaner majority. The Separate Representation of Voters Bill duly passed through the Assembly and then through the Senate, sitting separately. However, a group of Coloured voters contested the legislation on the grounds that under the constitution any changes to the franchise could only be approved by a two-thirds majority of both Houses sitting in joint session. The Appeal Court upheld their claim and declared the legislation invalid. Determined not to be thwarted by 'six old men in Bloemfontein', as one minister described the Appeal Court, the government introduced a new bill making parliament itself a High Court, higher in authority than the Appeal Court, with power to give the final judgement on constitutional matters. The High Court of Parliament was duly formed and declared the Separate Representation of Voters Act to be valid. But the Appeal Court then ruled that the High Court of Parliament itself was invalid. When Malan subsequently put the legislation before joint sittings of parliament, he failed to obtain a two-thirds majority. In 1954, when he retired from office, the Coloured voters in the Cape were still on the common roll.

The next prime minister, Hans Strydom, an aggressive Transvaal politician, was determined to force the issue. First, he changed the Appeal Court by adding five more judges and by passing regulations requiring a full quorum of eleven judges to hear constitutional appeals. Next he enlarged the Senate from forty-eight to eighty-nine members elected on a basis which ensured the government could obtain a two-thirds majority in a joint session of parliament. In 1956 the government finally succeeded in obtaining legislation removing the Coloured vote, and the Appeal Court, filled with new government appointments, formally gave its endorsement. As compensation, four seats in parliament were set aside for whites elected by Coloured voters in a separate poll.

Before parliament, Strydom was frank about his intentions. There was only one way in which the whites could maintain their leadership of non-whites, he said, and that was by domination:

Call it paramountcy, *baasskap* or what you will, it is still domination. I am being as blunt as I can. I am making no excuses. Either the White man dominates or the Black man takes over. I say that the Non-European will not accept leadership – if he has a choice. The only way the Europeans can maintain supremacy is by domination. . . . And the only way they can maintain domination is by withholding the vote from the Non-Europeans. If it were not for that we would not be here in Parliament today. It is because the voting power is in the hands of the White man that the White man is able to govern South Africa today. Under the existing law it is not possible for the Natives, through merit or any other means, to get the government into their hands. The government of the country is in the hands of the White man as the result of the franchise laws, and for that reason the White man is *baas* in South Africa.

CHAPTER SIX

Facing the Onslaught

The opponents of apartheid formed a motley collection. There were liberals, communists, Trotskyists, Africanists, African nationalists, Indian and Coloured organizations and assorted priests like Trevor Huddleston, Michael Scott and Bishop Lavis of Cape Town. All were determined to stand firm against the steady encroachment of apartheid laws. But they were divided over what methods to employ and what ideology to pursue.

The pace was set by the Congress Youth League. Its members were mostly in their twenties, products of secondary schools and the University College of Fort Hare, now employed as teachers, articled clerks, journalists and trade unionists, all burning with ambition to establish a new nationalist ideology. 'We were never really young,' one of them, Oliver Tambo, recalled. 'There were no dances, hardly a cinema, but meetings, discussions, every night, every weekend.' Much discussion centred on the question of whether one of the Youth League's aims should be 'to drive the white man into the sea'. Many shared strong anti-white sentiment. But when drawing up its 'Basic Policy' in 1947 the Youth League endorsed more moderate thinking:

It must be noted that there are two streams of African Nationalism. One centres round Marcus Garvey's slogan 'Africa for Africans'. It is based on the 'Quit Africa' slogan and the cry 'Hurl the Whiteman into the sea'. This brand of African nationalism is extreme and ultra-revolutionary. There is another stream of African National- ism (Africanism) which is moderate, and which the Congress Youth League professes. We of the Youth League take account of the concrete situation in South Africa, and realize that the different racial groups have come to stay. But we insist that a condition for inter-racial peace and progress is the abandonment of white domination, and such a change in the basic structure of South African society that those relations which breed exploitation and human misery will disappear.

The distrust of whites ran deep. Whites were not allowed to enlist as members of the African National Congress, partly for fear that they would seek to guide and control it for their own benefit. Not even the help of white liberals was thought to be of use. 'Their voice is negligible, and in the last analysis counts for nothing,' the Youth League decided. 'In their struggle for freedom the Africans will be wasting their time and deflecting their forces if they look up to the Europeans either for inspiration or help.' There was an equally hostile attitude towards the Communist Party, a small but influential group which included whites and blacks as members. Distrusting the Communist Party's long-term commitment to a socialist revolution, the Youth League believed it would try to use the nationalist movement for its own ends and warned of 'the need for vigilance against Communists and other groups which foster non-African interests'. Indian organizations were given similarly short shrift. At the heart of the Youth League's philosophy was a determination to assert an African identity, to give Africans control of their own future, to use African political power to change South African society. The African nationalist movement, said the Youth League, 'should be led by the Africans themselves'. But the extent to which other groups were to be excluded from the African struggle for power was an issue that was never resolved. At an early stage two rival schools of thought emerged: the 'Africanist' school, which put African interests above all others; and the 'Nationalist' school, which, mindful of the dangers of developing an extremist black nationalism, preferred a more flexible approach towards other groups. This division in African opinion was to be the cause of bitter clashes for years to come.

Confronted with an avalanche of apartheid legislation, however, the young radicals of the Youth League turned their attention to practical ways of combating it and in the process began to recognize the need for a wider circle of allies. In 1949 they succeeded in getting the African National Congress, at its annual conference, to endorse a 'Programme of Action'. The Programme was a statement of principles rather than a practical strategy, but it set the ANC on a more militant course. It called for civil disobedience, boycotts and 'stay-at-home' strikes on a mass scale. The objective now was 'national freedom', 'political independence' and 'self-determination'.

The leadership of the ANC also changed. A new national executive brought to the fore prominent members of the Youth League including Nelson Mandela, Oliver Tambo and Walter Sisulu.

Mandela was then a law student, studying part-time at the University of Witwatersrand. A tall, athletic man with a commanding presence, thirty-one years old, he had been born in the Transkei to a family belonging to the Tembu royal house. Expelled from Fort Hare university for participating in a student protest, he had moved to Johannesburg in 1941 where he had been drawn increasingly into political activity. Oliver Tambo was also a law student. He too had been expelled from Fort Hare university during a student strike. The son of a peasant farmer from the Transkei, a year older than Mandela, he had gained academic distinction at St Peter's Secondary School in Johannesburg and later returned there to teach, being drawn, like Mandela, into the circle of young radicals. Tambo and Mandela were soon to establish themselves as partners in a law practice in Johannesburg. Sisulu also came from the Transkei, but from rougher origins. He had worked in factories, in the gold mines, in a series of labouring jobs, clashing repeatedly with whites over their racial attitudes. In 1949, at the age of thirty-seven, he was elected as the ANC's secretary-general. In all six members of the Youth League joined the ANC executive, giving it a sharper sense of direction. But the leadership of the ANC still encompassed a broad spectrum of opinion, in which members of the 'Old Guard' together with a few hardcore communists were represented.

The government soon reacted to signs of growing opposition. Deeming that much of the dissent was caused by the activities of communists, it introduced the Suppression of Communism Act in 1950 giving itself sweeping powers. The Act was the first weapon in an arsenal of security measures acquired by the government over the next four decades that would provide it eventually with totalitarian control. The main target of the legislation was the Communist Party which had become increasingly effective in postwar years. Founded in 1921 by a group consisting mainly of foreign-born British radicals and eastern European Jews, it emerged from the Second World War with a small but efficient cadre of white, African, Indian and Coloured members who wielded considerable influence within multiracial trade unions and within the ANC and the South African Indian Congress. Three African communists were elected members of the ANC's National Executive Committee in the late 1940s. Communists had played a major role in the 1946 African mineworkers' strike. They were active in township politics, notably in Sophiatown, and they gained a voice in parliament in 1947 with the election of the communist Sam Kahn as a Native Representative. They also had the use of two communist-controlled newspapers, *The Guardian* and *Inkululeko*, which by 1945 claimed a weekly circulation of some 67,000. A government committee set up in 1949 to investigate communism proclaimed it 'a national danger'.

But in introducing the Suppression of Communism Act the government's purpose was to attack far more than communists. So wide was the Act's definition of communism that it could be used by the government to silence anyone who opposed government policy simply by 'naming' them. The Act defined communism to mean not only Marxist-Leninism, but also 'any related form of that doctrine' which sought to bring about 'any political, industrial, social or economic change within the Union by the promotion of disturbances or disorder', or which aimed at 'the encouragement of feelings of hostility between the European and non-European races of the Union'. In effect it equated communism with any determined form of opposition to apartheid. The government was empowered to ban any organization, to remove its members from public office, to place them under house arrest, to restrict their movements, and to prohibit them from attending public or even social gatherings. Such action could be taken, moreover, against anyone who had ever professed communism. Four days before the Act came into effect, the Communist Party dissolved itself. Of its membership of 2000 at the time, about 150 were white, 250 were Indian and the rest were African. Shortly thereafter, the government began to move against multiracial trade unions and communists within their ranks. By the end of 1953 some fifty union officials had been 'named' and forced to give up their posts.

The opposition against apartheid still sprang forth. Incensed by the government's willingness to tamper with the constitution in its attempt to remove Coloureds from the common roll in 1951, a group of ex-servicemen, led by a former war hero, Group Captain 'Sailor' Malan, organized a series of torch-lit processions through South African towns which drew widespread support from the white population. At its height in late 1952, the War Veterans' Torch Commando claimed to possess nearly a quarter of a million members. It hoped to use this following against the Nationalists in the 1953 election. But it soon reached the limits to which traditional liberals in South Africa were prepared to go. While supporting the campaign for the rights of the Coloured population, it failed to agree over the admission of Coloureds as members, with the result that Coloured ex-servicemen withdrew. After unsuccessfully backing opposition candidates in the 1953 election, the Torch Commando soon faded from view.

A far more effective challenge was initiated by the African National Congress in 1952. Joining forces with the South African Indian Congress (SAIC) and a Coloured organization, the Franchise Action Committee, the ANC launched a 'Defiance Campaign' aimed at the removal of particular grievances like the pass laws, the Group Areas Act and the Suppression of Communism Act. The plan was for groups of volunteers in major towns to flout apartheid laws with acts of defiance such as using railway coaches, waiting rooms and platform seats marked for Europeans only or by parading on the streets after curfew without permits, or by entering locations without permits. The volunteer corps were instructed to cooperate fully with the authorities. No attempt was to be made to conceal their intentions. In many cases the authorities were warned in advance of what action the volunteers were about to undertake. The idea was to fill the courts and prisons so they overflowed with petty offenders, thereby causing the system to break down.

The campaign opened on 26 June. In Port Elizabeth, a group of volunteers, wearing ANC armbands and shouting the slogan *'Mayibuye iAfrika'* – 'Let Africa Return' – marched through the 'Europeans Only' entrance to the railway station where they were arrested by police. The group's leader was sentenced to thirty days', the others to fifteen days' imprisonment. Near Johannesburg, a group of Indians and Africans walked into the African location at Boksburg without permits, holding up their thumbs in the Congress salute. They were arrested. That night in Johannesburg, the ANC held a meeting in the Garment Workers' Hall which dispersed at 11 p.m., the curfew hour after which Africans required special passes to move about. The volunteers marched out of the hall into Anderson Street where they were then arrested. The campaign quickly caught the popular imagination. *'Mayibuye iAfrika'*, with the thumbs-up sign, became a common greeting on the streets. During July, more than 1500 people were arrested for acts of civil disobedience. In five months, more than 8000 people went to prison for periods of one to three weeks. Some volunteers made persistent efforts to get arrested.

One Natal group, informing the police well in advance, defied the curfew law but failed to interest the police. The next night they marched past the police station itself, but still the police ignored them. Only at their third attempt, when they entered a railway booking hall reserved for Europeans, did they succeed in being arrested. A handful of whites joined in the protest. The end of the campaign was marred by a series of riots in Port Elizabeth and several smaller towns in which twenty-six Africans and six whites, including a Dominican nun, were killed. By November the campaign was on the wane. But its main result was to transform the ANC into a mass movement. The sight of Africans defying the government won it new prestige. Its membership rose from 7000 to perhaps as much as 100,000.

There was considerable optimism about what could be achieved by such protests. Nelson Mandela, appointed national volunteer-in-chief, later recalled:

> I visualized that if the Defiance Campaign reached the stage of mass defiance, the government would either say to the ANC . . . we will repeal these laws, we will remove discrimination and from now on everybody in this country . . . is entitled to vote for members of Parliament . . . or, if the government refused to take this attitude, we would expect the voters, because of the situation, to say, we can't go on with a government like this; we think that this government should make way for a government which is more sensible, more responsible; a government which will change its policy and come to terms with these people; and then they would vote it out of power.

The government, however, responded in a more traditional manner. In July, police raided the offices of the ANC and SAIC and the homes of their officials, and then arrested thirty-five leaders of the campaign, including Mandela and Sisulu, charging them with promoting communism. All were found guilty of what was termed 'statutory communism', though as the judge in the case admitted, 'this has nothing to do with communism as it is commonly known'. They were given suspended sentences. Banning orders were imposed on some fifty leaders and organizers preventing them from participating in any ANC or SAIC activity for life. For years to come, political activists were harassed by police raids, surveillance, banning orders, restrictions, arrests and banishments. Informers and agents provocateurs penetrated their inner ranks. Bribery and intimidation became commonplace. Ever more stringent measures were added to the security arsenal. In 1953 the Criminal Law Amendment Act laid down severe penalities of fines, imprisonment and corporal punishment for anyone inciting others to commit civil disobedience offences. A Public Safety Act in 1953 empowered the government to declare a state of emergency over any part of South Africa whenever 'the maintenance of public order was endangered' and to employ emergency regulations to deal with any contingency that might arise.

In retrospect, the Defiance Campaign marked a high point in ANC activity. Never again was the ANC, in its legal form, able to mount successfully such organized resistance against the government. Deprived of leaders, fearful of reprisal, short of funds and poorly organized, the movement lost much of its momentum. Officials found it increasingly difficult to obtain permission to hold meetings. The membership fell away in droves. Seeking ways of making the ANC more effective, Mandela drew up a new plan of organization. Because he was subject to a banning order at the time, prohibited from participating in ANC activity, the plan was referred to as the 'M Plan'. Mandela was critical of attempts to bring about mass action through public meetings, press statements and leaflets and proposed a more effective local organization by establishing cell structures in black townships, based first on single streets, then 'zones' and 'wards', which would improve cooperation between different levels of leadership and enable the ANC to resist further government harassment. But the 'M Plan' made little headway. In few areas was it ever implemented.

Hemmed in by difficulties on every front, the ANC drew closer to other opposition groups which it had once spurned. The help of sympathetic whites was now considered an advantage. A new ANC president, Chief Albert Lutuli, elected in December 1952, was strongly in favour of turning the ANC from an all-African movement into a multiracial front, believing that with white help the iniquities of apartheid could be overturned. A deeply committed Christian, Lutuli placed great faith in the moral impact of the African struggle and the willingness of whites to undergo a change of heart once they discovered the true nature of apartheid. He actively supported the civil disobedience campaign. Thirty years of his life, he explained in

1952, had been spent 'knocking in vain, patiently, moderately and modestly at a closed and barred door'. Now the time had come to join the revolt against injustice. Lutuli's support for civil disobedience cost him his position as chief of a small reserve in Natal which he had held for seventeen years. Soon after his election as ANC president, he was served with orders banning him from public gatherings and prohibiting him from all main towns in the country. But Lutuli held fast to a liberal vision of South Africa. He did not share the radical ambitions held by some black activists. The ANC's goal, he was to write in his autobiography, 'is not that Congress shall rule South Africa, but that all Africans shall fully participate in ownership and government'.

In an attempt to revive mass political activity, the ANC in 1953 devised the idea of holding a Congress of the People, comprising delegates from every corner of the land, to draw up a new covenant, a Freedom Charter, and point the road ahead towards a multiracial society. Support for the idea came from SAIC which had remained in close contact since the Defiance Campaign and from the recently formed South African Coloured People's Organization (SACPO) based in Cape Town. Whites were also invited to participate. After initial misgivings, an enthusiastic response came from the Congress of Democrats (COD), a small but influential group set up in Johannesburg in 1953 by radical whites, many of them former members of the outlawed Communist Party with long experience of political activity. The newly formed Liberal Party, launched by whites in 1953 to act as a multiracial opposition group, was also approached, but declined to participate mainly because its members resented the prominent role that COD activists were allowed to play in the planning of the Congress. The opposition United Party, which was also invited, did not trouble to reply. Thus in 1954, four groups – the ANC, SAIC, SACPO and the COD, later joined by the multiracial South African Congress of Trade Unions – agreed to form a Congress Alliance to sponsor the proposed assembly. The date fixed for it was 16 June 1955. In the meantime, committees across the country were asked to contribute ideas to be included in the drafting of the charter.

The Congress of the People duly opened on a bare stretch of ground near Kliptown, a ramshackle collection of houses and shacks ten miles to the southwest of Johannesburg. Some 3000 delegates arrived – lawyers, doctors, clergymen, trade unionists, peasants, city workers – though several prominent ANC figures, like Lutuli and Mandela, were absent, forced to stay away by banning orders. Everywhere the ANC colours of black, green and yellow were on display. For two days the meeting continued, with speeches, songs and hymns. The text of the Freedom Charter was read out, in English, Sesotho and Xhosa, and clause by clause approved by a show of hands. Towards the end of the second day the police arrived in force, surrounded the meeting and announced that treason was suspected. They searched delegates, demanded their names, took photographs and confiscated documents, posters and banners. As they continued their work, the organizers resumed reading out the Freedom Charter to the crowd.

It was a document which became the subject of endless controversy, though much of its content was relatively modest. The Freedom Charter affirmed the right of all citizens to vote, to hold office and to be equal before the law. It promised equal status for 'all national groups' and an end to discriminatory legislation. It went on to declare that the mines, banks and monopoly industry would be transferred into public ownership and that land would be redivided. Other promises concerned free compulsory education, minimum wages, free medical care, and welfare for the aged. The tone throughout was idealistic, at times naive. 'Rent and prices shall be lowered, food plentiful and no one shall go hungry,' the Freedom Charter proclaimed. 'Slums shall be demolished, and new suburbs built.' No suggestions were put forward as to how all this would be achieved. In the South African context, however, such sentiments were dangerous. White liberals deplored the 'socialist' character of the Freedom Charter, arguing that left-wing activists in the Congress of Democrats had clearly got the upper hand. The government deemed the Charter to be subversive. Mandela himself later acknowledged: 'It is a revolutionary document precisely because the changes it envisages cannot be won without breaking up the economic and political set-up of present South Africa.'

A new round of harassment soon began. Three months later, police conducted dawn raids on an unprecedented scale, searching the homes and offices of some 500 men and women. More banning orders were issued. The climax came in December 1956 when 156 people were arrested on charges of high treason. Among the accused were prominent ANC figures, including Lutuli, Mandela, Sisulu and Tambo and white activists like the advocate Joe Slovo and his wife, Ruth First, both former members of the banned Communist Party. In all some twenty-three whites were put on trial.

The prosecution asserted that the accused had been preparing 'for the overthrow of the existing State by revolutionary methods, involving violence and the establishment of the so-called People's Democracy'. The main evidence provided in support of its case was the Freedom Charter. According to the prosecution, it envisaged steps in the direction of a Communist state. Altogether some 12,000 documents were produced to the court in the first month – pamphlets, speeches, books, banners and flags – all items diligently accumulated by the security police in two years of searches. Among the haul were two signs seized from the kitchen at the Congress of People, one proclaiming 'Soup with Meat', the other 'Soup without Meat'.

The Treason Trial gave the ANC greater national prominence than ever before. For many blacks it meant that the ANC had emerged as a real force capable of challenging the government. Overnight the accused became popular heroes. The Drill Hall in Johannesburg, where preliminary hearings were held, became a new centre of political activity. The presence of so many whites on trial was seen by many blacks as evidence that whites too were beginning to turn against the government. White liberals raised their own voice of protest against the trial, fearing that its real purpose was to intimidate the government's opponents of any kind. 'Unless white South Africans defend under all circumstances the democratic values which they cherish,' said Alan Paton, chairman of the Liberal Party, 'the day may soon come when they lose them.'

Yet the cost to the ANC was high. The trial, held at first in Johannesburg then moved to Pretoria, was to drag on for more than four years, sapping the energy of the movement and its leaders. The accused were eventually allowed bail, despite the nature of the charges, the case against fifty-nine of them, including Lutuli and Tambo, was withdrawn in 1958, but many others lost their livelihoods during the proceedings and suffered much personal hardship. Deprived of effective leadership, the ANC fell into disarray. Disputes and dissension, never far beneath the surface, broke out anew, threatening to wreck the movement from within.

It was remarkable in these circumstances how much optimism

survived. ANC leaders, convinced that the handful of whites who supported them represented something more than a fringe of white politics, placed inordinate hope in the notion that eventually enough whites would have a change of heart about apartheid to bring about the downfall of the government. 'As far as the Nationalist Party is concerned,' wrote Sisulu in an article published in January 1957, 'any serious analysis will reveal that it has reached its high-water mark. There is no possibility of the Nationalists growing stronger than they are at present.' In his essay on the 1950s, which he called 'The Fabulous Decade', the Johannesburg journalist, Lewis Nkosi, wrote of how the cause of racial justice and intellectual freedom seemed to be gathering strength. 'It was a time of infinite hope and possibility; it seemed not extravagant in the least to predict then that the Nationalist Government would soon collapse, if not from the pressure of extra-parliamentary opposition, certainly from the growing volume of unenforceable laws.' For those seeking them, signs of a more tolerant era could be found everywhere. In the winter of 1956, white audiences flocked to the City Hall in Johannesburg to hear performances of *Township Jazz '56* given by African musicians. In some quarters, mixed parties where white and black danced together were much in vogue. It even became fashionable for some whites to invite one or two of the more respectable ANC leaders – like Chief Lutuli or Professor Zachariah Matthews – to the rich northern suburbs of Johannesburg, for quiet discussion.

Yet all this obscured a harsher reality. In power was a government determined not only to curb dissent with whatever measures it deemed necessary but which had set its sights on reconstructing South African society on a scale that would involve upheaval and hardship for millions of its people. By comparison to what lay ahead, the 1950s in retrospect did indeed seem an enlightened era. Yet it was to become a common failing of the government's opponents continually to underestimate its strength and its ruthlessness. Time and again they were to believe they had the government on the run, only to suffer defeat and disappointment. 'Alas,' Nkosi wrote later of 1950s, 'we didn't realize how small and powerless we were.'

CHAPTER SEVEN

Verwoerd's Grand Design

The architect of grand apartheid was not a true Afrikaner. Hendrik Frensch Verwoerd had been born in a small village near Amsterdam, Holland in September 1901 to Dutch parents who emigrated to South Africa when he was two years old. His family thus bore none of the scars of the Anglo-Boer war which afflicted so much of the Afrikaner population. For Verwoerd there were no tales of family heroism, no link to the *voortrekkers* of the past, no personal sense of anguish at the fate of a defeated people. In view of the importance that Afrikaner nationalists attached to their own history, it was a considerable irony that the most powerful leader they were ever to find had no place in it.

From an early age, however, Verwoerd had been integrated into the Afrikaner community and absorbed much of its thinking. On leaving school, his ambition had been to become a minister in the Dutch Reformed Church and he chose to study at Stellenbosch University because of the theological training it offered. A brilliant scholar, he spent six years at Stellenbosch, eventually deciding on an academic career. After studying at universities in Germany in the mid-1920s, he returned to Stellenbosch at the age of twenty-six to take up the Chair in Applied Psychology. Appointed Professor of Sociology and Social Work in 1933 he found himself drawn into the problems of white poverty, and from there into the world of politics. By the mid-1930s he had decided to devote his career to promoting the cause of Afrikaner nationalism. Moving rapidly to the centre of influence, he became a key figure in the Broederbond, directly involved in plans to achieve Afrikaner unity and domination. As editor of the Nationalist paper, *Die Transvaler*, for more than ten years he played a prominent role in shaping nationalist doctrine and theories about apartheid as well as making regular attacks on the English, Jews and blacks. Though defeated as a National Party candidate in the 1948 election, he was awarded by Malan with a seat in the Senate and lost no time in propounding his views there.

Verwoerd's impact on South Africa was profound. For sixteen years, first as Minister of Native Affairs, then as prime minister until his death in 1966, he constituted the main driving force within the government. Believing that his own rise to prominence was as much a matter of divine inspiration as the policies he propounded, he set his mind on achieving a new racial order in South Africa, allowing nothing to deflect him from his purpose. Whereas Afrikaner leaders like Malan and Strydom were daunted by the prospect of converting the theories of grand apartheid into practice, Verwoerd forged ahead supremely confident of the importance of his own mission. At heart an autocrat contemptuous of criticism and public opinion, he could nevertheless appear outwardly benign. He preferred a different language to the one used by abrasive politicians like Strydom in proclaiming *baasskap*. The cruder professions of apartheid he disdained. Given to making long, didactic speeches, he would explain how apartheid – or separate development, as he chose to call it – would benefit the blacks as much as the whites. 'Separation,' he declared, 'does not envisage oppression. It envisages full opportunities for all . . . it is designed for happiness, security and . . . stability.' With such comforting words he proceeded to construct a social system bringing hardship and misery to much of the population.

Verwoerd's ultimate objective, as he explained it, was total territorial separation between white and black. He acknowledged that this 'ideal' could not be reached for many years. The journey there would be arduous. But it was essential that the goal should be clearly stated. Unless white and black were separated as far as possible, the future would hold nothing but 'rivalry and clashes' between them. The solution lay in giving each race 'mastery' over its own area. Thus the Native reserves would become the homelands of the blacks – or Bantu, as Verwoerd insisted upon calling them – where they would enjoy full social and political rights under a system of government suited to their own tribal background. Those blacks living in white areas would be accorded rights in the homelands too, which was where their real roots lay, and otherwise treated as 'visitors' and assigned separate locations. For a period of twenty years or so, according to Verwoerd's calculations, the flow of Africans to urban areas would continue to increase. But in the meantime, the reserves would be properly developed, and in white areas the government would endeavour to separate white and black in every sphere of life. The time would then come when the flow would be reversed. At the end of this grand design, Verwoerd confidently expected, South Africa would consist of flourishing black homelands living side by side in peace with an ever prosperous white territory.

Verwoerd's plans for separate development were far removed from the previous strategy of white *baasskap*, but his purpose was essentially the same: it was to relegate the African population to a permanently inferior status. The key to his policy was tribalism. By reviving tribal authority and by placing greater power in the hands of tribal chiefs beholden to the government, he intended to establish a new administrative structure for the reserves which would restore traditional customs and practices and keep African advancement in line with what the reserves themselves required. For most of the century, the system of government in the reserves had largely bypassed the chiefs. Their status had long since declined. Verwoerd's objective henceforth was to use the chiefs as the allies of white government, creating small centres of tribally-based power on the periphery of South Africa. By emphasizing tribal loyalties, he would keep the black population divided. Division of the blacks became a central part of Verwoerd's strategy: it was division that would counter the challenge mounted by African nationalists, destroy the notion of black majority rule and guarantee the supremacy of the whites.

Another crucial part of Verwoerd's scheme was his intention to reorganize black education.

> Bantu education [he said] should stand with both feet in the reserves and have its roots in the spirit and being of Bantu society. . . . There is no place for him in the European community above the level of certain forms of labour. . . . Until now he has been subject to a school system which drew him away from his own community and misled him by showing him the green pastures of European society in which he is not allowed to graze. . . . What is the use of teaching a Bantu child mathematics when it cannot use it in practice? That is absurd. Education must train people in accordance with their opportunities in life. . . .

Verwoerd set to work on his grand design with inexhaustible energy. As Minister of Native Affairs, placed in command of a vast bureaucracy, he wielded enormous power over the lives of the

African population. The laws at his disposal made him in effect their absolute ruler. As he told his wife after receiving news of his appointment in October 1950, 'I am now actually the Great Induna.' The idea clearly appealed to him. As part of his plan to revive tribal authority, he paid a series of visits to African kraals at which white officials were instructed to organize traditional ceremonies of welcome fit for a great chief, though such pageantry had long ago fallen into disuse. With elaborate courtesy, gifts would be exchanged with chiefs and headmen, then Verwoerd would join his hosts in a meal, squatting around a common pot of porridge, drinking beer, and patronizing them with tribal parables.

A torrent of legislation soon followed. It was under Verwoerd's auspices that tougher pass laws and labour controls were introduced. New methods were devised to prohibit African admittance to schools, hospitals and clubs in white areas and to prevent them from attending church or religious services there. And, stage by stage, the foundations were laid for establishing grand apartheid.

Verwoerd began in 1951 with the Bantu Authorities Act which replaced the existing European model of administration in the reserves with a structure of tribal authorities staffed by African chiefs and officials appointed and paid by the government. It made no provision for any form of elected representatives. In the case of the Transkei, tribal authorities were installed in place of a partly-elected District Council system. Chiefs were made responsible for the maintenance of law and order and the implementation of government measures. Those who refused to cooperate were deposed.

In 1953 Verwoerd introduced the Bantu Education Act under which the government assumed control over African education hitherto run mainly by missionary societies. He was blunt about its purpose: 'Natives will be taught from childhood to realize that equality with Europeans is not for them,' he told the House of Assembly. 'Racial relations cannot improve if the wrong type of education is given to Natives. They cannot improve if the result of Native education is the creation of a frustrated people who . . . have expectations in life which circumstances in South Africa do not allow to be fulfilled.' New syllabuses for primary schools, introduced in 1956, emphasized obedience, tribal loyalty, rural traditions and use of the vernacular. Vernacular instruction was made compulsory in all African primary schools and later extended to the first class of secondary schools. Expenditure on African education was pegged to the level of African taxes together with a fixed annual contribution from government revenue. In 1959 the government announced that future expansion of secondary education would be concentrated in the reserves. The government also moved to put an end to integrated university education. Hitherto, black students had been allowed to enrol for degree courses at the 'open' universities of Cape Town and the Witwatersrand. They were admitted to the same lectures and the same student societies as whites. Now the Extension of University Education Act, introduced in 1959, provided for separate colleges for Coloureds, for Indians and for Africans. In the case of Africans, they were to be given their own 'ethnic' universities sited in isolated rural areas – one in Natal for Zulu students, one in the Transvaal for Sotho, Tsonga and Venda-speaking students, one in Cape Province for Xhosa students. The university college of Fort Hare, the principal centre of higher education for Africans, which had a distinguished record in producing graduates since the 1920s, was to be reduced to the status of a Xhosa tribal college.

Verwoerd's determination to press ahead with his schemes was fortified by the findings of a government commission which spent five years investigating ways of rehabilitating the reserves. The Tomlinson report, published in 1956, warned that despite government restrictions Africans were leaving the reserves in ever greater numbers to settle permanently in white areas. If this process continued, millions more blacks would become established in white areas by the end of the century. The ultimate outcome would be that political power would pass into the hands of blacks. The only alternative to integration, said the report, was to promote 'the establishment of separate communities in their own separate territories where each will have the fullest opportunity of self-expression and development'. If the reserves were properly developed they would be capable of carrying a higher black population and providing it with a reasonable standard of living. Scattered as they were at present in 264 sections across the country, they formed no foundation for common growth. They were congested, unproductive and poverty stricken. They possessed no cities, no industries and few sources of employment. The report recommended therefore that the reserves should be consolidated into seven blocks, that a minimum sum of £104 million should be allocated for a ten-year development programme, and that industries should be set up both in the reserves and in border areas adjoining them to provide the reserve population with jobs. It argued strongly in favour of using white capital investment in black areas to provide 'the necessary stimulus to development'. Above all, said the report, a sense of urgency was needed.

> Circumstances demand a speedy, definite and unambiguous decision. The Commission is convinced that the separate develop-ment of the European and Bantu communities should be striven for as the only direction in which racial conflict may possibly be eliminated and racial harmony possibly be maintained. . . . There is no midway between the two poles of ultimate total integration and ultimate separate development of the two groups.

An Afrikaner *volkskongres*, called to discuss the Tomlinson report and attended by some 800 delegates representing 540 organizations, resolved in June 1956 to support territorial separation on the grounds that 'there is no possibility of the peaceful evolutionary development of White and Black in South Africa into an integrated society'.

Elected prime minister in September 1958 after the death of Hans Strydom, Verwoerd possessed a clear field in which to implement his ideas more fully, casting himself in the role of a leader chosen by God. On the day of his election by National Party colleagues, he declared: 'I believe that the will of God was revealed in the ballot.' Initially, many of Verwoerd's colleagues had doubts about some of his ideas. But Verwoerd mastered every detail of his policies and was always prepared with answers when sceptics challenged him. He retained supreme confidence in himself, dismissing all proposals that were at variance with his own. 'I do not have the nagging doubt of ever wondering whether perhaps I am wrong,' he said.

In 1959, consulting only a handful of his closest advisers, Verwoerd unveiled his master plan. His aim was to turn South Africa into a 'multi-national state' by fragmenting the African population into separate ethnic groups. The Promotion of Bantu Self-Govern-ment Act provided for the establishment of eight black 'homelands', one for each of the major ethnic groups – North Sotho, South Sotho, Swazi, Tsonga, Tswana, Venda, Xhosa and Zulu. No previous attempt had ever been made to implement territorial segregation on this tribal basis. Hitherto the whole emphasis of government policy had been simply to segregate black from white. Now Verwoerd decreed that the African people were not homogenous but a collection of separate national groups divided by language and culture. Their roots lay in separate homelands; there they would be accorded 'separate freedoms'. This principle applied not only to rural blacks but to urban blacks, regardless of how many generations they had lived in towns; they were all deemed citizens of the new homelands. Accordingly, the right of Africans to have representation in parliament was to be abolished.

In the beginning the role of the Bantu Authorities in homelands would be mainly administrative. They would be given no opportunity to formulate policy, on education, health, employment or any other subject. They would have powers to levy taxes, control public works and allocate licences and trading rights. But the government would retain the right to choose, depose or veto any territorial authority. At some distant and unforeseen stage, however, Verwoerd held out the possibility that the homelands might be granted some form of independence.

Verwoerd was also much taken with the idea of establishing new industries, under white ownership and control, in white areas close to the borders of reserves, thus providing employment for Africans living in the reserves. White businessmen, he said, would receive government subsidies to induce them to develop 'border industries'. But he adamantly rejected suggestions that white private capital and government money should be used to develop the homelands, as Tomlinson had recommended, on the grounds that this was based on 'the old system which this government inherited of doing everything for the Native: the system of spoon-feeding'. Instead a government-controlled Bantu Investment Corporation would suffice. Verwoerd, in fact, was interested not so much in the development of the reserves, as he claimed, as in finding ways of slowing down the flow of blacks to the main urban centres. The concept of border industries was ideally suited to this purpose. If the policy worked, fewer migrants would find their way to the towns. While still continuing to work in 'white' areas, they would keep 'their anchor in the homelands'.

Verwoerd's 'new vision', as it was called, was hailed by the National Party as providing a lasting solution for South Africa. The advantages to whites seemed conclusive. The whites maintained unfettered control over their own areas, while claiming to permit blacks equivalent rights in the homelands. The blacks meanwhile were divided into separate ethnic groups, inhibiting their ability to act as a single community against outnumbered whites. Because each national group was a minority of the whole, no one 'nation' could claim rights on the basis of its numerical strength. Thus the demands for majority rule by African nationalists were irrelevant. The problem of urban blacks was solved by denying them any permanent place in towns. At an economic level, white businessmen were given continued access to cheap black labour through the 'border industries' scheme, but without increasing the flow of rural Africans to existing industrial areas. In the long term there was the prospect that the number of urban Africans might be reduced. On the basis of Verwoerd's calculations, the reverse flow back to the homelands would begin in 1978. All this was to be set in motion in the name of racial harmony, peace and security. 'The development of South Africa on the basis of this Bill,' said Verwoerd, 'will create so much friendship, so much gratitude, so many mutual interests . . . that there will arise what I call a commonwealth, founded on common interests.'

The reality, however, was different. In less than a year, South Africa was beset by its greatest upheaval since the Union was founded fifty years before.

CHAPTER EIGHT

The Sharpeville Crisis

As the tentacles of apartheid penetrated to every level of African society, African protest against the government steadily mounted. In rural areas opposition to apartheid measures like the Bantu Authorities Act flared into open revolt. There was prolonged violence in the Hurutshe Reserve in the western Transvaal, in Sekhukhuneland and in Pondoland. Chiefs and councillors resisting government authority were deposed and deported. Armoured units and aircraft had to be deployed to crush the Pondoland revolt. When the government decided to compel African women to carry reference books from 1956, there were protest marches in almost every major town. Boycotts and demonstrations against apartheid continued throughout the late 1950s. But the effect of all this agitation was limited. For the most part, the protests were isolated from each other and sporadic. Attempts by the African National Congress to organize mass support were largely unsuccessful. Not once was the government deflected from its central purpose.

The ANC's failure to provide a more effective challenge to the government contributed to a growing crisis within the nationalist movement. Since 1953 the Africanist wing had become increasingly critical of the direction taken by the ANC, in particular its policy of seeking alliances with other racial groups. The rift had taken shape in the aftermath of the Defiance Campaign and it had widened when the ANC joined forces with whites and Indians in the Congress Alliance. The Africanists claimed that the ANC, by accepting the Freedom Charter, with its emphasis on multiracial objectives, had yielded to the influence of other racial groups like the Congress of Democrats and the Indian Congress. The clause declaring that South Africa belonged to 'all who live in it, Black and White' aroused particular resentment. In the Africanist view, the only true 'owners' of South Africa were Africans. Others had merely 'stolen' the country. Instead of the Freedom Charter, the Africanists wanted the ANC to revert to the goals of the 1949 Programme of Action which emphasized 'freedom from white domination'. Nothing could be gained, they insisted, by trying to appease white opinion. The only way by which white domination would be broken was by black force.

The other wing of the ANC – the Charterists, as they were known – reacted to this overt appeal to African race-consciousness with a mixture of alarm and disgust, dismissing it as nothing better than a black version of Afrikaner ideology. For both moral and practical reasons, the Charterists argued, the ANC needed the help of whites and other groups. Therefore African demands would have to be moderated to take account of their interests.

The gulf widened. In November 1958, the Africanists broke away from the ANC to form their own group. At a three-day conference in April 1959 at the Orlando Communal Hall, south-west of Johannesburg, the Pan-Africanist Congress was launched amid placards proclaiming 'Africa for Africans' and 'Imperialists Quit Africa'. Hoping to tap the undercurrents of anger and resentment at white rule rising among the younger generation of urban blacks, the PAC set out to project an aggressive image. Its goal specifically was African rule. Explaining the party's policy at its inaugural conference, the PAC president, Robert Sobukwe, a thirty-five-year-old lecturer in African languages at the University of Witwatersrand, announced:

> We aim, politically, at government of the Africans, by Africans, for Africans, with everybody who owes his only loyalty to Africa and who is prepared to accept the democratic rule of an African majority, being regarded as an African. We guarantee no minority rights because we think in terms of individuals not groups.

By setting African rule as its objective and by promising militant action to achieve it, the PAC leaders were convinced they would attract huge support. The target they set themselves was to enlist 100,000 members within three months. Once the masses were given bold, decisive leadership, then the fires of rebellion, they believed, could soon be lit. The pace at which the rest of Africa was changing set a heady example. Everywhere European colonial powers were on the retreat. Black Africans were rising to positions of political power. Ghana had won its independence in 1957. Other states in West Africa were following suit. Pointing to the growing momentum towards independence in Africa, Sobukwe predicted in December 1959 that South Africa too would be free within four years.

Yet from the outset, the PAC, like the ANC, possessed no coherent strategy. It was poorly organized, short of funds and trained leaders, and relied on little more than the notion that the time was ripe for militant action. After six months, its membership officially had reached less than 25,000 and the true figure was probably far lower. Still determined to force the pace and establish the PAC's credentials as the leading nationalist group, Sobukwe in December 1959 announced plans for a campaign of mass protest against the pass laws. On an appointed day, Africans would leave their reference books at home, boycott work, present themselves *en masse* for arrest at their local police stations and opt for imprisonment. The slogan chosen was 'no bail, no defence, no fine'. By swamping the prison system, they would make the pass laws unworkable. The campaign, he hoped, would disrupt the economy and eventually inspire a popular uprising. In a parallel move, the ANC announced its own campaign of protest against the pass laws, but one that was far less ambitious. It proposed a series of demonstrations on days of symbolic importance during 1960.

Little more than three months was given for the PAC to prepare its campaign. Though scant effort had been made to organize mass support for the protest, Sobukwe decided on 21 March as the launching date, partly in order to preempt an ANC demonstration scheduled for 30 March. His final instructions sent to PAC branches stressed the need for non-violent protest. A letter he wrote to the police commissioner, Major General Rademeyer, informing him that PAC members would surrender themselves for arrest on 21 March, also emphasized the non-violent purpose of the campaign. If PAC crowds were given adequate time in which to disperse, he said, then they would comply with any police orders to do so; but he acknowledged that there was considerable potential for violence and warned Rademeyer of 'trigger-happy, African-hating' police.

The events of 21 March 1960 were to leave an indelible stain on South Africa and to make a lasting impact around the world. For the most part, the PAC campaign was a failure. Sobukwe and other members of the PAC executive, together with about 150 volunteers, presented themselves for arrest at police stations in Johannesburg townships. Crowds gathered outside police stations in Evaton and Vanderbijlpark, towns in the southern Transvaal. But in Durban, Port Elizabeth and East London there were no demonstrations at all. In one place, however, a brutal tragedy occurred that for years to come stood as a symbol of the evil of apartheid and the suffering it brought to African people.

Sharpeville, by the standards of the time, was a model township. Built as a black suburb for the steel manufacturing centre of Vereeniging, fifty miles south of Johannesburg, it had remained largely immune from the wave of demonstrations and occasional disorder which afflicted other African towns during the 1950s. Municipal officials there were proud to point out how 'peace-loving and law-abiding' the local population was. The facilities provided by the municipality were relatively advanced and included street lighting, a brewery, a clinic and weekly film shows; houses there boasted running water, sanitation and in some cases bathrooms. By the end of the 1950s, however, grievances over influx control, unemployment and rising poverty had provided fertile ground for political activists.

The PAC made extensive efforts to prepare for the campaign in Sharpeville. From early in the morning, PAC pickets were active on the streets telling residents they should not go to work. By mid-morning, a crowd of several thousand Africans had gathered outside the police station. Their mood, according to most accounts, was relaxed and amiable. But they showed no signs of dispersing. Police reinforcements were called in. At 1.15 p.m., by which time nearly 300 police were facing a crowd of some 5000 Africans, a scuffle broke out near one of the gates to the police compound. A police officer was pushed over. The crowd surged forward to see what was happening. According to police witnesses, stones were thrown at them. No order was given to shoot. No warning shots were fired. In a moment of panic, the police opened fire indiscriminately into the crowd. The crowd turned and fled. But the firing continued. Sixty-nine Africans were killed and 186 wounded. Most were shot in the back.

Later in the day, a similar incident, though on a smaller scale, occurred in Langa, a black township outside Cape Town occupied mainly by migrant workers. Confronted by a crowd of 6000 Africans police mounted baton charges to break it up. The crowd retaliated by throwing stones. The police opened fire, killing two Africans and injuring forty-nine others. That night rioting broke out in the township. The Langa protest then turned into a major confrontation with the authorities in Cape Town. A strike which began that day eventually spread until almost all African workers in Cape Town joined it, bringing industry to a standstill. After several unsuccessful attempts to break the strike, the police raided Langa on 30 March, smashing down doors, pulling inhabitants out of bed, beating them up and throwing them into the streets. This police brutality provoked a mass march by some 30,000 workers into the centre of Cape Town. Their original intention had been to reach parliament, but on the way the local PAC organizer, Philip Kgosana, a former university student, was persuaded to lead them instead to police headquarters in Caledon Square. There, in negotiation with the local police commander, Kgosana agreed to send the marchers home in return for the promise of an appointment with the Minister of Justice at Caledon Square later that day. When Kgosana turned up for the appointment, he was arrested.

The Sharpeville massacre produced a storm of African protest. The ANC president, Chief Lutuli, called on workers to stay at home and observe 28 March as a day of mourning. The response in many large towns was overwhelming. In demonstrations across the country, thousands of Africans burned their pass books. Violence broke out in Johannesburg's black suburbs. Many blacks there believed they were on the verge of liberation.

To much of the white population it seemed that South Africa had indeed reached a critical turning point. The sight of massed ranks of blacks marching on the centre of a white city suggested that black patience had finally snapped. As fear and alarm about the defiant mood of the black population spread, whites rushed to gunshops in the Transvaal and in Cape Town, clearing out their stocks. Foreign embassies were inundated with inquiries about immigration. House prices and the stock market slumped. An outburst of international protest against the Sharpeville killings added to the atmosphere of crisis. Liberal whites were convinced that the government would now have no alternative but to change its policies.

The government at first appeared uncertain as to how to react. For a brief period it suspended the pass laws; but soon enough it reverted to type. On 30 March it declared a state of emergency and began to round up hundreds of anti-apartheid dissidents. Officials were empowered to arrest suspects without warrants and to detain them indefinitely. Large-scale police raids were conducted in one township after another. In Langa, police units threw a cordon around the township, cut off water and electricity supplies, then staged house-to-house raids, dragging men and women on to the streets and assaulting them with clubs and whips. Four days of continuous brutality eventually broke the strike.

In parliament, the government introduced new security legislation, the Unlawful Organizations Act, empowering it to proscribe the ANC, PAC and any other organization attempting to further their aims. Government spokesmen claimed that the nationalist parties were determined on the violent overthrow of the government. 'Their aim,' said the Minister of Justice, François Erasmus, 'is to bring to its knees any White Government in South Africa which stands for White supremacy and for White leadership. . . . [They] do not want peace and order . . . what they want is our country.' Armed with this new legislation, said Erasmus, the government would be able to protect innocent Africans and bring an end to the ANC-PAC 'reign of terror'.

On 8 April, the ANC and PAC were declared illegal organizations. For several weeks afterwards, police continued their round-up of suspected activists. By the beginning of May, more than 18,000 people had been arrested. Subjected to mass raids and arrests, the PAC became virtually leaderless. Sobukwe was imprisoned for three years on a charge of incitement. In Johannesburg the PAC's headquarters were left in the hands of a student who previously had been working as an office manager. Within weeks the back of African resistance had been broken. An attempt by the underground ANC to organize a week-long strike in April proved a failure. By mid-April workers were queuing at government offices to obtain replacements for their burned passes.

But for the shooting at Sharpeville, the day might have marked no more than another abortive episode in the annals of African protest. The poor response to the PAC's call for mass civil disobedience showed how few were ready to seek the confrontation with white power that Sobukwe told them would result in the government's downfall. Not only did Sobukwe misjudge popular reaction to his campaign, he entirely underestimated the government's real strength. Though the government was pitched into a political crisis of unprecedented magnitude, it was never in danger of losing control. Its ability to use repression was far more formidable than Sobukwe and other nationalists ever supposed. Indeed, the main result of his ill-prepared campaign was to give the government the opportunity to crush the nationalist movement in the name of law and order.

Nevertheless the cost to the government was high. White confidence in the apartheid system was seriously shaken. Black activists now began to think in terms of revolutionary strategy. And abroad, South Africa faced universal condemnation.

CHAPTER NINE

Against the World

The name of Sharpeville reverberated around the world provoking such outrage and indignation that South Africa's reputation was left permanently damaged. Photographs of the shooting, published by newspapers everywhere, made a sharp impact on millions of people who saw them. In the following days, as reports of police brutality, mass arrests, emergency laws, demonstrations and marches accumulated, the impression gained abroad was of an evil regime in the throes of crisis so severe that it might not survive. Comparisons with Nazi Germany were common. Though the storm of condemnation was eventually to recede, from Sharpeville onwards South Africa was marked out as one of the world's pariah states.

The tide of opinion against South Africa had been mounting since the Second World War. While South Africa held fast to its system of white supremacy, everywhere else in the world the era of white hegemony was drawing to a close. In Asia and Africa, Europe's colonial powers were on the retreat. In the United States, segregation was under challenge. Racist suppositions prevalent before the war were no longer fashionable. In forums like the United Nations, South Africa came under constant attack from Afro-Asian states. General Smuts, given a foretaste of such action over South Africa's treatment of its Indian population, was moved to complain of 'a solid wall of prejudice against the colour policies of South Africa'. Nearly every year after 1946, United Nations resolutions were drafted criticizing South Africa's treatment of its Indian population. From 1952 the whole policy of apartheid came under attack. As the number of Asian and African members of the United Nations multiplied, so the volume of condemnation rose and, with it, calls for sanctions and boycotts.

The South African government attempted to fend off the criticism by claiming that it was based on ignorance, or that it amounted to interference in South Africa's internal affairs or, when coming from Afro-Asian states, that it was merely intended to draw attention away from their own misconduct. The government concentrated its efforts on trying to win the support of Western powers by portraying South Africa as a bastion of Western civilization dedicated to resisting communist encroachment which it was in their own interests to defend. During the cold war era this ploy had considerable effect. But as South Africa moved further along the road to apartheid while Western powers became increasingly committed to ideas of racial equality and colonial freedom, South Africa's policies proved an embarrassment to its allies in the West which they were no longer prepared to ignore so readily.

The clearest signal of this change in attitude was given in February 1960 by the British prime minister, Harold Macmillan, during a visit he paid to South Africa as part of an African tour. In long private discussions with Verwoerd, Macmillan made little headway.

It was only during these days [he recalled in his memoirs] that I began to realize to the full extent the degree of obstinacy, amounting really to fanaticism, which Dr Verwoerd brought to the consideration of his policies. . . . I had the unusual experience of soon noticing that nothing one could say or put forward would have the smallest effect upon the views of this determined man.

With his speech to parliament in Cape Town on 3 February, however, Macmillan achieved a more profound impact. He said nothing new, but by addressing his remarks on South Africa's racial policies to South Africans in their own parliament, on an occasion intended to celebrate its fiftieth anniversary, the full import of his message was no longer lost, even on Verwoerd.

Taking as his theme the rise of nationalism since the days of the Roman Empire, Macmillan drew attention to 'the wind of change' now blowing through Africa with which Western powers had to deal. Britain's answer, he said, in colonies for which it was responsible, was to create societies which allowed citizens an increasing share in political power and responsibility, societies in which individual merit, and individual merit alone, was the criterion for a man's advancement, whether political or economic. Since it was not possible to isolate one part of Africa from another, British policy might therefore create difficulties for South Africans. But that would not prevent Britain from fulfilling its duty. While the British government would endeavour to give South Africa its support and encouragement, there were aspects of South Africa's policies which made it impossible for it to do this without contradicting its own convictions about the political destinies of free men.

At the end of a fifty-minute speech, notable for the broad sweep of history on which Macmillan enjoyed dwelling, the burden of his message was unmistakable. The growth of African nationalism could not be stopped. Britain, as a major Western power and as leader of the Commonwealth, had decided to come to terms with it. If South Africa persisted with its policies of white supremacy, then it could no longer rely on British support.

As Verwoerd sat listening to this message, his face grew slowly more pale and tense. Clearly angered by what Macmillan had said, he rose to give an impromptu rebuttal, speaking for thirty minutes, warning of the dangers inherent in British policies and demanding 'justice for the white man'. If the survival of the white race seemed to warrant it, he said, then South Africa would abandon accepted values.

The following month, in the wake of the Sharpeville massacre, Western attitudes, became markedly more hostile. A United Nations Security Council resolution blamed South Africa's racial policies for causing 'international friction'. In a General Assembly debate, British delegates, who had previously stuck to the argument that South Africa's racial policies were its own internal affair, now openly attacked apartheid. The United States added its own condemnation. For the first time the General Assembly approved a resolution not just expressing abhorrence of South African policies but asking for action to be taken. Foreign investors, meanwhile, fearing imminent upheaval, took their own action. A sharp outflow of capital from South Africa hit the value of the currency and halved its foreign exchange reserves.

Yet however strongly Western governments felt about Sharpeville, beyond expressions of outrage they were uncertain about what action to take. South Africa was still valued for its strategic position on the Cape sea routes, for its vast mineral resources, and for its thriving economy. It possessed the world's largest deposits of gold, chromium, platinum group metals, manganese, vanadium and asbestos as well as large deposits of iron, coal, uranium, diamonds and copper. With the help of foreign investors it had developed important manufacturing, mining and agricultural industries which offered high returns. In the case of United States investment at the time, the average annual return was running at more than 17 per cent, a figure exceeded only by West Germany. More than 60 per cent of South Africa's trade was linked to Western Europe and North America. For Britain there were not only strong economic and cultural ties but a defence agreement which entitled the Royal Navy to use facilities at the Simonstown base in the Cape. Indeed, most Western states, however deep their sense or moral indignation at South Africa's racial policies, found they had a far greater interest in preserving their links with South Africa than in agitating for change. There was much debate, therefore, but not much action.

Nevertheless South Africa was now propelled into an era of isolation from which there was to be no escape. United Nations resolutions condemning South Africa's policies wholesale were regularly passed with massive majorities and almost no defending votes. In most countries in the world, boycott movements sprang up. Several governments imposed official boycotts on South African goods. Demands for Western sanctions were frequently made. All this added to the sense of insecurity that many South African whites now felt about their future. Internally they were besieged by African unrest, externally they encountered a hostile world. An attempt by a deranged white farmer to assassinate Verwoerd three weeks after the Sharpeville massacre added a new element of uncertainty. Never before, it seemed to many whites, had they faced such a combination of dangers.

CHAPTER TEN

Walls of Granite

In the aftermath of the Sharpeville crisis many doubts were voiced among the white community about the wisdom of continuing with apartheid, even within the inner circles of Afrikanerdom. Four weeks after the shooting, a senior cabinet minister, Paul Sauer, proclaimed that 'the old book' of South African history had been closed at Sharpeville. 'For the immediate future,' he said, 'South Africa will reconsider in earnest and honesty her whole approach to the Native question. We must create a new spirit which must restore overseas faith – both white and non-white in South Africa.' A prominent Afrikaner institution, *Die Suid Afrikaanse Buro vir Raase Aangeleenthede* (the South African Bureau of Racial Affairs) which had once campaigned vigorously for 'total' apartheid, now proposed that Coloureds should be brought closer to the white community and given direct representation in parliament. The Nationalist newspaper, *Die Burger*, also spoke out in favour of direct representation for Coloureds.

The sharpest rebuff came from the Dutch Reformed Church. Throughout the 1950s it had given the government spiritual and moral support, providing theological justification for every step it took on the road to apartheid. But when in December 1960 DRC delegates attended a conference at Cottesloe Hall in a Johannesburg suburb organized by the World Council of Churches for its eight member churches in South Africa, a different mood prevailed. Leading figures in the *Nederduitse Gereformeerde Kerk*, the principal Dutch Reformed Church, accepted decisions which rocked the very foundations of the apartheid system. The conference declared that any political system which deprived men of the right to own land wherever they were domiciled and the right to participate in the government of their country could not be justified. It concluded that there were no scriptural grounds for the prohibition of mixed marriages. And it criticized the migratory labour system, job reservation and restrictions placed on the freedom of worship. In effect the conference decisions amounted to an indictment of the whole policy of apartheid.

To all such criticisms, Verwoerd remained impervious. Neither Sharpeville nor the physical and mental shock of the attempt on his life altered his outlook. Nothing was to shake his faith in apartheid. His advice to Nationalist leaders was that they needed to stand by their racial policies 'like walls of granite'. It was an image that he cultivated for himself – indomitable, iron-willed, supremely confident in his own ability and judgement. All suggestion of reform was dismissed. Every adverse event was explained away. While Verwoerd was confined to hospital for six weeks, recovering from bullet wounds to his head, his Minister of Bantu Administration and Development, Daan de Wet Nel, reaffirmed the government's total commitment to apartheid.

> I am convinced that the policy of apartheid will serve as a model to the world for the establishment of good race relations [he declared]. Never before in the history of South Africa has the Bantu shown so great a spirit of cooperation with, and trust in, the white man. What of the recent disturbances? Let me point out that barely 2 per cent of the Bantu population were involved in the disturbances, and most of them were victims of organized gangs who forced them into these actions at the point of the knife and the pistol.

Verwoerd's own response was given in a long and carefully-worded statement read to parliament on his behalf in May.

> The government sees no reason to depart from the policy of separate development as a result of the disturbances. On the contrary, the events have more than ever emphasized that peace and good order, and friendly relations between the races, can best be achieved through this policy. . . . It is regrettable that the Government is being so hindered by misrepresentations here and abroad in its efforts to promote as quickly as possible the process of separate development.

His critics were soon routed. At Verwoerd's insistence, the Federal Council of the National Party, its highest authority, issued a statement pledging total support for him and denouncing all idea of concession. Dissidents in the South African Bureau of Racial Affairs were driven out of the fold. *Die Burger* was forced to halt its campaign on Coloured representation. Strong pressure was brought to bear on provincial synods of the Dutch Reformed Church which duly recanted the Cottesloe declarations and reaffirmed support for government policy. Most of the DRC leaders who participated in the Cottesloe conference were ousted.

Verwoerd showed equal determination in pursuing the Afrikaners' cherished goal of turning South Africa into a republic. Neither Malan nor Strydom had felt strong enough to confront the electorate with such a controversial issue. Though the National Party had won an increasing number of parliamentary seats during the 1950s, it had never gained an overall majority of votes cast in an election. In the 1958 election the Nationalists had won 103 seats against the United Party's fifty-three seats, but they had collected only 48.9 per cent of the poll against the United Party's 50.36 per cent. Several of Verwoerd's colleagues doubted the wisdom of trying to resolve the republican issue at such a difficult time. Not only was it bound to alienate the English-speaking population which valued South Africa's link to the British crown, but, in view of the election record, there was a danger that the government might suffer a defeat at the hands of the United Party which opposed a republic.

Ever since becoming prime minister, however, Verwoerd had treated the republican issue as a priority. A republic, he argued, would unite white South Africa rather than divide it. Once the imperial connection was broken, the whites would forget their divided heritage instead of looking back to it. Ignoring the views of more cautious colleagues, he announced abruptly in January 1960 that there would be a referendum on the issue the following October. Even if the result was a majority of only one, he said, a republic would be declared. And if there was an adverse vote, then he would let members of parliament decide the matter, which would mean that a republic was guaranteed.

As soon as Verwoerd had recovered from his injuries, he threw himself into the republican campaign with undiminished zeal. Hoping to woo the English-speaking population away from its traditional loyalties, he now emphasized the importance of white nationalism rather than Afrikaner nationalism, urging whites to stand together in the face of growing internal and external dangers, and making great play of the way in which Britain and other European powers were abandoning white communities in Africa to the mercy of black rule. Time and again, the chaos in the Congo, which followed the departure of the Belgians in June 1960, was used as an example of what was likely to happen to them. As the *Rand Daily Mail* commented: 'The whole republican referendum is reduced to the simple question of whether you want your daughter to marry an African, or, more to the point, be ravished by a Congolese soldier.'

On 5 October 90 per cent of eligible voters gave their verdict on the matter. In English-speaking Natal, an overwhelming majority voted against a republic. In the Cape, where half a million votes were recorded, the majority in favour of a republic was fewer than four thousand. But the Afrikaner strongholds of the Transvaal and the Free State gave Verwoerd the victory he sought. Overall there were 850,458 votes in favour of a republic to 775,878 against. Verwoerd pronounced himself delighted with the result.

There remained the question of South Africa's membership of the Commonwealth. Verwoerd had no liking for the Commonwealth. The days when it served as a forum for the old white dominions of the British Empire, which he found acceptable, were clearly over. It had become instead a multiracial association of states many of which were openly scathing about South Africa's racial policies. During the republican campaign he had promised that South Africa would remain a member of the Commonwealth in order to allay the fears of the English-speaking population. But the change in South Africa's status to a republic, scheduled for 31 May 1961, meant that Verwoerd had to make a formal application for South Africa to continue its membership of the Commonwealth, and when he did so, he ran into a barrage of opposition from other Commonwealth prime ministers who demanded reform of the apartheid system. As Harold Macmillan recalled, Verwoerd's performance at a Commonwealth meeting in March 1961 in London was unbending: 'The Prime Minister of South Africa made it abundantly clear, beyond all doubt, that he would not think it right to relax in any form the extreme rigidity of his dogma, either now or in the future.' Rather than retreat an inch on apartheid, Verwoerd withdrew South Africa's application for membership. 'I was amazed and shocked by the spirit of hostility . . . even of vindictiveness towards South Africa shown in the discussions,' he said.

Verwoerd was to turn South Africa's departure from the Commonwealth to good use. On his return to South Africa he portrayed it not as a defeat but as a victory. 'We have freed ourselves from the

Afro-Asian states,' he proclaimed. Finally South Africa's independence was complete. The response of most Afrikaners was jubilant.
For them, a republic outside the Commonwealth was an even greater
triumph than one that was obliged to remain inside it. In the
English-speaking community there was much resentment. 'We have
been thrown out of the Commonwealth, out of the group of the most
tolerant, the most civilized, the most fair-minded peoples in the
world,' complained the *Cape Times*, 'because of the narrow-minded,
inflexible doctrines of racism.' But Verwoerd's granite-like stand
against critics abroad and the 'black peril' within impressed a
growing number of whites, including English speakers, once the
shock of Sharpeville began to recede. In the October 1961 election,
the National Party again improved its position. For the first time
since the Nationalists gained office in 1948, they won more votes
than opposition parties. Their share of parliamentary seats also rose
from 102 to 105, giving them an unassailable majority of two-thirds
of the seats in the House of Assembly.

Verwoerd now used his commanding position to take the grand
design for apartheid a stage further. He viewed the matter with some
urgency. The outburst of international criticism against South
Africa had made him anxious to prove that his strategy for devolving
power upon the African population in their own Bantustans had as
much merit as the plans that European powers had devised for giving
independence to their African colonies. Moreover he needed a device
that would counter the threat posed by African nationalists and that
would win for itself local African support. He therefore proceeded
apace to set Bantustans on the road to self-government, promising
that the eventual goal for them would be independence.

Verwoerd's proposals amounted to a radical change in his own
thinking. In the early 1950s he had dismissed all notion that Native
reserves might lead a separate existence. 'It stands to reason,' he said
in 1951, 'that white South Africa must remain their guardian.
[When] we talk about the Natives' right of self-government, we
cannot mean that we intend by that to cut large slices out of South
Africa and turn them into independent states.' By 1959, when
introducing the Promotion of Bantu Self-Government Act, he had
come to acknowledge that the ultimate consequence of giving
political rights to Africans in their own areas might involve some
form of independence, an idea that few Nationalist politicians had

ever contemplated. But while conceding the possibility of independence, Verwoerd considered it at the time to be no more than a remote
prospect. By 1961 he had been forced to consider a new timetable. A
few days after Britain and the United States had voted for a United
Nations resolution calling on member states to take action to bring
about an end to apartheid, Verwoerd countered with a new
commitment. 'The Bantu will be able to develop into separate states,'
he declared. 'That is not what we would like to see. It is a form of
fragmentation that we would not have liked if we were able to avoid it.
In the light of pressure being exerted on South Africa, there is
however no doubt that eventually this will have to be done, thereby
buying for the white man the right to retain his domination in what is
his country.' As he explained it the following year, the choice for South
Africa was to become either a multiracial state in which blacks would
eventually predominate or a country partitioned so as to provide for
separate and independent Bantustans. His own view on the matter was
clear, 'I choose division,' he told parliament.

To those traditionalists in the National Party worried about the
implication of black *baasskap* and the possibility of losing access to
cheap black labour, Verwoerd emphasized that he was not departing
from apartheid principles, but merely making 'adjustments' to take
into account changing world circumstances and the emancipation of
Africans elsewhere on the continent. It would have been better, he
told them, if whites could have continued to rule the country as
undisputed masters, treating blacks as before as a community under
white guardianship; but events had impelled him 'to seek a solution in
a continuation of what was actually the old course, namely separation.'

The key to Verwoerd's Bantustan policy was the Transkei.
Covering an area of some 16,000 square miles north of the Great Kei
river, it was the only African reserve which constituted a coherent
piece of territory. Its black population numbered about 1.5 million,
enough to represent a 'nation'. Its settled white population was
insignificant – some 1400 people, mostly farmers, traders and their
dependents living in areas designated 'white spots' which could
eventually be removed if necessary. Furthermore, Verwoerd had
found in the Transkei an ambitious and ruthless local politician more
than willing to fall in with his plans.

Kaiser Matanzima was a chief from the western district of Emigrant
Tembuland who saw in apartheid a means both of restoring hegemony
for the Xhosa-speaking people of the Transkei and of satisfying his

own aspirations for power. A graduate from the University of Fort Hare who liked to describe himself as a Xhosa nationalist, he had already proved useful to Verwoerd by helping to persuade the old General Council, or Bunga, of the Transkei, to vote itself out of existence and accept Verwoerd's Bantu Authorities Act which gave chiefs an enhanced role. Matanzima was duly rewarded. In 1958 he was appointed Regional Chief of Emigrant Tembuland, and three years later he became chairman of the Transkei Territorial Authority. The Transkei Territorial Authority had little power. Most of the business at its annual meetings consisted of 'humble requests' to government department to look into grievances for which replies would sometimes take years to arrive. But for Matanzima it was a useful vantage point from which to further his career.

The Transkei, however, was soon engulfed in trouble. While its chiefs enjoyed their new status under the Bantu Authorities Act, the mood of much of the population there became increasingly restless. Resentment against the role of chiefs as 'allies' of the white government was widespread. In Pondoland dissent flared into open rebellion. Police and troops had to be used to crush an underground resistance movement. Emergency regulations were introduced empowering police to detain suspects without trial and impose tight control over public meetings. Chiefs were given the right to try and punish any African accused of subverting their authority. Any attempt to treat chiefs with disrespect or to refuse to obey their orders was deemed an offence. The result was that many chiefs came to be regarded no longer as leaders of their people but as 'stooges' of the government.

It was in these circumstances that Verwoerd decided to press ahead with his plan for converting the Transkei into a self-governing Bantustan. In 1961 an official committee of twenty-seven members was appointed under the chairmanship of Chief Kaiser Matanzima to examine the implications of self-government and to draft a new constitution. From the outset, certain guidelines were made clear to committee members. The constitution, they were told, would have to conform to apartheid principles. It could not include multiracial objectives. The criterion for deciding citizenship was to be race, not place of birth or residence. Thus whites and Coloureds living in the Transkei were to be excluded from citizenship. Only Africans were to be eligible. Transkei citizenship would extend not only to Africans living there, but to all Africans of Transkei origin, including those resident in 'white' areas of South Africa. In effect, about one million Africans were to be deprived of rights to South African citizenship and accorded citizenship in the Transkei, an area many had never even seen.

Another guideline laid down for the constitution was that it would have to secure the power of the chiefs. On this point Matanzima was even more emphatic than Verwoerd. He wanted to keep down the number of elected members in the future legislative assembly to thirty, compared to the sixty-four seats allocated to chiefs. Verwoerd, mindful of the need to gain international approval, insisted however that the number of elected members should be raised to forty-five. This still left the chiefs entrenched as a permanent majority in the assembly.

When members of the committee were given the opportunity to discuss their findings at tribal gatherings, they encountered strong opposition, notably in Tembuland and Western Pondoland. But under Matanzima's skilful guidance, the draft constitution was soon cleared through the Transkei Territorial Authority, most of whose members were chiefs and headmen. As chairman, Matanzima decided at a meeting in May 1962 to read out the constitution clause by clause and obtain approval for it then and there. According to an account in the *Rand Daily Mail*, 'the clauses shot through at the rate of one every fifteen seconds'. By the lunch break, it was almost all over.

A general election followed in November 1962, the first to be held in a homeland. The central issue over which it was fought revolved around the question of whether the Transkei should accept Verwoerd's version of separate development or whether it should attempt to pursue a multiracial course. Matanzima stood as a champion of separate development. His main opponent, Chief Victor Poto of Western Pondoland, advocated a multiracial solution for both the Transkei and South Africa and wanted chiefs to be removed from the hurly-burly of politics and placed in a second chamber.

The election verdict was a clear rejection of apartheid. Three out of every four members elected were candidates who favoured Poto's multiracial solution. But once again Matanzima moved deftly. Relying on the support of ex officio chiefs in the legislative assembly, he managed to wheedle enough votes there – fifty-four to forty-nine – to ensure his own election as Chief Minister. He then proceeded to claim he had a mandate to implement separate development policies. 'The people of the Transkei,' he told the assembly, 'have, through the ballot box, expressed their uncompromising rejection of the policy of multi-racialism.' Verwoerd could not have wished for a more dependable ally.

Thus, through a process of chicanery and manipulation, with emergency regulations still in force, the Transkei was transformed from a fledgling Bantustan into a self-governing one. It possessed a flag, a national anthem, a legislative assembly and a cabinet. But its powers were strictly limited. Among the portfolios it was given were finance, justice, education, agriculture, forestry and roads and works. But the South African government retained control over the most important functions including internal security, defence, railways, currency, banking, immigration, posts and telegraphs, national roads, and customs and excise. In Pretoria too lay the right to veto legislation, to cut off funds and to revoke the constitution. As an exercise in self-government it was but a poor imitation.

Yet for Verwoerd, the mere fact of the Transkei's existence as a self-governing territory represented a triumph. It provided proof that the government was fulfilling its promise to allow Africans to be masters in their own areas, without incurring any real cost. It enabled the government to deny citizenship rights in South Africa to Africans of Transkei origin living in 'white' areas on the grounds that they now exercised them in the Transkei. And it created a new stumbling block in the way of African nationalists attempting to unify blacks against their white rulers.

CHAPTER ELEVEN

The Sabotage Campaign

Despite being driven underground, the outlawed African National Congress still held fast for a while to the notion that mass action might yet shake the government. ANC leaders, released from detention after the state of emergency was lifted in August 1960, decided to launch yet another protest campaign in the hope of forcing the government to change course. Assembled at what was called an 'All-in' conference at Pietermaritzburg in March 1961, ANC delegates were told of plans to stage a three-day strike timed to coincide with South Africa's proclamation of a republic on 31 May, to be followed by a campaign of 'mass non-cooperation' if the government refused to heed ANC demands for a national constitutional convention. The belief that such conventional tactics might still work was given new impetus in March 1961 by the government's humiliating defeat in the marathon treason trial which ended after more than four years of hearings in the acquittal of thirty of the defendants. The case against the remaining sixty-one accused was withdrawn. Not one of the original 156 accused had been convicted. The courts thus demonstrated that, despite attempts to manipulate them, they were willing to take an independent stand against the government.

The key figure in the new campaign was Nelson Mandela. Abandoning his legal practice and forsaking all chance of a family life with his young wife Winnie and their two children, he had decided to commit himself wholeheartedly to working as an underground leader. For ten years his movements and activities had been restricted by government banning orders; he had made no speech in public since 1952. Much of his time in the previous four years had been taken up with the proceedings of the treason trial in Pretoria at which he was one of the accused. By chance, his banning order preventing him from attending gatherings had expired shortly before the 'All-in' conference at Pietermaritzburg was due to begin. His sudden appearance there proved to be the highlight of the meeting. Elected head of a National Action Council, he insisted that real action had to be taken. A few days later he was present in court in Pretoria to hear Mr Justice Rumpff terminate the treason trial. Then he disappeared underground, travelling furtively around the country, assuming disguises, avoiding police traps and informers, organizing support for a general strike.

The threat of a general strike provoked the government into ordering a further bout of repression. A new law – the General Law Amendment Act – was introduced in 1961 enabling the police to detain anyone without trial for twelve days. Night after night police raids were conducted in African townships. Some 10,000 Africans were arrested and jailed for pass-law offences. Political meetings were banned throughout the country. Armed police units were deployed in townships to 'encourage' Africans to ignore the call to strike. Employers threatened mass dismissals. Army reservists were called up. For the first time since the end of the Second World War, troops camped in the heart of Johannesburg, ready for action. It was the biggest show of strength the Nationalist government had ever mustered.

In the event, the strike achieved greater results than the government expected. In Johannesburg, Cape Town, Durban and Port Elizabeth there was considerable disruption to commerce and industry. At least half of the African workforce in Johannesburg stayed away. But overall the ANC found the response disappointing. After the first day, Mandela called off the strike: 'It was not the success I had hoped for.'

At a secret meeting of the ANC national executive in June 1961, Mandela put forward proposals for a new strategy. As the failure of the May strike had shown, there was little further to be gained from continuing with conventional methods of protest. Years of demonstrations, boycotts, strikes and civil disobedience had achieved nothing. Each occasion had been met with punitive government action. The mood of the African population, meanwhile, had become increasingly restless and resentful. There was a danger that small, inexperienced groups would break away. Mandela proposed therefore the use of violent tactics. A campaign of sabotage, he believed, would scare off foreign investors, disrupt the economy and eventually cause white opinion to change. Providing there was no loss of life, then race relations in the long term would not be impaired. If nationalist leaders failed to take decisive action, the undercurrents of hatred rising among the African population would eventually surface in outbreaks of terrorism which would have far more damaging consequences.

Mandela's arguments now prevailed. The meeting agreed that while the ANC itself would remain a mass political organization adhering officially to a policy of non-violence, its members would be free to join a separate military wing. The military wing was subsequently given the name *Umkhonto we Sizwe*, meaning The Spear of the Nation. Unlike the ANC which still restricted its membership to Africans, *Umkhonto* opened its ranks to whites, Indians and Coloureds. It was to be an elite group, with a membership of no more than a few hundred.

Among those who played a prominent role in establishing *Umkhonto* were members of the banned Communist Party. After dissolving itself in 1950, to conform to the Suppression of Communism Act, the party had been re-formed secretly in 1953. During the 1950s its members operated clandestinely under cover of other organizations like the Congress of Democrats, the African National Congress and Indian Congress, and through radical publications such as *Advance* and *New Age*. It was only during the 1960 emergency that the Communist Party publicly announced its existence. A leaflet issued at the time called on communists to work in alliance with the Congress movement in preparing for revolution. The party's theory on revolution in South Africa, which was formally adopted at an underground conference in Johannesburg in 1962, envisaged two stages. In the first stage, 'a united front of national liberation', consisting of a Communist Party alliance with the ANC through the military wing of *Umkhonto*, would set out 'to destroy white domination'. In the second stage, South Africa would be transformed into a socialist state. Mandela welcomed the help of communists. As he explained at his trial in 1964:

> For many decades communists were the only political group in South Africa who were prepared to treat Africans as human beings and their equals; who were prepared to eat with us, talk with us, live with us and work with us. They were the only political group which was prepared to work with the Africans for the attainment of political rights and a stake in society. Because of this, there are many Africans who, today, tend to equate freedom with communism.

The operational headquarters of *Umkhonto* was a farmhouse on a smallholding of twenty-eight acres in a peri-urban area north of

Johannesburg known as Rivonia. It was purchased with the aid of funds provided by the Communist Party. From there, members of a national high command, headed by Mandela, determined tactics and targets, organized training and established a network of regional commands. White communists, some with military experience, were prominent as planners and instructors. The Rivonia property also served as a useful hiding place. Mandela lived there for a time while police scoured the country searching for him.

The date set for the start of the sabotage campaign was 16 December 1961, a day then known as the Day of the Covenant which whites celebrated to mark their victory over the Zulu chief, Dingane, at the Battle of Blood River in 1838. Bombs exploded that night at government buildings in Johannesburg, Durban and Port Elizabeth. Leaflets left behind on the streets announced the formation of *Umkhonto* with the warning: 'The time comes in the life of any nation when there remains only two choices: submit or fight. That time has now come to South Africa.' Over the course of the next eighteen months, more than 200 attacks were made, mostly on public buildings, railway lines and power installations in major towns. Most of the sabotage attempts were clumsy and ineffectual. One white activist was arrested in Port Elizabeth after he had tested his homemade bombs by setting them off in his backyard on quiet Sunday afternoons. Despite Mandela's injunction against bloodshed, a score of attacks were made on policemen and Africans thought to be collaborators; other actions endangered lives. But overall the damage caused was minor.

Preparations were also laid for guerrilla activity. Recruits were sent abroad for training to countries sympathetic to the nationalist cause, like Algeria, Cuba, Ghana, Ethiopia, Tanzania and China. In all, some 300 men were dispatched for guerrilla training. Mandela himself left South Africa surreptitiously in January 1961, crossing the border into Bechuanaland, then touring African states to arrange for training facilities. In Addis Ababa, he met his old law partner Oliver Tambo who had left for exile shortly after the Sharpeville shooting to set up an ANC structure abroad. He addressed a meeting of the Pan-African Freedom Movement of east, central and southern Africa. Then he underwent a course of military training in Algeria. 'If there was to be guerrilla warfare,' he said later, 'I wanted to be able to stand and fight with my people and to share the hazards of war with them.' After six months abroad, he returned in secret to South Africa.

Mandela's skill in evading police capture, his daring in leaving the country, making contact with African leaders, then returning to pursue a clandestine existence, turned him into a legendary figure. In the press he became known as the 'Black Pimpernel' and as 'Verwoerd's most wanted man'. But seventeen months after going underground, he was betrayed. Returning by car to Johannesburg from a trip to Natal in August 1962, he was stopped by police and arrested. Whatever suspicions the police may have had, however, they still possessed no evidence to link Mandela with *Umkhonto* and the sabotage campaign. In court he was charged with no more than inciting African workers to strike, and leaving the country without valid travel documents.

Mandela's trial attracted worldwide attention. He conducted his own defence and his manner and bearing before the court in Pretoria marked him out as a leader of distinction. Found guilty on both charges in November 1962, he took the opportunity, when speaking in mitigation of sentence, to deliver a powerful indictment of the government. Every attempt the ANC had made seeking peaceful solutions to the country's ills had been treated with contempt and met with force, he said. 'They set the scene for violence by relying exclusively on violence with which to answer our people and their demands.' And he warned of more violence to come.

He spoke too of his decision to leave home and family and live as a fugitive continually hunted by police. 'No man in his right senses would voluntarily choose such a life in preference to the one of normal, family social life which exists in every civilized country. But there comes a time, as it came in my life, when a man is denied the right to live a normal life, when he can only live the life of an outlaw because the government has so decreed to use the law to impose a state of outlawry upon him.' Mandela was sentenced to five years' imprisonment with hard labour, taken to the maximum security prison on Robben Island, near Cape Town, and held in solitary conditions.

The government, meanwhile, faced a new and more alarming threat. A second underground movement was established by the Pan-Africanist Congress with aims that included the murder of whites. Given the name '*Poqo*', a Xhosa expression meaning 'alone' or 'pure' to emphasize its African origins, it was poorly organized but inspired a large following, notably in the Western Cape, with visions of an imminent black uprising. A leaflet left in a black township outside Cape Town in December 1961 declared: 'We are starting again Africans . . . we die once. Africa will be free on 1 January. The white people shall suffer, the black people will rule. Freedom comes after bloodshed. *Poqo* has started.'

Poqo developed into the most sustained insurrectionary movement that South Africa had ever known. In random, haphazard operations, *Poqo* supporters were responsible for the killing of African policemen and informers, for an uprising in Paarl in November 1962 in which a mob of 250 men attacked the police station and rampaged through the town killing two whites, and for the murder of five whites in a road-builder's camp in the Transkei in February 1963. *Poqo* was also involved in plots to assassinate the Transkei leader, Kaiser Matanzima. In 1963, plans for a more general uprising were prepared by a group of PAC leaders based in exile in Maseru, the capital of Basutoland. Instructions were sent to *Poqo* supporters to manufacture their own weapons with whatever materials were to hand and to collect food and clothing. On a given date, they were to launch simultaneous attacks on strategic points such as police stations and power installations before turning their attention to massacring whites indiscriminately. The plan began to go wrong when Potlake Leballo, an ambitious and wayward figure who had inherited the PAC's leadership from Robert Sobukwe, gave warning of the uprising two weeks before it was due to start at a press conference in Maseru, claiming that 100,000 armed followers were waiting for his signal. As a result of Leballo's impetuous announcement, the colonial authorities in Maseru raided the PAC's premises, seized lists of 10,000 names, arrested PAC officials and closed down their office there. In South Africa, police, probably assisted by the lists of names obtained in Maseru, began to round up hundreds of PAC supporters. The date set for the uprising passed by with only a few incidents recorded. Most activists were either in detention or too demoralized to take action.

A small white sabotage group called the African Resistance Movement also joined the fray. Consisting mainly of young left-wing intellectuals based in Johannesburg and Cape Town, some of them members of the Liberal Party, it added to the toll of attacks on railway lines, power installations and telephone kiosks, aiming to 'inconvenience and confuse, disrupt and destroy'. One of its final acts of sabotage was carried out by a teacher, John Harris, a member of the Liberal Party, who filled a suitcase with explosives and a detonator and left it in the main concourse of Johannesburg station. It exploded, killing an old woman and injuring fourteen other people. Harris was subsequently hanged, the only white saboteur ever to be executed in South Africa.

At each stage of this violent confrontation, the government reacted with increasingly ruthless counter measures. In 1961, Verwoerd appointed a new minister of justice, John Vorster, with instructions to root out all resistance. Vorster, a former *Ossewa Brandwag* general who had been imprisoned without trial by the Smuts government during the Second World War for pro-Nazi activities, took to the task with enthusiasm. Recalling the meeting at which Verwoerd appointed him, he said, 'I remember saying to Dr Verwoerd that he should let me deal with the threat of subversion and revolution in my own way. I told him that you could not fight communism with the Queensberry rules, because if you did then you would lose. He agreed with me and said that he would leave me free to do what I had to do – within reason.' Vorster appointed a new head of the security police, Hendrik van den Bergh, who had been interned with him at Koffiefontein in the Orange Free State during the war and who shared his views about how to tackle the problem. As van den Bergh recalled, 'For me the choice was between revolution, violence and a bloodbath and the so-called rule of law, about which there was all the noise. I looked at my children and those of others and said: "To the devil with the rule of law".' The partnership between Vorster and van den Bergh was to have a devastating effect.

Vorster put into operation new laws which gave him virtually unlimited powers and wiped out a whole range of individual rights and liberties. Under the General Law Amendment Act of 1962, or the 'Sabotage' Act, as it was usually called, Vorster was empowered to order the 'house arrest' of anyone he believed was a threat to security. He could prohibit persons banned or listed under the Suppression of Communism Act from preparing anything for publication, from communicating with each other, from having visitors, from joining organizations, from attending social gatherings. Nothing written or spoken by banned persons was allowed to be published or reproduced in South Africa. In 1962, Vorster silenced 103 people by such means. He also listed 437 people as communists, placed eighteen people under house arrest, outlawed the left-wing Congress of Democrats, banned the radical weekly paper *New Age*, and prohibited meetings on the steps of the Johannesburg City Hall.

He also gave new definitions to the meaning of sabotage. Acts of sabotage henceforth included such offences as tampering with property, possessing firearms, hindering essential services, putting up a poster and unlawful entry. The minimum penalty laid down for offences under the Sabotage Act was five years imprisonment; the maximum was death.

More draconian measures followed in 1963. The General Law Amendment Act in May that year empowered the police to arrest without warrant and detain any person suspected of having committed sabotage, or any offences under the Suppression of Communism Act or the Unlawful Organizations Act, or any person suspected of possessing information about such offences. Detainees could be held in solitary confinement without access to lawyers and family, until they had replied 'satisfactorily' to all questions put by police interrogators. The initial period for which they could be held was ninety days. But the police were entitled to renew the order again and again – 'until this side of eternity', according to Vorster. The Act expressly prohibited the courts from ordering the release of a detainee.

Scores of men and women vanished into jails, to be subjected to solitary confinement and prolonged interrogation. They were allowed no reading material except the Bible, no writing material, no visitors; and their interrogators constantly taunted them with the threat of holding them without trial indefinitely. Their 'cracking point' varied. Writing of her own experience of being held incommunicado for 117 days, Ruth First, a Communist Party member, noted: 'Men holding key positions in the political movement, who had years of hard political experience and sacrifice behind them, cracked like egg shells. Others, with quiet, reticent, self-effacing natures, who had been woolly in making decisions and slow to carry them out, emerged from long spells of isolation shaken but unbroken.' When interrogation methods failed, the police resorted to physical assaults and torture. At first torture was reserved for Africans alone. Later whites were included. In September 1962 an ANC member became the first political detainee to die while under police interrogation.

With information obtained from detainees, the Security Police soon broke the back of underground resistance. On 11 July 1963 they raided *Umkhonto* headquarters at Rivonia, capturing Walter Sisulu and other key figures in the National High Command and acquiring an immense haul of incriminating documents. Among the documents was a draft plan for guerrilla warfare and foreign intervention entitled *Operation Mayibuye*. The Rivonia raid marked the end of *Umkhonto*'s campaign, eighteen months after it had begun. *Poqo* too was broken by mid-1963. The following year the African Resistance Movement was crushed. The Communist Party as well was wiped out in 1964 after a police agent infiltrated its ranks. Its leader, Bram Fischer, a prominent defence lawyer from a distinguished Afrikaner family, was sentenced to life imprisonment. Those activists who evaded arrest soon fled the country. By the end of 1964 hardly any active revolutionaries remained at large in South Africa.

A series of trials followed showing how widespread resistance against the government had been. Nearly 8000 people were charged with offences linked to political defiance. Most were convicted and imprisoned, some for life, some for fifteen or twenty years, others for lesser periods. Nearly fifty men were sentenced to death. Most of the trials were held in relative obscurity. But the Rivonia trial, in which Nelson Mandela, Walter Sisulu and other *Umkhonto* leaders were charged with sabotage and conspiracy to overthrow the government, stirred interest around the world. Lasting for nine months from October 1963 to June 1964, the trial was made all the more memorable by the bearing of the accused and by an impassioned statement from Mandela about the reasons for his participation in *Umkhonto*.

> It was only when all else had failed, when all channels of peaceful protest had been barred to us, that the decision was made to embark on violent forms of political struggle, and to form *Umkhonto we Sizwe*. We did so not because we desired such a course, but solely because the Government had left us with no other choice.

Mandela explained that the initial plan was based on careful analysis of South Africa's political and economic situation.

> We believed that South Africa depended to a large extent on foreign capital and foreign trade. We felt that planned destruction

of power plants and interference with rail and telephone communications, would tend to scare away capital from the country, make it more difficult for goods from the industrial areas to reach the seaports on schedule, and would in the long run be a heavy drain on the economic life of the country, thus compelling the voters of the country to reconsider their position.

Attacks on the economic life of the country were to be linked with sabotage on Government buildings and other symbols of apartheid. These attacks would serve as a source of inspiration to our people. In addition, they would provide an outlet for those people who were urging the adoption of violent methods and would enable us to give concrete proof to our followers that we had adopted a stronger line and were fighting back against Government violence.

In addition, if mass action were successfully organized, and mass reprisals taken, we felt that sympathy for our cause would be roused in other countries, and that greater pressure would be brought to bear on the South African Government.

At the end of a four-hour speech, Mandela declared:

> During my lifetime I have dedicated myself to this struggle of the African people. I have fought against black domination, and I have fought against white domination. I have cherished the ideal of a democratic and free society in which all persons live together in harmony and with equal opportunities. It is an ideal which I hope to live for and achieve. But if needs be it is an ideal for which I am prepared to die.

On 12 June 1964, Mandela, then forty-five years old, was sentenced to life imprisonment. Sisulu and seven others were given the same sentence. That night they were flown to Cape Town and taken by ferry to Robben Island. Known as prisoner no. 466/64, Mandela spent his time labouring in the island's lime quarry, collecting seaweed for fertilizer and studying economics and Afrikaans.

In terms of the objectives that Mandela listed in court, *Umkhonto*'s sabotage campaign was a total failure. The impact on the economy was negligible. Foreign investors, far from being frightened away during the early 1960s, became more deeply involved. Foreign governments, while vociferous in condemning apartheid, were still content to sit on the sidelines. The white electorate, on the rare occasions when it was alerted to the danger of sabotage attacks, reacted in support of the government not in opposition to it. The government, meanwhile, was spurred into taking ever more repressive counter measures, obliterating fundamental civil rights, on the grounds that it was dealing with a communist-inspired conspiracy to overthrow the state. Following the ninety-day detention law came the 180-day detention law, introduced in 1965, and then two years later, the Terrorism Act which allowed the government to detain anyone without trial and in secret for an indefinite period. Once again, nationalist leaders underestimated the power of the government and the way in which it was willing to use it. As a former saboteur, Ben Turok, noted: 'Having talked of fascism for a decade and more, the movements were nevertheless caught by surprise when the police behaved like fascists.' The conspirators also tended to underestimate the effectiveness of police techniques. Joe Slovo, a key *Umkhonto* strategist, who escaped the dragnet, observed in retrospect how 'a mood of carelessness and bravado' had overtaken the conspirators. Few had been prepared to commit themselves to the rigours of a real underground existence. Meanwhile, the site of the Rivonia headquarters had become known to so many activists that it represented a security weakness to the whole movement. 'Under torture,' wrote Turok, 'many victims found to their regret that they knew too much and that the police knew that they knew.' The end result for the nationalist movement was disastrous. With its leaders imprisoned and its internal organizations destroyed, a silence descended for more than a decade.

CHAPTER TWELVE

Heyday of the Whites

White society after two decades of Nationalist rule had become increasingly prosperous and secure. Throughout the 1960s South Africa experienced one of the highest rates of economic growth in the world, second only to that of Japan. Its mines produced record amounts of gold and other minerals. Its factories boomed as domestic consumption soared. Foreign trade with Western countries rose in leaps and bounds. Foreign investors, after recovering from the shock of Sharpeville, found South Africa to be an increasingly lucrative proposition. With returns on investment as high as 20 per cent, British and American companies competed vigorously for positions in new industries. In 1970, according to the *Wall Street Journal*, 260 United States corporations reported their South African ventures to be their most profitable investments abroad. German and French companies joined the throng. The annual net inflow of foreign capital in 1970 rose to a level six times higher of the pre-Sharpeville era. The economic boom also brought to South Africa a flood of white immigrants, mainly from Europe. Between 1960 and 1970 there was a net gain of 250,000 white immigrants. All this gave white South Africans a growing sense of confidence about the future. Black resistance had been crushed. The security net was capable of meeting any contingency. A vast bureaucracy existed to ensure government control. Military strength was being developed. Above all, the government had the resources to make white supremacy a success.

The benefits of Nationalist rule were noticeable particularly among the Afrikaner community. With government assistance, a new class of Afrikaner financiers, businessmen and managers had moved into commanding positions in industry, commerce and banking, areas once the preserve of English-speaking whites. Afrikaner entrepreneurs were now familiar figures on the Johannesburg stock exchange and in international business. Some Afrikaner enterprises, like the Rembrandt Tobacco Company founded by

Anton Rupert, had established world-wide interests. Though English-speaking whites continued to dominate the world of business, industry, mining and the professions, the Afrikaner share of it had steadily increased. Before the war, Afrikaners had controlled less than 10 per cent of trade and commerce, 5 per cent of finance, 3 per cent of industry and less than 1 per cent of mining. In 1945 only one Afrikaner company had a capitalization of £1 million, in contrast to 116 other companies quoted by the Johannesburg stock exchange which had at least that amount. By the mid-1960s, the Afrikaner share of commerce had increased to more than 25 per cent; of finance, to 21 per cent; of industry, to 10 per cent; and of mining, to 10 per cent. A notable advance in the mining sector had occurred in 1964 when Federale Mynbou, an Afrikaner company seeking a way into the goldfields, hitherto the domain of English-speaking enterprise, succeeded in buying out the General Mining and Finance Corporation, one of seven traditional houses which controlled the gold industry.

The public sector was greatly expanded under National Party rule, giving the Afrikaner establishment greater control over the economy and the means to promote Afrikaner business interests. From an average of 6.2 per cent in 1946–50 the public sector's share of fixed investment nearly doubled to 11.5 per cent in 1971–3. The range of state enterprises extended from railways and harbours to iron and steel production, electric power generation, heavy engineering and oil production from coal. At a senior level they were manned almost exclusively by Afrikaners and used as training fields for Afrikaner scientists and business leaders. Government contracts and concessions were frequently steered towards Afrikaner companies. Afrikaner participation in industry was also fostered by parastatal organizations like the Industrial Development Corporation which set up joint ventures with private Afrikaner companies. By 1968 twice as many Afrikaners were employed in government jobs than before the 1948 election that brought the National Party to power.

Out on the *platteland*, Afrikaner farmers were also well served by Nationalist rule. Though the white rural population had continued to shrink – by 1970 more than 80 per cent of the Afrikaner population were living in towns and cities – the influence of the farming community, and in particular Afrikaner farmers, who made up 82 per cent of the total number, remained strong. White farmers were assisted at every turn by favourable prices fixed by state marketing boards, by government subsidies, tariffs, huge research funds, modernization programmes and official controls to ensure a regular supply of cheap black labour. In the five-year period from 1965–70 government aid to white farmers amounted to one fifth of their income. One Afrikaner historian, Leo Marquard, noted that South African agriculture had many of the characteristics of a gigantic system of outdoor relief.

The Afrikaner working class also prospered. The years of Nationalist rule had brought full employment and growing protection of white jobs from black competition. Almost every skilled trade and craft was reserved for white workers. When unskilled whites felt threatened by black competition, the government was ready to make use of legislation introduced in 1956, the Industrial Conciliation Act, enabling it to reserve any occupation for whites only. Between 1956 and 1970 twenty-six job reservation orders were issued. Some orders applied only to small, specific areas protecting a handful of employees; other orders affected entire industries. Thus the jobs of traffic policemen in Cape Town and passenger lift operators in Johannesburg, Bloemfontein and Pretoria were reserved for whites, along with production jobs in the clothing, building, metallurgical and mining industries. By 1970 more than 200,000 jobs were covered by reservation orders. At a more general level, white workers were protected by two cardinal principles the government used to determine its labour policy: firstly, no white worker could be replaced by a black worker in the same job; secondly, no white worker could work under a black. Government employment was also used to shelter a growing number of whites. By 1968, one in five economically-active whites was employed in official agencies at central, provincial and local level. To help unskilled whites move up the employment ladder, the government built secondary, technical and vocational schools specifically for Afrikaners lacking skills. Engineering and medical faculties were established at Afrikaans universities. Compared to English-speaking whites, Afrikaners were still largely confined to lower-paid, less skilled employment; but the gap was steadily narrowing. In 1946 Afrikaner incomes on a per capita basis were just under half that of English-speaking incomes. By 1970 they had passed the two-thirds mark.

The English-speaking community, of course, shared in the prosperity; few other communities in the world possessed such a high standard of living. The northern suburbs of Johannesburg, where many English congregated, were said to have the greatest concentration of swimming pools outside Beverly Hills. Whatever reservations English speakers held about the nature of Nationalist rule, the success it enjoyed made it easier for them to bear. The English response to apartheid in any case had always been ambiguous. English objections to Nationalist rule tended to focus more on the way the Nationalists rode roughshod over the constitution, over the judiciary, the universities and the rule of law than on the iniquities of apartheid. As the voice of English speakers in parliament, the United Party kept alive the notion of opposition to apartheid but never offered any clear alternative to it. The slogan frequently used by the party to sum up its policies was 'White leadership with Justice'. But what this meant in practice was that the United Party voted in favour of residential and social separation and the industrial colour bar; it supported legislation like the Suppression of Communism Act and the Unlawful Organizations Bill which was used to ban the African National Congress and the Pan-Africanist Congress; and it also backed the introduction of ninety-day detention without trial. The party's loyalty to the cause of white supremacy eventually caused a split with its more liberal wing. In 1959, eleven MPs seceded to launch the Progressive Party which opposed the colour bar and advocated a gradual extension of the franchise; but when it came to the test at the polls in 1961, only one Progressive Party candidate, Helen Suzman, was returned by the electorate. She remained the only Progressive MP for the next thirteen years, carrying on a parliamentary struggle single-handed, despised by the Nationalists and ostracized by the United Party. As the Nationalist newspaper, *Die Burger*, once noted with some measure of accuracy, the English 'joined the Progressives, voted for the United Party and thanked God for the Nationalists'.

Nationalist leaders, for their part, saw some advantage in adopting a more conciliatory approach towards the English-speaking community. As the African challenge grew stronger and the outside world became more critical, Verwoerd sought to draw English-speaking whites into the Nationalist fold, portraying it as the rightful home for all whites threatened by the menace of black nationalism and hostile foreigners. His emphasis now was less on Afrikaner nationalism, more on the need for white nationalism. Addressing a National Party congress in Pretoria in August 1961 he declared: 'I see the Nationalist Party today not as an Afrikaans or English or Afrikaans-English party in the future, whatever it might have been in the past; I see it as a party which stands for the preservation of the white man, of the white government in South Africa.' In keeping with this new approach, Verwoerd appointed two English-speaking members to his cabinet. He also authorized the recruitment of white immigrants, including those from Britain, to bolster white numbers. Verwoerd was duly rewarded. In the 1961 election, the National Party for the first time won more votes than opposition parties. In the 1966 election, it won 126 of the 170 parliamentary seats, leaving the United Party with only thirty-nine, increasing its shares of the overall vote from 53.5 per cent to 58.6 per cent. Its share of the English-speaking vote rose to an estimated 16 per cent.

But while welcoming English support, particularly at election times, Verwoerd had no intention of relaxing Afrikaner hegemony. Every opportunity was used to protect and enhance Afrikaner institutions and to ensure that Afrikaner values prevailed. White society had become accustomed to the barriers which separated Afrikaners from English-speakers. By tradition they tended to go to different schools, universities and churches; they supported their own professional organizations, charities, learned societies, savings banks and insurance companies; they held fast to a separate culture and language. Verwoerd sought not only to preserve all this but to impose even more rigid controls.

Nowhere was this more evident than in the field of education. The guidelines for Nationalist thinking on education had been drawn up by a group of university professors and Nationalist politicians in 1948. The aim was to make what was called Christian National Education – *Christelijk Nationaal Onderwijs* – the basis of the public education system. One of its key features was separation between English and Afrikaans education. White children were to be compulsorily divided into two sets of schools, English-medium and Afrikaans-medium. As Professor van Rooy, chairman of the Broederbond, explained in a pamphlet in 1948: 'Our Afrikaans schools must not merely be mother-tongue schools; they must be places where our children will be saturated with the Christian and National spiritual cultural stuff of our nation. . . . We want no mixing of languages, no mixing of cultures, no mixing of religions, and no mixing of races.'

In Nationalist terminology, 'Christian' was equated specifically with the Calvinist creed articulated by the three Afrikaner churches; 'National' was equated, in effect, with Afrikaner nationalism. 'By Nationalist, we mean imbued with the love of one's own language, history and culture.' The thinking that lay behind Christian National Education (CNE) had changed considerably from the time when it had first emerged in the 1900s, in the grim days of Lord Milner's administration. Then it was part of the fight for recognition and equality. Now it was part of the plan for domination. Its most striking aspect was the fundamentalist doctrines put forward as principles on which to base education. The theory of evolution was condemned as opposed to predestination; history and geography were accorded a divine purpose; the task of history teachers was to show that God 'willed separate nations and people, and has given to each separate nation and people its special calling and task and talent'. Educational establishments were to be rigidly controlled. Teachers who were not prepared to subscribe to CNE doctrines would not be appointed.

Under Nationalist rule, CNE ideas gradually took root. From 1951 schoolchildren in the Transvaal and the Orange Free State were required by law to receive their education in their home language. Then in 1967 the government decreed that all Afrikaner and English children, at both primary and secondary level, should attend separate schools. The medium of instruction henceforth would be the home language only. Dual-medium schools were to be gradually disestablished. The Broederbond wanted to go a stage further. At a secret meeting in 1965, its executive committee resolved 'to investigate the possibility of Afrikanerizing English-speakers'.

With similar fixity of purpose, the Nationalists took control of broadcasting. Ostensibly, the South African Broadcasting Corporation functioned as an independent organization. But in 1959 the government appointed a new chairman, Piet Meyer, with plans for a thorough transformation. Meyer was a leading member of the Broederbond; indeed, from 1960 to 1972, while employed as chairman of the SABC, he was also, in secret, chairman of the Broederbond. He soon filled senior management and editorial posts with members of the Broederbond or personnel acceptable to them. In short order, the national radio network was turned into a propaganda arm of the National Party. Each commentary, each news bulletin conveyed the government's view of the world. Independent voices were rarely heard. 'No useful purpose can be served by causing the public distrust of our leaders' policies,' remarked one former Director-General. Programmes were often influenced by Calvinist morality and cultural values. All attempts to introduce television were blocked partly through fear that it would be weighted in favour of English-speaking culture to the disadvantage of Afrikaans culture, partly because of the effect it might have on the black population. The minister responsible for broadcasting, Albert Hertzog, reported to parliament in 1967: 'Friends of mine recently returned from Britain tell me one cannot see a programme which does not show black and white living together, where they are not continually propagating a mixture of the two races.'

An equally tight grip was kept on literature and entertainment. Up until 1962 the government had relied on the Customs Act to keep out of the country what it deemed to be undesirable publications. Over the years more than 9000 titles had been banned from importation, most of them during Nationalist rule. Then in 1963 Verwoerd's government set up a Publications Control Board with power to ban any publication, film, record or art show, including the work of South African writers, artists and sculptors. Besides the usual tests for obscenity and blasphemy, a publication could be banned if it brought the country into ridicule or contempt; if it was harmful to relations between sections of the community; or if it was prejudicial to the safety of the state, the general welfare, or peace and good order. Over the next ten years, the board prohibited 8768 publications. The list ranged from Karl Marx to *Playboy*. Books with titles which included the words revolt, socialism or black were usually suspect. Anna Sewell's children's story about a horse, *Black Beauty*, was embargoed for a time. Books by contemporary Western writers like Mary McCarthy, Philip Roth, John Updike, Jean-Paul Sartre and John Steinbeck were kept out. South African writers like Nadine Gordimer, Lewis Nkosi and Ezekiel Mphalele found their works suppressed in South Africa. The second volume of the *Oxford History of South Africa* could be bought in South Africa only in a special edition, with fifty-three blank pages substituting for a chapter entitled 'African Nationalism in South Africa' which contained policy statements by African leaders. Films like *Bonnie and Clyde*, *Belle de Jour*, *Guess Who's Coming to Dinner* and *Easy Rider* all fell foul of the censor. No film which showed 'scenes of intermingling of

Europeans and non-Europeans' was allowed. In defending the frequent use of censorship laws, government ministers were given to explain that behind many prohibited works lurked the menace of communism. 'When we think of literature containing filth, then we must think of the communist tactic behind it,' said the Minister of Education, Arts and Science, Jan de Klerk. 'It is known to the Government that it is a communist tactic throughout the world to use filth to break the backbone of the nations; to use filth to attack a nation on the cultural and social front, to paralyse people and make them an easy prey for communism.'

The press was exempted from the clutches of the Publications Control Board, but otherwise forced to steer its way through a minefield of legislation. The laws affecting press freedom were complex and ill-defined but rarely invoked, for their real purpose was to intimidate journalists rather than to stifle them. For the Afrikaans press this presented little difficulty. Afrikaans newspapers all identified closely with the government, seeing themselves as representatives solely of Afrikaner interests. But the English press, though being primarily concerned with English interests, frequently drew attention to the plight suffered by the rest of the population under apartheid laws and consequently were obliged to run the gauntlet of government harassment. The government's method for dealing with left-wing publications like *Guardian*, *Advance*, *New Age* and *Fighting Talk* was simply to close them down, using security legislation. Individual critics were silenced by banning order. By 1968 the list extended to some 600 people, none of whose statements or writings could be published. But with the main body of the English press the government was more cautious, reluctant to damage South Africa's claim to possess the 'freest press in Africa'. From Malan onwards, Nationalist prime ministers sought to 'discipline' the press by threatening new statutory controls rather than by resorting to overt censorship. Under constant official pressure, newspaper proprietors and editors slowly gave way. As the price for avoiding inclusion in the 1963 Publications and Entertainments Act, authorizing direct censorship, the main newspapers agreed to operate their own 'code of conduct'. Often unsure of what they could print, editors resorted more and more to self-censorship. Outright attacks on apartheid were rare. The English press continued to expose the worst excesses of government policy, but the costs both for newspaper proprietors and for editors and reporters involved were usually high. In 1965, the *Rand Daily Mail*, a persistent critic of the government, published a series of articles on brutal prison conditions. The government responded by raiding the offices of the *Rand Daily Mail* and by banning the informant on whose evidence the articles were largely based. The chief editor, Laurence Gandar, a reporter, Benjamin Pogrund, and several of the newspaper's informants were then hauled before the courts accused of contravening the Prisons Act. After a series of trials lasting more than four years, the *Rand Daily Mail* and others accused were found guilty. Gander and Pogrund were given light fines. But the legal costs for the newspaper were huge.

Apart from the English language press only a small minority within the white community kept alive the voice of dissent. Many liberal whites ceased to be active in the face of government persecution. The price too often was police harassment, social ostracism, and unwelcome attention – threatening and abusive telephone calls, slashed tyres, shots from passing cars, petrol bombs. There were also doubts about the cause. As Archbishop Denis Hurley noted about white liberals in 1966: 'There is always that paralysing fear that a benevolent attitude towards non-whites must culminate in black Government, and the end of the white man in South Africa.'

The small multi-racial Liberal Party soldiered on for several years, adopting a more radical programme as its black membership increased. By 1960 it accepted universal adult suffrage and endorsed tactics like boycotts and passive resistance, conceding that white supremacy would never yield 'to mere verbal persuasion'. Some Liberal Party members, like John Harris, the Johannesburg bomber, participated in the sabotage campaign, making it easier for the government to discredit and harass other Liberal Party members who abhorred such activity. As Justice Minister, John Vorster was already moving in for the kill:

> No matter what can be said of liberalism in other parts of the world, it is my conviction that liberalism, as manifested in South Africa, is, according to my lights, nothing other than the precursor of communism. It is typical of the communists that they use liberalism as a screen behind which they can hide. . . . The

difference between the communists and the liberals is getting smaller and smaller, so that a person will eventually need to use a magnifying glass to see those differences.

The end for the Liberal Party came in 1968 when the government passed the Prohibition of Political Interference Act making interracial political activity illegal. It became a criminal offence for any South African to belong to any political organization with a membership of different races. In addition it became illegal for any person to address a political meeting if the majority of the audience belonged to a race other than his or her own. Unable to function as a multiractial party, the Liberal Party decided to disband. In terms of its membership – numbering less than 4000 – it was insignificant. But it had nevertheless served as a platform for leading white liberals like Alan Paton and had provided one of the few areas of racial contact left in the country.

A body of liberal opinion survived in the multiracial 'English-speaking' churches, notably in the Methodist, Anglican and Roman Catholic churches, and in organizations like the South African Institute of Race Relations, the National Union of South African Students and the Black Sash, a women's group concerned with civil rights whose most characteristic form of protest was to stand in public places in silent vigil, wearing black sashes. The churches frequently spoke out against the injustices of apartheid, passing resolutions, organizing deputations, publishing pastoral letters, belabouring the government over incidents like the Sharpeville shootings, the state of emergency, the detention laws. Yet there was always a degree of ambivalence about the position they took. The protests were mostly confined to church leaders; their white parishoners remained largely unmoved. Most congregations were segregated. The churches' leadership, moreover, was kept firmly in white hands, even though their membership was predominantly black. Internal practices tended to reflect society outside. Black ministers, for example, were invariably given far lower stipends than white ministers. To many blacks, the ringing condemnations of apartheid sounded hollow.

The Dutch Reformed Church, meanwhile, stood as a bulwark behind the government, defending its actions at every turn, binding the Afrikaner people to its Calvinist dogma, providing theological justification for apartheid whenever necessary. More than half of the white population belonged to its three denominations. The principal church, the *Nederduits Gereformeerde Kerk*, contained within its membership most leading politicians, civil servants, military and police officials, provincial and local councillors and academics, indeed most of the Afrikaner establishment – the National party at prayer, it was often said. Again and again, from one pulpit to another, the same biblical texts were used to explain the folly of attempts to unify mankind and to confirm that the leaders of Afrikanerdom alone had been appointed by divine sanction to guide South Africa's destiny.

A handful of Afrikaner clergy dared to defy the creed of apartheid, drawing upon themselves the wrath of the entire Afrikaner establishment. In 1961, eleven Dutch Reformed Church theologians published an attack on racial discrimination entitled *Vertraagde Aksie* (*Delayed Action*). One of the principal contributors, Professor Albert Geyser, who held the chair of New Testament Theology at Pretoria, became the target of a sustained vendetta. Refusing to accept a *Hervormde Kerk* law which placed a racial restriction on church membership, Geyser was called to account before the *Hervormde Kerk* Commission of the Assembly and given one week in which to resign his chair. Simultaneously three of his students charged him with heresy and insubordination. After a protracted trial he was convicted of heresy and defrocked. Taking the matter to the South African Supreme Court, he was subsequently reinstated as a minister. But he and his wife had to endure ostracism from the Afrikaner community and physical threats.

Another prominent rebel, Beyers Naudé, came from within the very heart of Afrikanerdom. The son of a legendary Boer War chaplain, a distinguished minister in the Transvaal Synod of the *Gereformeerde Kerk* and a member of the Broederbond, Naudé had begun to question apartheid doctrine after the Sharpeville shooting. As a delegate to the Cottesloe conference in 1960 he approved decisions attacking the whole basis of apartheid. In 1962, along with Albert Geyser and other liberal figures, he helped to launch a new monthly journal, *Pro Veritate*, hoping to keep alive a dialogue on Christian issues within the Dutch Reformed Church. The journal was immediately attacked in the Afrikaner press as a 'propagandist newspaper', and its list of subscribers eventually dwindled to less than a dozen. In 1963 Naudé was offered a position as director of a new ecumenical organization, the Christian Institute, set up to promote a dialogue between Afrikaans and English-speaking Christians and to work for reconciliation between the races in South Africa. The church warned that if he accepted the post, he could no longer hope to remain a minister. After agonizing over the matter, Naudé decided to give up his position in the church. He also broke with the Broederbond, knowing full well the cost to himself and his family: 'The Afrikaner who deviates is apt to be labelled a traitor, to be accused of falling for "the bribes of the English", a sell-out of his people, and a political renegade.'

From outside South Africa, foreign critics kept up a barrage of attacks on the government. Much of the anti-apartheid activity abroad was organized by South African exiles who had left the country after Sharpeville and during the wave of repression that followed. London became the main centre for attempts to influence international opinion. Western governments took note of anti-apartheid activity but tended to confine their actions to a minimum. South Africa was forced to withdraw from the Food and Agricultural Organization, the World Health Organization and other technical and scientific bodies. In 1963 the United Nations Security Council resolved to ban the sale of arms to South Africa. The United States and Britain complied, but France, West Germany and Canada did not. South Africa was excluded from the Olympic Games and barred from international championship competition in sports ranging from basketball to weightlifting. Gestures of support were made to the African nationalist movement. In 1961, the ANC leader, Chief Lutuli, was awarded the Nobel Peace Prize. There was also much debate about economic sanctions. Ronald Segal, writing on sanctions in 1964, noted: 'Those who wanted sanctions dismissed all arguments against them as trivial or irrelevant, while those who opposed such action denounced it as illegal, impractical and economically calamitous. It was a dialogue of pulpits, with the phrases of revolution.' Little was to change over the next twenty years.

Verwoerd remained as uncompromising towards foreign criticism as to domestic criticism, refusing to permit any kind of variance. When in the early 1960s the British Embassy in South Africa decided to mark the Queen's official birthday by holding a single reception open to all races instead of giving two separate receptions as the convention had been before – one for whites only in the morning and a racially mixed one in the afternoon – Verwoerd's cabinet solemnly decreed that no minister or official could henceforth attend a racially mixed diplomatic function. A planned visit to Cape Town in 1965 by the aircraft carrier, the USS *Independence*, had to be cancelled because Verwoerd ruled that no black American airmen would be allowed to land at South African airfields. In sport, even though many white South Africans were dismayed at the way their international sporting links were being broken one by one, Verwoerd insisted upon strict segregation: no racially mixed teams from abroad would be allowed to tour South Africa; no mixed South African teams would be permitted to compete abroad; no concessions would be made, whatever the cost.

Under Verwoerd's rule, then, white society became increasingly insular and inbred, kept in isolation from the views and lifestyles of the modern world as well as from the majority of the population. It was a society which expected conformity and which regarded dissent, however trivial, as a form of treachery. 'Opposing apartheid,' observed a prominent Afrikaner member of the Progressive Party, 'is worse than murder to some Afrikaners. You endanger the nation by refusing to conform.' Through rigorous control of the media, Verwoerd had little difficulty in convincing most whites that the coalition of forces ranged against South Africa – communist states, the Afro-Asian bloc, 'leftists' and 'liberals' in Western countries, and revolutionaries from within – was sufficiently threatening to warrant any action the government took to protect the nation. Each new piece of legislation strengthening the government's hand, each inroad made into civil liberties, evoked less and less protest from within the white community. Those advocating concessions or conciliation were simply accused of endangering white survival. Though government action was often taken in the name of defending Western civilization, there was never any doubt about what the ultimate purpose was. 'Our motto,' declared Verwoerd in 1965, 'is to maintain white supremacy for all time to come over our own people and our own country, by force if necessary.'

To virtually the entire white population – totalling more than 3.5 million in the mid-1960s – white rule was an unquestionable virtue. Whatever differences may have separated Afrikaans and English speakers, the prosperity that white South Africa enjoyed was considered by both communities to be a mark of its success. Outwardly, South Africa could claim many of the trappings of a Western democracy: a parliamentary system of government, an independent judiciary, an outspoken press, a market economy, full churches, generous charities. All this helped to reassure whites that, whatever faults they possessed, South Africa had a rightful place in the Western camp. If harsh police methods were sometimes employed, then they were needed, so it was said, solely to deal with a troublesome minority of the population stirred up by paymasters in Moscow. When defending their system of racial rule, white South Africans were also apt to point to the turmoil which afflicted black African states as a far worse alternative. The fact that the benefits of white rule were confined largely to whites themselves was taken for granted.

A notable celebration of white rule took place in 1966 at the Voortrekker Monument, a massive granite temple built on the heights overlooking Pretoria to commemorate the deeds of the Boer trekkers who broke away from British rule to found their own republic. Its foundation stone had been laid in 1938 to mark the centenary of the Great Trek and since 1949 it had been open to the public, albeit on a segregated basis. In front of the main entrance was a bronze statue of a *voortrekker* mother with her two children, and carved on the wall behind were four black wildebeest. According to the official guide in use at the time, both were symbolic.

> The statue of the Voortrekker Mother and her children symbolizes white civilization while the black wildebeest portray the ever threatening dangers of Africa. The determined attitude and triumphant expressions on the women's face suggest that the dangers are receding and that the victory of civilization is an accomplished fact.

The celebration in 1966 was held to mark the fifth anniversary of the founding of the Republic. A crowd of 500,000 whites attended. Though it was mainly an Afrikaner affair, large contingents of children from both English and Afrikaans schools were assembled to give the occasion a 'national' flavour. At the end of a spectacular military display, Verwoerd rose to make the main speech.

> We seek peace and friendships with the great nations of the world [he said]. But we will not sacrifice this Republic and its

independence. If we are forced to by aggression, we will defend it with all we have at our disposal. This republic is not to be taken away from this new nation which has come so far and is so proud of what it does.

Three months after that celebration, on 6 September 1966, Verwoerd lay dead, stabbed to death by a parliamentary messenger as he sat on his bench in the National Assembly waiting for the day's session to begin. His assailant, Demetrio Tsafendas, the illegitimate son of a Greek father and a mother of Portuguese and African descent, had a long record of mental instability and was later found to be insane and unfit to stand trial. Verwoerd at the time was at the peak of his power. He had endured the Sharpeville crisis, crushed African resistance, established a republic, defied world opinion and laid the foundation for a system of racial domination that many whites thought would be indestructible. That year he had been rewarded with the greatest electoral victory ever won by the National Party. No other Afrikaner leader in this century, not even Smuts, had gained such ascendancy among his own people and among the English-speaking community. No other Afrikaner leader wrought such harsh and terrible change. In the circumstance, therefore, it was a considerable irony that Verwoerd met his death at the hands of an assassin who claimed no motive.

The white community took Verwoerd's death in its stride. The system by now was strong enough to take such shocks. Nor were there any fears about the future. Verwoerd's successor chosen by the National Party was John Vorster who, as minister of justice, had made such a success of smashing black opposition. Immediately upon being elected, Vorster declared: 'My role is to walk further along the road set by Hendrik Verwoerd.'

CHAPTER THIRTEEN

The Black Underworld

In the terminology commonly used in South Africa, the rest of the population other than white was known as 'non-white'. It was a term which symbolized the subordinate status accorded to four-fifths of the population. Wherever possible, non-whites were kept separate from the white caste. In public buildings, on trains and buses, at airports and railway stations, at race courses and sports grounds, in restaurants, hotels, cinemas and theatres, on the beaches, in graveyards, the non-white population was shunted into separate facilities. Signs declaring *'Blanke'* and *'Nie-Blanke'* proliferated on park benches, elevators, libraries, liquor stores and taxis. The white obsession with separate facilities reached in every direction. In 1970 a string quartet composed of Africans entered a musical competition organized by the South African Broadcasting Corporation to commemorate the two hundreth anniversary of Beethoven's birthday. When it was discovered that the players were black, the quartet was barred from participating in the competition. A spokesman explained: 'Different races perform best in their own idiom.'

To keep the non-white population confined to its subservient role, a vast apparatus of laws and regulations was employed, giving the government control of every aspect of its existence – employment, residence, domicile, movement. No section of the population was left untouched. Whenever the need arose, new laws were added. No less than 231 different measures were introduced between 1948 and 1971, by which time the apartheid machine was reaching its zenith. At every turn the non-white population endured greater restriction and greater hardship.

The foundation stone of the system was the Population Registration Act of 1950 under which every citizen was classified according to race and required to carry an identification document recording it. A large bureaucracy was created to determine on which side of the colour line everyone should stand. Initially the government specified three racial groups: white, Coloured or African. The criteria used for deciding who was white and hence destined for a privileged existence was that the person in question should either be 'obviously white in appearance' or 'white by general repute and acceptance'. The criteria were subsequently tightened. In 1962 the definition of a 'white' person was altered, making it obligatory for appearance and acceptance by the community to be considered together. A further amendment in 1967 made descent of primary importance: a person might appear to be white and might be accepted as white but first had to prove that his parents were white. Some of the early classification procedures used by white officials were crude in the extreme; on occasion the 'pencil in the hair' technique was allowed to determine a person's fate. On payment of a prescribed fee, anyone could object to the racial classification he or she had been given. But so were members of the public entitled to object to a particular classification, making life for those on the border line especially hazardous, never free from the risk of being denounced. If officials had reason to believe a wrong classification had been made, they were empowered to reopen a case. At the stroke of a pen, a white could be turned into a Coloured, and a Coloured into an African, changing their entire existence. By 1961 the Population Registration Appeal Board had tried some 3000 white-Coloured cases and 42,000 Coloured-Asian-African cases. By 1968 the number of appeals had dropped to about 100 a year. But the procedures became more complex after the government decided to divide the Coloured classification into seven further categories: Cape Coloured, Cape Malay, Griqua, Indian, Chinese, 'Other Asiatic' and 'Other Coloured'. Under another law, the African population was subdivided into eight tribal groups. Whites, of course, whether Portuguese, Greek, English or Afrikaners were all considered to belong to the same group, though their cultural and language differences were often more marked than those of the African population.

The suffering caused by racial classification laws was particularly severe for Coloureds at the white end of the spectrum. Many 'Coloureds' were fair enough of skin to be able to 'pass' for white. They had established themselves as whites, acquired white jobs, white salaries and white lifestyles. Subjected to the scrutiny of government officials, however, hundreds failed to stay on the white side of the line. Families lost homes and property; children were obliged to leave white schools and accept an inferior education; jobs were forfeited. Some families found themselves divided into different groups, their whole lives thrown into turmoil. Couples married for years were forced to live apart. In 1966 it was estimated that 148,000 Coloureds on the borderline had avoided applying for identity cards, despite the risk of prosecution, for fear that they would jeopardize their employment, their children's education, their property, their social status. Lower down the scale there were thousands with an African ancestry but light enough skins who had managed to pass into the Coloured world. Many were summarily reclassified and consigned back to the African underworld.

Another mainstay of the system, the Group Areas Act, described by Malan as 'the kernel of apartheid' also caused severe hardship. In the name of preserving racial harmony, the government apportioned towns and cities throughout South Africa on a racial basis, uprooting whole communities that stood in the way. By 1968 more than 1000 group areas had been proclaimed – nearly 600 for whites, 300 for Coloureds and 130 for Indians. The pattern was nearly complete. In only three urban centres with populations exceeding 20,000 had group areas not yet been demarcated. Once again, the Coloured community bore the brunt of the changes. By tradition and by law, Coloureds in Cape Province had been free to live anywhere they could afford. Under the terms of the Group Areas Act, however, tens of thousands of Coloureds were compelled to leave areas where they had settled for generations. Compensation was paid to families forced to leave but usually at derisory rates.

The symbol of this great upheaval became District Six, an area close to the centre of Cape Town occupied by Coloureds since 1834. As its residents admitted, District Six was largely a slum. 'It was drab, dingy, squalid and overcrowded,' wrote Richard Rive, a distinguished author who lived there. 'Those who could moved out for reasons of upward social mobility.' But it also had immense vitality. 'District Six had a mind and soul of its own. It had a homogeneity that created a sense of belonging.' In 1966, District Six was proclaimed a white area and the 40,000 Coloureds living there were ordered to remove to a bleak tract of land ten miles from the centre of Cape Town. A similar fate befell the Indian community in Durban which once owned a quarter of the total area of the city. In the Transvaal, hundreds of Indian businessmen and traders were expelled from central business districts, to the considerable advantage of white shopkeepers. By the end of 1972, the total numbers forced to move by orders under the Group Areas Act comprised 44,885 Coloured families, 27,694 Indian families and 1513 white families. A further 27,694 Coloured families, 10,641 Indian families and 135 white families had been given notice to move. In all that amounted to one quarter of the Coloured and Indian communities. White property speculators were able to amass fortunes out of the forced sale of many of their houses.

The treatment meted out to the Coloured population stirred the conscience of some moderate Afrikaners. No other population group had such close ties to the Afrikaner people. Descended partly from Afrikaner ancestors who had interbred first with slaves brought to the Cape from Malaya, India and Ceylon as well as parts of Africa and then with indigenous tribes, the Coloured population, numbering 2 million by 1970, largely spoke Afrikaans, often bore Afrikaner names and worshipped at their own branch of the Dutch Reformed Church. Under Nationalist rule, they had been deprived of voting rights, subjected to discriminatory laws and uprooted from their homes. The loss of churches to Coloured communities under Group Areas Act orders aroused deep misgivings among Afrikaner clergy in the *Nederduitse Gereformeerde Sendingkerk*. A church report in 1967 spoke of 'suffering too deep to understand' caused to Coloureds forced to leave District Six. The government, however, was impervious to such views. In 1968, when it appeared likely that Coloured voters would elect members of the opposition Progressive Party to represent them in parliament for the four seats still left to them, the government abolished Coloured representation altogether, thus severing the last link that the non-white population had with the main political process. As compensation, the Coloureds were given a partly-elected Coloured Persons' Representative Council. But the Council possessed no real power nor any credibility. When anti-apartheid candidates gained a majority in the first elections in 1969, the government used nominees, many of whom had been defeated in the election, to ensure that a pro-apartheid party emerged in control.

For the African population, the greatest daily burden of life under apartheid was the pass law system. It governed the movement of Africans throughout South Africa encompassing their entire existence. Every African over the age of sixteen was required to carry a passbook proving that he or she was 'entitled to be, remain, work or reside' in a 'white' area. Passbooks contained an African's photo-graph, tribe, identity number, tax stamp and employer's signature which had to be renewed each month to prove that the holder was still employed. If an African failed to produce a passbook on demand, he was sent to prison. If an African failed to prove his right to be present in a white area, he was 'endorsed out' – ordered to return to a homeland. Under Section 10 of the Bantu Urban Area Consolidation Act of 1952, the only Africans entitled to remain longer than seventy-two hours in a white area were those who could prove either continuous residence in the area since birth or continuous work in the area for the same employer for ten years or continuous lawful residence in the area for at least fifteen years. In criminal prosecutions under Section 10, an accused person was presumed to be unlawfully present within an area until proved otherwise. The operation of the pass laws meant that no African in an urban area was secure from police questioning and harassment at any time of day or night, even in his own home. It also meant that families were split apart, wives prevented from living with their husbands and children separated from their parents.

The impact of the pass law system was described vividly by Lewis Nkosi in an article in the *Golden City Post* in 1959 entitled 'I am a Reference Book'. Commenting on the death of two Africans who crept under blazing factory walls to rescue their passbooks, Nkosi wrote:

It is not heroism – and certainly nothing like bravado – that can make a man go to his death in an attempt to save a Pass Book.

The motive is simply FEAR – the realization of what his life will be worth without a reference book.

For a reference book has ceased to be a mere form of identification. It is interchangeable with the man himself. . . .

I do not live apart from my own reference book any more. In fact I have decided I AM THE REFERENCE BOOK.

It stands for my personality. It delineates my character. It defines the extent of my freedom. Where I can live, work and eat.

Whenever I see a police constable looking at me, the lifting of his eyes is at once adequate to make me understand that my right to walk the streets, to be about in a White area, even to confront my White fellow being with the sheer physical fact of my existence is now being called into question.

And the only answer equally adequate is the production of a reference book.

An African lawyer, Godfrey Pitje, writing in 1961 about 'The effect of the Pass Laws on African Life', had this to say:

> There is a rancid smell of slavery – chattel slavery – about it. Under the reference book system you are either employed or a vagrant or an idler or an undesirable element. . . . The reference book is an instrument for socio-economic regimentation, dragooning and control. It creates a pattern with machine-like efficiency, and brings each and every individual throughout life under the direct eye and vigilance of the State machinery. It is an instrument for economic exploitation, social control and regimentation, forced labour and political persecution. It is more than a badge of inferiority. It is a merciless fetter strangling the life of the Black millions of South Africa.

During the 1960s, as the government worked systematically to stem the flow of Africans from rural to urban areas and to destroy all notion that urban Africans could have a permanent place in 'white' towns, ever greater use was made of the pass law system and other control measures. A new sense of urgency prevailed. By 1960, according to the census taken that year, the total African population had risen to nearly 11 million. It was continuing to grow at a rate of 3.5 per cent a year. In urban areas, despite influx control, it was increasing twice as fast as the white population. By 1960, some 3.5 million Africans lived in urban areas, nearly 1 million more than the number of whites. In rural areas, where the white population was constantly preoccupied with *die beswarting van die platteland* – the blackening of white countryside – the African population totalled 3.5 million, outnumbering whites by seven to one. In many districts supposedly 'white' areas were almost entirely black.

With remorseless vigour, the government set about reducing the urban African population wherever possible, stripping urban Africans of what few rights they possessed, and ridding white rural areas of vast numbers of blacks. Government ministers stressed that all Africans in white areas – whether urban or rural – were there purely on a temporary basis.

> It is accepted government policy that the Bantu are only temporarily resident in European areas of the Republic for as long

as they offer their labour there, [declared a government paper, General Circular 25 in 1967]. As soon as they become, for some reason or another, no longer fit for work or superfluous in the labour market, they are expected to return to their country of origin or the territory of the national unit where they fit in ethnically if they were not born or bred in the homeland. . . . It must be stressed here that no stone is to be left unturned to achieve the settlement in the homelands of non-productive Bantu at present residing in the European areas.

Among those whom the circular defined as 'non-productive' were 'the aged, the unfit, widows and women with dependent children'. A government minister estimated that of 6 million Africans in white areas, 4 million were 'surplus appendages' suitable for deportation to black homelands.

As the policy took effect, the number of prosecutions under pass laws rose sharply. In 1968 they reached a peak of 700,000, affecting one in twenty Africans. Countless thousands found themselves 'endorsed out' of urban areas. In the Transvaal and the Orange Free State a massive urban relocation programme was carried out. African townships considered to be within commuting distance of a home-land were 'deproclaimed' and their residents moved to new rural townships built in the homelands. In some cases, such as Nelspruit and Lichtenburg, the entire African population was moved. In other cases, government officials concentrated on removing the unemployed, the elderly and disabled, women and children, leaving behind African workers to live in all-male hostels and visit their families on a weekly or monthly basis. Wherever possible the boundaries of homelands were redrawn to include existing townships. By such means the government deprived Africans of their right to live and work in urban areas.

In place of a stable, urban population, what the government wanted was a workforce composed principally of migrant labour. A government minister explained to the House of Assembly in February 1968: 'We are trying to introduce the migratory labour pattern as far as possible in every sphere, that is in fact the entire basis for our policy as far as the White economy is concerned.' With migrant workers circulating continuously between black homelands and white-owned enterprises in urban areas, the government saw a means of reconciling the white need for labour with its own determination to prevent permanent black urbanization. African workers could be turned into commuters, if they lived in homelands close enough to urban areas, or migrants if the distance was too far. The basis on which government planners made their calculations was that daily travel to work was possible within a distance of seventy miles and weekly travel was possible within four hundred miles. Alternatively, African workers could be engaged in the traditional manner on annual contracts, housed in all-male compounds, and released to visit their families in the homelands at the end of a year.

To reinforce the migrant labour system, new measures were introduced during the 1960s. The network of government labour bureaux, previously confined to the towns, was extended in 1968 to the homelands to control the flow of African labour at its source. Henceforth all work seekers were required to register there and obtain labour contracts before leaving for white areas. Labour contracts were now limited to a period of one year only, after which workers had to return to their homeland to reregister. In effect, the regulations prevented workers from gaining residential rights in urban areas. In 1970 it was estimated that more than 2 million men spent their lives circulating as migrants between their homes and urban employment. Many of them were deprived of all normal family and social life, confined for months on end to a bleak and barren existence in overcrowded barracks notorious for high rates of drunkenness and violence. Others spent hours each day travelling long distances to work in packed buses and trains, rising before dawn and returning home late into the night.

As part of its influx control policy, the government also set out to keep black townships as unattractive places as possible. Few urban amenities were ever provided. Black businessmen were prevented by government restrictions from expanding their enterprises there. Regulations issued in 1963 stated that no African could carry on more than one business and that African businessmen were to confine their activities to providing 'the daily essential necessities of the Bantu'. These did not include businesses such as dry cleaners, garages and petrol-filling stations. No new licences for them would be granted. 'Existing dry cleaners, garages and petrol-filling stations may, however, be allowed to continue until the opportunity arises to close them or to persuade their owners to transfer their businesses to a Bantu town in the Bantu homelands.' Nor were Africans allowed to establish companies or partnerships in urban areas, or to construct their own buildings. These had to be built and leased from the local authority. By such means the growth of an African entrepreneurial class in 'white' urban areas was deliberately obstructed.

The provision of housing was also affected. Initially, the government's aim was to eradicate black slums and black freehold areas like Sophiatown and regroup the African population in new townships. With his customary eye for detail, Verwoerd declared that black townships had to be 'an adequate distance from the white township . . . preferably separated by an area of industrial sites . . . [with] suitable open buffer spaces around . . . and a considerable distance from the main, and more particularly, national roads.' The need for security was a constant theme in the government's housing policy; most townships were built with a limited number of entrances which could be easily sealed off by police. The new townships duly took shape. In Johannesburg's South Western Townships, an area ten miles from the city centre, known from 1963 as Soweto, nearly 50,000 family houses for Africans were built between 1948 and 1966. The housing was mostly identical four-room brick 'matchboxes', as residents called them, stretching in monotonous rows across a bleak landscape. Only a small proportion had electricity or adequate plumbing. Houses were allocated on a tribal basis: Sotho in one area, Xhosa in another, in an attempt to perpetuate tribal divisions, a policy which caused widespread resentment. Few paved roads or proper pavements were built in Soweto. There were no modern shopping centres or office blocks, not a single pharmacy or bakery. Because of restrictions placed on African trading rights, three-quarters of the groceries consumed by Sowetans were purchased in white shops in Johannesburg. But for all that conditions in new townships like Soweto were a considerable improvement on the scattered slums from where many residents came. Moreover, from 1949, Africans were entitled to build houses on thirty-year leasehold plots. A small group of Africans were wealthy enough to afford to construct luxury mansions for themselves. Then in the 1960s, after the government decided to divert the African population increasingly towards homelands, black townships were deliberately neglected. From the mid-1960s the construction of family housing in urban areas virtually came to a halt. Priority was given instead to building housing in the homelands and hostels in urban areas for migrant labour. In 1968 the government decreed that the thirty-year leasehold schemes would be discontinued.

Thirty-year leases could no longer be transferred and improvements could be sold only to local authorities. Slum conditions began to reappear in many urban locations. By 1970 an average of thirteen people lived in each house in Soweto. By 1972 the housing backlog in Johannesburg was even larger than it had been during the 1940s.

Through the use of harsh and arbitrary measures, the government succeeded in reducing the rate of African urbanization. But it still failed to halt the increase. Though the population of nearly two-thirds of African townships in white areas was reduced during the 1960s, the proportion of Africans living legally in towns rose from 31.8 per cent in 1960 to 33.1 per cent in 1970. The actual numbers grew from 3.5 million to 5.1 million, nearly two million more than the number of urban whites. Thousands more, possibly as many as 250,000, lived in urban areas illegally, finding employment as peddlars, small-scale merchants, backyard mechanics and in other low-paid jobs. In every one of South Africa's major cities, non-whites outnumbered whites, forming roughly two-thirds of the population of Johannesburg, Cape Town and Durban. Whatever action the government took, the trend continued upward. A special effort was made to eliminate the African population from the Western Cape, in particular from the Greater Cape Town area, on the grounds that it was 'the natural labour field of the White man and the Coloured man'. Under the Coloured Labour Preference Area policy, thousands were deported to homelands. But the African population in Greater Cape Town still increased between 1960 and 1970 from 65,000 to 110,000. The government's determination, however, did not wane. 'It remains Government policy,' said the minister in charge of the Bantu Affairs Department in 1970, 'that our white cities, our metropolitan areas, will, in future, become whiter and not blacker.'

The disadvantages under which the African population laboured in the 'white' economy were legion. Africans were barred by law from skilled work, from forming registered unions, from taking strike action. In industrial disputes, armed police were often called in by white employers to deal with the workforce. If Africans lost their jobs, they faced the possibility of deportation. Job reservation measures were extended in 1970 making it possible for the authorities to prohibit the employment of Africans in any job, in any area, or in the service of any employer. The extent to which the government was prepared to go was illustrated in 1970 when the Minister of

Bantu Administration gave notice of his intention to ban the employment of Africans as counter assistants in shops and cafés; as professional or commercial receptionists; as telephone operators in shops, offices and factories and hotels; or as clerks, cashiers or typists in shops, offices and factories, except in municipal African townships, homelands and border areas. After a public outcry, the Minister was forced to think again.

Throughout commerce and industry wage rates were kept low. On the gold mines, black wages between 1911 and 1971 actually fell in 'real' terms. The gap between white and black wages in the mines meanwhile steadily increased: in 1911 white miners earned on average eleven times more than Africans; in 1971 they earned on average twenty times more than Africans. Black workers in manufacturing fared better, earning by 1966 more than two and a half times as much as black mineworkers. The ratio of white wages to African wages in manufacturing in 1970 was no more than six times higher. But a considerable proportion of the workforce still received wages which fell short of providing the costs of family subsistence. In 1970 an employers' organization, the Associated Chambers of Commerce, calculated that the average industrial wage was 30 per cent below the minimum monthly budget needed for a Soweto family of five. The overall comparison between white and black wage increases was striking; between 1948 and 1973 white workers' wages rose by 416 per cent – black workers' wages by 36 per cent.

There were similar disadvantages in the field of education. Though more schools were built and the number of pupils increased from 1 million in 1955 to 2.7 million in 1970, African education suffered from low standards, crowded classrooms and poorly-trained teachers. It was markedly inferior to white education. In 1970 the government spent sixteen times more on white education per capita than on black education. A survey that year showed that of 1 million South Africans who had completed a full school programme, some 88 per cent were white, 7 per cent were African, 3 per cent were Coloured and 2 per cent were Indian. In 1970 less than 5 per cent of African pupils had places in secondary schools and very few completed the fifth and final form successfully. The number who obtained a passmark entitling them to proceed to a degree course at university in 1969 was no more than 869. A similar disparity occurred at university level. In 1970 there were only 1400 African graduates in South Africa compared to 104,500 white graduates.

In white farming areas, conditions for African workers were even more meagre. Wages were pitifully low. A study of agriculture between 1866 and 1966 concluded that cash wages and the general standard of living for African farm labourers in selected areas rose little for the whole of that century. Housing conditions were poor and facilities like schools, clinics and hospitals were sparse in the extreme. Life for many workers amounted to a semifeudal existence. More than 3 million Africans lived in white farming areas. But their presence there during the 1960s came increasingly under threat. With the government's encouragement, white farmers adopted more mechanized production methods and began to replace permanent black workers with casual employees and single migrant workers. Between 1960 and 1971 an estimated half a million full-time black workers lost their employment on white farms. Together with their families, this meant that at least 1.5 million blacks were displaced. About 1 million appear to have moved into urban areas; the remainder went to homelands. African labour tenants who had survived numerous government attempts to eliminate them from white farming areas also came under renewed pressure. By January 1969 labour tenancy had been abolished throughout the Orange Free State and the Transvaal. In 1970 the government announced that it would be 'finally abolished' everywhere. Thousands of 'squatters' were also turned off white land. The only Africans whom the government wanted in white farming areas were hired labourers, preferably migrants.

The impact of all these changes in 'white' South Africa was felt with dramatic force in black homelands. Already overcrowded and impoverished, homelands had to cope with an endless flow of displaced Africans – tenants, squatters, redundant farm labourers, urban dwellers – 'superfluous' people, all clambering for survival. During the 1960s the homeland population nearly doubled, from four million to 7.4 million, its proportion of the total African population increasing from 37 per cent to 47 per cent. Once in the homelands, most African men had no alternative but to offer themselves up to the migrant labour treadmill or to try for work as illegals. The homelands, confined to 13 per cent of South Africa's land area, were no longer capable of sustaining the population there. Poor farming techniques and high population densities kept most agriculture to a subsistence level. In the period between 1918 and 1975, while the population steadily grew, the output from African agriculture was virtually stagnant. By 1970 only 5 per cent of South Africa's total agriculture output came from the African sector.

The government's own efforts to develop the homelands, despite Verwoerd's grandiose pronouncements, produced few results. The border industries plan, under which Africans living in homelands would find employment by crossing into white areas to work in white-owned factories built with government assistance at selected 'growth points', made only a limited impact. In the thirteen years from 1960 to 1972 the number of new jobs for Africans in border areas amounted to 85,500 and most of these would have been created anyway through normal development. One calculation was that only 11,600 jobs had been established by the border area policy during the whole of the 1960s. In an attempt to divert more white enterprises to border areas, the government resorted to new legislation, the Physical Planning and Utilization of Resources Act of 1967, empowering it to curb African employment required for new industrial development in established white areas. But neither threats nor inducements had much effect. In the homelands themselves, little development occurred except for housing and the construction of new settlements. 'The White State,' said a government minister, 'has no duty to prepare the homelands for the superfluous Africans because they are actually aliens in the White homelands who only have to be repatriated.'

For the vast majority of blacks in the homelands, the only means of survival remained the migrant labour system. In 1970 it was estimated that more than half the adult men normally resident in the homelands were absent as migrants, in some areas as many as two-thirds, leaving behind mostly women, children, the old and the sick, people described in government circulars as being 'nonproductive labour units'. What the homelands were being turned into, in effect, were labour dormitories for the white economy.

The catalogue of suffering was to grow still further. Leaving 'no stone unturned' in its drive for racial separation, the government turned its attention to excising scores of African settlements surrounded by white farming areas where Africans had lived in relative peace and quiet for generations. In the government's terminology, these settlements were known as 'black spots', small fragments of land in what was deemed to be 'white' South Africa which stood out as irritating blemishes on the apartheid map. Some was land held by title deed, purchased by African farmers in the nineteenth and early twentieth century; some was mission land, occupied by generations of African tenants; some was land scheduled for African use under the Natives Land Act of 1913, small African reserves which had survived the era of white occupation but which were now considered to be 'badly situated'. In all there were an estimated 350 black spots in the early 1960s, 250 of them in Natal, comprising about half a million acres. The government's aim was to be rid of them all by removing them to new areas linked to black homelands. A senior official in the Bantu Affairs Commission, G. F. van L. Froneman, explained in 1968:

> The policy of the present Government is to consolidate as far as possible all Bantu land into consolidated blocks, i.e. by excising smaller scattered areas out of scheduled or released areas and giving compensatory land of equal value contiguous to the larger Bantu blocks. . . . When all these 'Black spots' and isolated scheduled and released areas are once removed, the chess board pattern of Bantu Areas and White Areas in South Africa will also to a great extent be eliminated.

The elimination of 'black spots' began in earnest in the 1960s. Much of what occurred was hidden from public view. Then in 1971 a graphic account of the effects of the forced removal of African communities was published by a Franciscan priest, Father Cosmas Desmond, whose interest in the subject was stirred when his own parishoners on farmland around Maria Ratschitz Mission in the Dundee district in northern Natal were ordered to leave in 1968. The first to be moved were tenants on three African-owned farms at Meran, a well-established community with neat mud-and-thatch houses. They were taken away in government trucks to a resettlement camp twenty miles away called Limehill. Desmond recorded the scene: 'We found the first arrivals sitting in the bare veld, surrounded by their belongings, lost and still bewildered. There was a water tank a little distance away and a pile of folded tents; these people had never erected a tent in their lives. There was nothing else.' Later, the inhabitants of other local 'black spots', including tenants from Maria Ratschitz Mission, were sent to Limehill. Each family was allocated a tiny plot, fifty yards square. No livestock, except chickens, were allowed. There was no land for ploughing. Neither were there any shops or any medical services. Even elementary sanitation was lacking. Water supplies were scarce.

There was no industry and no work within daily reach. The nearest town was twenty miles away. So most men had to find work far away as migrant labour in Johannesburg and Durban. As more and more Africans were moved there, Limehill rapidly took on the appearance of a slum, 'a wretched and desolate place', wrote Desmond, whose inhabitants gave it the name *mshayazafe* meaning 'beat him until he dies'.

Desmond's experience at Limehill led him to make a journey across the length and breadth of South Africa for five months in 1969 trying to ascertain the full extent of the forced removals policy. It was a journey, he wrote, which took him into a 'labyrinth of broken communities, broken families and broken lives'. There were, he discovered, scores of Limehills, unmarked on any map, far from towns and main roads, out of reach of hospitals or clinics, frequently lacking in water supplies, often unsuitable for cultivation, beset by malnutrition and starvation. The families forced to move mostly met their fate with an attitude of resignation and helplessness. Protests were to no avail. The police, armed if necessary, were always on hand to deal with any resistance. The government, meanwhile, maintained that the removals were carried out only with the cooperation of the people concerned. In the words of the Minister of Bantu Administration, Michiel Botha, in 1969: 'We get their cooperation in all cases voluntarily. As a matter of fact, sometimes it is necessary to do quite a lot of persuasion, but we do get them away.' When Father Desmond's account of African resettlement, *The Discarded People*, was published in 1971, the government reacted in characteristic manner. Desmond was issued with a five-year banning order, placed under house arrest, and his book was proscribed.

Between 1960 and 1970, nearly 100,000 Africans lost their homes during the elimination of black spots in rural areas, finding themselves like others tossed into the maelstrom that apartheid created for its hapless victims. Many more were to follow. Throughout the 1970s and beyond, the same policies were pursued. By the end of two decades, the number of non-whites uprooted in order to satisfy the requirements of apartheid amounted to more than 3 million. The government, for its part, pronounced itself well pleased with the results of its removals policy. In 1969 the Deputy Minister of Bantu Administration and Development, Piet Koornhof, declared the 'elimination of the redundant non-economically active Bantu in our White areas' to be 'a tremendous achievement'.

CHAPTER FOURTEEN

The Soweto Revolt

The years of silence were broken by a new generation of black activists. It was a generation which drew its inspiration not from the concept of multiracial struggle that the African National Congress once championed but from a sense of black assertiveness more in line with the Africanist tradition of black politics. The black consciousness movement which emerged in South Africa in the early 1970s dominated black political activity for the rest of the decade. It found an articulate spokesman in Steve Biko, a young intellectual from the eastern Cape whose short life had a profound impact on black thinking and whose lonely death was to stand as a permanent monument to police brutality. Within a few years, black consciousness activists succeeded in transforming the outlook of a large part of the black population, arousing a new mood of defiance which culminated in sustained revolt against the government. The revolt was eventually to fade out. But what it showed was that no matter what tactics the government employed, black nationalist protest against apartheid could not be erased.

Steve Biko was a medical student at the University of Natal when he began to develop his ideas on black consciousness. The son of a government-employed clerk, born in 1947 in King William's Town, his initiation into political life had come at the age of sixteen when he was interrogated by police about the activities of his elder brother, a suspected *Poqo* supporter, and subsequently expelled from school. Influenced by writers like Frantz Fanon, Biko started from the premise that oppression was most immediately a psychological problem and that what was needed was a massive effort to reverse the negative image that blacks held of themselves and to replace it with a more positive identity. Biko's contempt for the cowed and submissive attitude of the black population was given full vent in a student newsletter published in September 1970.

The type of black man we have today has lost his manhood.

Reduced to an obliging shell, he looks with awe at the white power structure and accepts what he regards as the 'inevitable position'. . . . In the privacy of his toilet his face twists in silent condemnation of white society but brightens up in sheepish obedience as he comes out hurrying in response to his master's impatient call. In the home-bound bus or train he joins the chorus that roundly condemns the white man but is first to praise the government in the presence of the police and his employers. . . . All in all, the black man has become a shell, a shadow of man, completely defeated, drowning in his own misery, a slave, an ox bearing the yoke of oppression with sheepish timidity. . . .

The first step therefore is to make the black man come to himself; to pump back life into his empty shell; to infuse him with pride and dignity. . . .

The initial action that Biko urged was for blacks to sever their links with the white liberal establishment which hitherto had dominated apartheid opposition endeavouring to represent black interests but never prepared to go beyond certain limits.

The biggest mistake the black world ever made was to assume that whoever opposed apartheid was an ally. For a long time the black world has been looking only at the governing party and not so much at the whole power structure as the object of their rage.

White liberals believed that the answer to apartheid was multiracial organizations and parties. Yet this was no more than a diversion.

. . . It never occurred to the liberals that the integration they insisted upon as an effective way of opposing apartheid was impossible to achieve in South Africa. . . . The myth of integration as propounded under the banner of the liberal ideology must be cracked and killed because it makes people believe that something is being done when in reality the artificially integrated circles are a soporific to the blacks while salving the consciences of the guilt-stricken white . . . [who] possesses the natural passport to the exclusive pool of white privileges.

Using the slogan 'Black man you are on your own', Biko and other student colleagues broke away from the multiracial National Union of South African Students (NUSAS) in 1968 to form their own South African Students' Organization (SASO). NUSAS had constantly spoken out against racial injustice, making itself the target of government harassment. Vorster, when minister of justice, had been sufficiently irritated by NUSAS activities to describe it in May 1963 as a 'cancer in the life of the nation'. But with a membership consisting mainly of white English-speaking university students, NUSAS tended to reflect white liberal interests and their concern for the erosion of civil liberties rather than to confront the problems facing black students for whom civil liberties were an unknown luxury. SASO and its ideas on the need to promote black awareness, black pride, black achievement and capabilities met with a ready response from students in Verwoerd's new segregated universities. Those to whom it appealed included Coloureds and Indians, for SASO defined the word 'black' not as a colour but as a term covering all victims of racial oppression. 'We are oppressed not as individuals, not as Zulus, Xhosas, Vendas or Indians,' wrote Biko. 'We are oppressed because we are black.' Students in high schools and seminaries were soon caught up in the movement. An 'adult' wing, the Black People's Convention (BPC), was launched in 1972. As it gathered momentum, black consciousness found outlets in poetry, literature, drama, music, theology and in local community projects promoting education, health and welfare. A host of youth clubs, discussion groups and cultural organizations sprang into existence. Black consciousness lacked a clear strategy. It constituted not so much a political movement as, in SASO's words, 'an attitude of mind, a way of life'. Its underlying purpose, nevertheless, was to set blacks on the road to economic and political power. 'Black Consciousness,' wrote Biko in 1972, 'is more than just a reactionary rejection of whites by blacks. The quintessence of it is the realization by the blacks that, in order to feature well in this game of power politics, they have to use the concept of group power and to build a strong foundation for this.'

The mood of restlessness among black students in the early 1970s also affected black workers. The economic boom which had lasted throughout the 1960s, providing a decade of slowly increasing real wages for African workers, came to an end in 1971, with a sharp increase in the inflation rate. Food prices rose steeply. In 1973 a wave of strikes broke out over demands for higher wages and improved conditions. Between January and March there were 160 strikes in the Durban area involving 61,000 workers. The strikes, though illegal, spread to East London and the Rand. In the period from January

1973 to June 1974 there were more than 300 strikes involving some 80,000 workers. By comparison, the number of African workers involved in strike action in the 1960s had not risen above 2000 a year. The strikers won substantial improvements in wages and conditions and also stimulated new interest in the black trade union movement. Between 1970 and 1974 the number of African trade unions increased from thirteen to twenty-two, with a membership growing from 16,000 to 40,000. The level of strikes fell from 1974 as workers became preoccupied with the growing threat of unemployment. In 1970 an estimated 1 million blacks were without work; by 1976 the number had risen to 2 million. The other hazards facing black workers – police action, imprisonment, banishment – remained severe. Nevertheless, the strikes of 1973 had brought about a revival of trade union activity and began to give workers a sense of their potential strength.

The stirring of black discontent eventually prompted the government to take reprisals. In March 1973 it issued banning orders on Biko and seven other leaders of the black consciousness movement. Biko, having given up his medical studies in 1972, had been working as a full-time political organizer. He was now restricted to King William's Town, forbidden to speak in public or to write for publication or to be quoted or to be present with more than one person at a time. For two years he worked on black community programmes in King William's Town until barred from such work in 1975. The government's action, however, came too late to stop the spread of black consciousness. A dramatic boost to black morale occurred in 1974 when Portuguese rule in Mozambique and Angola collapsed, paving the way for African liberation movements there to take control. Frelimo's victory in neighbouring Mozambique in particular had a profound impact on the black population in South Africa. Both SASO and BPC called for nationwide 'Viva Frelimo' rallies in September 1974 to mark Frelimo's advent to power. The government banned all meetings. But despite the ban, crowds gathered in Durban and students at the black university at Turfloop in the Transvaal responded to the call. A senior black lecturer at Turfloop recalled: 'What had happened in Mozambique had excited them: they were beginning to feel that change was possible – and in their lifetimes.' When South African troops were obliged to withdraw from Angola in early 1976, having failed to prevent the Marxist MPLA movement from gaining power there, black students again

celebrated the defeat of white power. The government's response to
the call for 'Viva Frelimo' rallies was to order the arrest and detention
of SASO and BPC activists. By March 1975, some fifty prominent
members were in detention; another fifty had fled the country. A
group of nine leaders was brought to trial in 1975 on charges under
the Terrorism Act, accused of conspiring to transform the state by
'unconstitutional, revolutionary and/or violent means' and of attempting 'to create and foster feelings of racial hatred, hostility and
antipathy by the Blacks towards the White population'. No physical
acts of terrorism were included in the indictment. The prosecution's
intention was to establish that black consciousness philosophy as
enunciated by SASO and BPC was a danger to public safety in that it
was likely to lead to a mobilization of black opinion against the
established white order. The evidence consisted mainly of black
consciousness literature, including poetry and plays. In effect, it was
black consciousness itself that was on trial as much as the nine
accused. The trial ended after seventeen months in the conviction of
the accused who were given sentences of either five or six years'
imprisonment on Robben Island. Yet far from intimidating black
consciousness activists, as the government had hoped, it seemed to
provide greater stimulation. The trial became a platform for black
consciousness ideas. The accused men took every opportunity to
show their defiance, regularly entering the courtroom singing
freedom songs, raising clenched fists in the black power salute and
shouting '*Amandla*' – the Zulu for 'power'.

The rising anger of the black population was fuelled by old
grievances over pass laws, police harassment, job reservation, low
wages and insecurity of tenure and by fears over unemployment and
inflation. Conditions in black townships were steadily deteriorating.
As a result of the government's policy of deliberately restricting
urban development, the housing shortage had become acute. A
survey of housing conditions in ten urban centres which accounted
for half of the total urban African population showed that in the five-
year period up to 1975 only 20,000 houses had been built, an increase
of 15 per cent, while in the same period the African population there
had grown by 900,000, an increase of more than 50 per cent. The
average number of people per house had risen from thirteen in 1970
to seventeen in 1975. A new system of township administration
brought further burdens. Determined to enforce tighter controls
over township life, the government removed local authorities

previously responsible for their administration and replaced them with new Bantu Affairs Administration Boards under direct government supervision. The new boards, introduced from 1972, were told from the outset that they would have to be entirely self-financing, receiving no subsidies. For most African townships this made little difference since only twenty-one of some 450 local authorities had contributed subsidies to township budgets. But for Soweto, the largest township in the country with a population of more than 1 million, the loss of its subsidy from Johannesburg's rates meant higher rent charges and deteriorating services for sewerage, refuse removal and roads. A survey in 1976 indicated that 43 per cent of households in Soweto, ten miles from the richest city in Africa, were living below the Poverty Datum Line.

Black school pupils, who formed the backbone of the revolt in 1976, possessed their own particular grievances. The system of Bantu Education, designed by Verwoerd to educate Africans only to the point at which they served the labour needs of the white economy, had produced a legacy of inferior schooling, poorly-trained teachers, overcrowded classrooms and inadequate equipment. Government expenditure on African education had always been kept to a minimum. Because of deliberate restrictions on places in middle and higher schools, hundreds of thousands of children – 'push-outs', as they were known – left school with no greater prospects than menial work or unemployment. In the early 1970s, the government was forced to expand secondary schooling for Africans to meet a growing demand for skilled labour. Between 1972 and 1976 the number of secondary schools doubled. But the number of secondary pupils trebled, leading to even worse overcrowding. Those completing secondary school were then blocked by a whole range of apartheid restrictions affecting the kind of employment for which they could apply. The difficulties that school leavers faced in 1976 were particularly acute, for a large increase in the number of matriculants graduating that year coincided with a reduction of employment opportunities caused by economic recession.

Into this tense and potentially explosive atmosphere the government then stumbled with yet another new regulation. With the encouragement of government ministers, officials in the Department of Bantu Education decided to enforce an old ruling, originally made in 1958, that half of the subjects in secondary schools not taught in the African vernacular should be taught in Afrikaans and the other half in English. Because of the practical difficulties involved, the ruling had since been ignored. African teachers in training colleges continued to receive their instruction almost exclusively in English. Many teachers were unable even to converse in Afrikaans. In representations to the government, they argued that only one language should be used and expressed a strong preference for English. The government, however, remained adamant and in 1974 decided to force the issue. Orders were given that from the following year instruction in general science and practical subjects should be in Afrikaans. In one protest after another, teachers' organizations, school boards, principals and parents sought to persuade the Department of Bantu Education to change its mind. But the government persisted with its intransigence and thus precipitated a crisis even worse than Sharpeville.

In Soweto, the epicentre of the revolt, students, denouncing Afrikaans as the language of the 'oppressor', began to boycott classes in Afrikaans. As agitation spread, a students' organization, the South African Students' Movement (SASM), took the initiative in organizing protest. Formed originally in Soweto high schools in 1971, as interest in black consciousness was beginning to develop, SASM had since spread to schools in the Transvaal, Durban, the eastern Cape, Cape Town and the Orange Free State, functioning as a national student movement. Its nucleus was provided by three high schools in Soweto – Orlando West, Diepkloof and Orlando. On 17 May pupils at Orlando West junior secondary school came out on strike. Six other schools followed suit. Within a few weeks, several thousand pupils were involved. At a meeting at Naledi high school on 13 June, SASM formed an action committee, composed of two delegates from each school in Soweto, to organize a mass demonstration on 16 June in protest against the Afrikaans decree. It was this committee, later renamed the Soweto Students' Representative Council (SSRC) which was to provide much of the leadership of the revolt.

On 16 June a dozen columns of students marched through Soweto carrying placards, chanting slogans and singing freedom songs. Their plan was to converge on Orlando West junior secondary school and from there march to the Orlando stadium. As the students gathered at Orlando West school, in an orderly mood according to most witnesses, the police arrived. A white policeman threw a teargas canister into the crowd. The students retreated slightly then stood their ground, waving placards and singing. A white policeman drew his revolver and opened fire. In the first burst of shooting, a thirteen-year-old schoolboy, Hector Petersen, was killed. The students fought back, pelting the police with bricks and stones, forcing them to withdraw. As news of the shooting spread, students went on the rampage, attacking government buildings, beerhalls, bottle stores, vehicles and buses. Two whites were killed. For three days, Soweto was the scene of running battles between groups of students and riot police in armoured convoys, often firing indiscriminately. Clashes spread to other townships in the Transvaal and to black universities. After ten days, the death toll, according to the government, had reached 176 with more than 1000 wounded. Black organizations put the casualty figure far higher.

In July, the government finally retreated on the Afrikaans issue. But by then the students had set their sights on bringing down the whole Bantu Education system and on drawing parents and workers into their protest. Some believed that the government itself could be toppled. After a lull of several weeks in street activity, the SSRC called for a stay-at-home protest on 4 August and organized a march the same day along one of the main roads leading out of Soweto intending to reach police headquarters in Johannesburg to demand the release of political detainees. On the way, the marchers, numbering more than 20,000, were met by armed police. Once more shooting started, this time setting off weeks of violence and disorder which spread to every corner of the country. Cape Town and cities in the eastern Cape were caught up in the fray; even small rural towns were affected. By early September, the level of violence and arson had reached such proportions that the Minister of Justice, James Kruger, was forced to admit that the police on their own could no longer cope: 'The day is past when people can sit at home thinking the police will protect their property. There are not enough police. . . . The task of protecting business premises is primarily that of the owners.' Black workers added their weight to the protest. Three weeks after the first stay-away, workers in Soweto and other parts of the Witwatersrand participated in a second sympathy strike. In mid-September, a third stay-away involved three-quarters of Johannesburg's workforce. A simultaneous strike in Cape Town by Coloured and African workers brought much of commerce there to a halt for two days.

In the face of police firepower, student activists showed remarkable resilience. Time and again they returned to the streets to give battle to the police, displaying a level of defiance and hatred of the apartheid system rarely seen before. Hundreds were arrested, some of them dying in police custody. As soon as student leaders were detained or disappeared into exile, others stepped forward readily to take their place. Yet for all the courage shown, the student revolt lacked any sense of direction. Marches, demonstrations and arson attacks produced little discernible result other than a high cost in casualties and an endless series of police raids. From September onwards the momentum of the revolt began to ebb. Hoping to inflict economic damage on the government, student leaders called for a five-day strike from 1 November. But this time workers refused to pay heed, seeing nothing to be gained from it. Sporadic violence continued into December, but by then the revolt had virtually died out. According to official estimates, it had cost 575 dead and some 4000 wounded.

Student protest continued the following year, but it was now mostly directed towards opposing Bantu Education. The school system was constantly disrupted by boycotts. In Soweto, the SSRC launched a campaign to oppose high rents and forced the resignation of members of the Urban Bantu Council, an advisory body installed by the government in 1968. The Urban Bantu Council collapsed. The students then turned their attention to members of school boards in Soweto, demanding their resignation. The boards ceased to function. From mid-1977 the school boycott campaign steadily spread. By September some 250,000 students were on strike. In Soweto some 600 teachers showed their sympathy by resigning. Then on 12 September the news of Steve Biko's death unleashed a new wave of fury and violence.

Biko had been arrested at a police roadblock near Grahamstown in the eastern Cape caught breaking the banning order which restricted him to the King William's Town magisterial district seventy miles away. As subsequent police evidence disclosed, he was held in solitary confinement, kept naked, given no proper washing facilities and allowed no exercise. On 6 September he was taken from his cell to security police headquarters in Port Elizabeth for interrogation, still naked and now held in leg irons and handcuffs. The following day, after interrogation had been resumed, Biko suffered severe head injuries. According to police evidence, the injuries occurred when Biko's head hit a wall in the course of a scuffle that started after he had become violent. During the next four days, Biko's condition steadily deteriorated. By 11 September when he was nearly comatose, doctors concluded that he should be sent to hospital for treatment. Though he was close to collapse, he was put naked into the back of a Land Rover, provided with nothing more than a blanket and a bottle of water, and driven for 700 miles to a prison hospital in Pretoria. There, a few hours after arriving, he died lying on a mat on a stone floor. He was the forty-sixth detainee to die in police custody. Two days later, the Minister of Justice, James Kruger, provoked laughter among delegates to the Transvaal congress of the National Party when referring to the death: 'I am not glad and I am not sorry about Mr Biko. It leaves me cold. [*Dit laat my koud*.] I can say nothing to you. Any person who dies. . . . I shall also be sorry if I die. . . .'

As student violence spread once more, the government finally resolved to stamp it out with traditional methods of repression. On 19 October, it outlawed virtually every black conciousness organization in the country, including the South African Students' Organization, the Black People's Convention, the South African Students' Movement and the Soweto Students' Representative Council. It closed down the Christian Institute, a multiracial body of anti-apartheid churchmen, banned its outspoken director, Beyers Naudé and other officials and proscribed its monthly journal *Pro Veritate*. It stopped publication of two black newspapers, *The World* and *The Weekend World*, detained *The World*'s editor, Percy Qoboza, and banned the editor of the *Daily Dispatch*, Donald Woods, who had mounted a campaign of protest against Biko's death. In all, the government silenced eighteen organizations, took action against forty-seven black leaders and seven prominent whites. Justifying the crackdown, the Minister of Justice blamed 'a small group of anarchists and organizations bent on subversion that hid behind a smokescreen of "sweet-sounding names and aims"'.

In the short term, the government's tactics succeeded. A period of relative calm ensued. But the overall cost to the government of the Soweto revolt and its finale of murder and repression was nevertheless high. International opinion was once more outraged by the suppression of black organizations and, in particular, by the manner of Biko's death. Representatives from thirteen Western governments attended his funeral to mark their own form of protest. Calls for economic boycotts and sanctions resounded in Washington and Westminster. At the United Nations Security Council, members voted for a mandatory ban on arms sales to South Africa. Even more damaging to the government was the reaction of foreign investors who no longer looked at South Africa as such a stable or profitable haven for their capital. The extent of the revolt also shook white opinion, even though the white population was left largely untouched. White emigration increased; immigration fell. But in the long term what counted more was the mood of the black population. Soweto marked a turning point in the way that black youth were prepared to challenge the government. A whole generation was brought up on its legends. Never again was the government able to suppress black political activity as successfully as it had done in the past. Soweto also marked the beginning of an exodus of black youths in search of guerrilla training, providing a new corps of recruits for the exiled African National Congress. Both at home and abroad therefore the government faced new dangers.

CHAPTER FIFTEEN

The Homeland Strategy

Whatever setbacks the Nationalist government suffered as a result of the Soweto revolt, its plan to give African homelands a separate identity in accordance with the grand design of apartheid made rapid progress. Using the Transkei as a model, the government propelled other homelands along the road to self-government, determined that they should accept responsibility for the entire African population. One by one, the homelands were provided with legislative assemblies, cabinets, ministers, bureaucracies and budgets, and dispatched into self-government to exercise their 'separate freedoms'. Between 1972 and 1977 eight homelands joined the list of self-governing 'nations', as Pretoria liked to describe them: Bophuthatswana became the homeland for the Tswana people; KwaZulu for the Zulu; Lebowa for the North Sotho; QwaQwa for the South Sotho; Gazankulu for the Shangaan and Tsonga; KaNgwane for the Swazi; Venda for the Venda; and Ciskei for a second group of Xhosa-speaking people. In each case, homeland governments were required to accept as their citizens not only Africans resident in the homelands but Africans resident in 'white' areas, including those who had always lived there and who had no knowledge of any 'homeland' or any relatives there, but who were said to be associated with a homeland 'by virtue of their cultural or racial background'. Under the terms of the Bantu Homelands Citizenship Act, passed in 1970, every African was deemed to be a citizen of one of the homelands. Hence none could claim citizenship rights in 'white' South Africa.

The geography of the new homelands made little sense. Most were made up from scattered and fragmented pieces of land. In the case of two of the most important homelands, KwaZulu in 1975 consisted of forty-eight pieces of land and scores of smaller tracts and Bophuthatswana of nineteen major pieces of land spread across three of South Africa's provinces. Ciskei consisted of fifteen pieces of land, Lebowa of fourteen, Gazankulu of four, and Venda, KaNgwane and the Transkei of three each. Only one homeland, QwaQwa, an area of about 200 square miles, consisted of a single contiguous territory. The African populations living in the homelands in general represented only a minority of their citizens. The Venda homeland had the highest proportion, with about two-thirds of its citizens living there. The Transkei and KwaZulu had about half; Bophuthatswana, about one third. In the case of the South Sotho homeland, QwaQwa, less than 2 per cent of its citizens lived there, while 8 per cent lived in other African homelands and 90 per cent lived in 'white' areas. Every African 'nation', in fact, was scattered far and wide beyond their own 'homeland', living either in 'white' areas or in other African homelands. Nearly one third of Bophuthatswana's resident population came from ethnic groups other than Tswana. In an attempt to make the homelands ethnically purer, the government resorted to large-scale removals, adding thousands more victims to the population upheavals which apartheid had already caused. It also embarked on plans to 'consolidate' African homelands, attaching new bits of land, excising others, creating new upheavals in the process.

Where no homeland existed, the government, in its fanatical drive to implement apartheid to the full, was prepared to create one. The Ndebele people, numbering about 800,000, possessed no 'traditional homeland' of their own in South Africa. They were scattered across 'white' areas and throughout other homelands. So the government purchased nineteen white-owned farms fifty miles north-east of Pretoria, declared the area to be the 'homeland' of the Ndebele nation, installed a legislative assembly and in 1971 pronounced KwaNdebele to be a self-governing territory. The population grew rapidly. In 1970 the area contained about 32,000 Africans. With the influx of Ndebele expelled from white-owned farms, from urban areas, from other homelands and from 'black spots', it grew by 1980 to 150,000 people. KwaNdebele, concocted merely to satisfy the needs of apartheid, was even more of an artificial creation than the other nine homelands. But by mopping up 'surplus' Ndebele and by ridding 'white' South Africa of the problem of Ndebele citizenship, it served the government's purpose well enough.

The economic base supporting the homelands in their new life as self-governing nations was pitifully inadequate. The homelands contained few roads or railways, no major ports or cities, poor natural resources and land that was badly depleted by overpopulation and poor husbandry. When ranked against the 263 white magisterial districts of South Africa in terms of average output per head in 1970, the homelands filled nine of the ten places at the bottom of the list. Only a fraction of South Africa's total output was produced there; in 1975 it amounted to no more than 3 per cent. The average per capita gross domestic product for the homelands that year was less than one-twentieth of that for 'white' South Africa. The main source of income for homeland residents came from migrants or commuters working in South Africa: only a quarter of the income earned by the homeland population in 1975 was generated in the homelands. The main source of income for homeland governments remained the South African treasury: only a fifth of their total expenditure in 1975–6 came from local sources. Some endeavours were made by Pretoria to stimulate economic development in the homelands. In the late 1960s the government decided on a policy of industrial decentralization aimed at establishing growth points in the homelands. Regulations forbidding white capital there were relaxed in 1968; a number of concessions designed to attract white investors, such as low interest rates and transport rebates, were introduced in 1970. With the help of such measures, eight 'growth centres' were established between 1971 and 1978 and some 300 industries were launched. In the case of Bophuthatswana, substantial revenues were obtained from mining royalties. But otherwise whatever development occurred was invariably outstripped by population increase.

Between 1960 and 1970, as a result of forced removals, boundary changes incorporating townships into homelands and natural increase, the homeland population overall grew from 4 million to 7.4 million. By 1980 it had reached 10.7 million. Most homelands were unable to cope with the numbers. The chief minister of Gazankulu, Hudson Ntsanwisi, complained that the homelands had become a 'dumping ground for the dispossessed'. An economic research organization, Benbo, reported in 1977 that the authorities in QwaQwa, whose population grew from 25,000 in 1970 to an estimated 200,000 in 1977, were finding it 'almost impossible to surmount' the problems arising from resettlement and overpopulation. It had not been impossible, said Benbo, for QwaQwa to keep pace with the provision of housing, job opportunities, social services and other amenities. 'The effect of the resettlement can be seen in the often chaotic distribution of dwellings in the rural parts of QwaQwa, in the wasteful exploitation of fertile agricultural land and in the tensions that have arisen between new and old settlers.' For a homeland like KwaNdebele, devoid of all resources, the only means of survival for the resident population was to commute daily to work in white urban areas, whatever distance was involved. All but a few residents depended on jobs in Pretoria or Johannesburg, spending up to eight hours a day travelling to and from work in convoys of buses, rising long before dawn, returning late into the night. Throughout the homelands, the ranks of commuter workers steadily increased, much to the government's satisfaction. Between 1970 and 1980 the total number rose from 250,000 to 700,000. By 1980 it was estimated that about a third of the homeland labour force worked in white areas as migrants, another third worked as commuter labour, and the remaining third were either employed in the homelands, or, more likely, unemployed.

There were, nevertheless, beneficiaries of the homeland system. For an elite group of African politicians, chiefs, civil servants and traders, self-government in the homelands brought substantial rewards. Cabinet ministers, members of the legislative assemblies and civil servants gained increasingly from high salaries, loans, land and housing, as the South African authorities sought to establish a prosperous middle class that would underpin the homeland system and provide them with allies in the business of government. In the thirteen-year period that the Transkei remained a self-governing territory, the pay of members of the legislative assembly increased fivefold. The salary scales of civil servants were upgraded nine times. As more government functions were handed over by Pretoria to the Transkei administration, the civil service establishment became ever stronger. Between 1963 and 1976 the number of civil service posts rose from 2446 to 17,320. By 1976, the salaries, wages and allowances for civil servants and teachers consumed nearly a third of the Transkei's budget. Many civil servants earned ten times more than the average wage. The chiefs, forming an integral part of the system of government, also gained substantially. Chiefs sitting in the legislative assembly in 1976 were paid at least sixty times more than the minimum stipend provided for chiefs in 1963. In the field of trade and commerce, a new class of African entrepreneur emerged to take over trading enterprises from departing whites. The proportion of Transkei's population that benefited from self-government was tiny. One estimate put the figure at 35,000 or about 1.5 per cent. Within this group, a far smaller number, totalling perhaps 1000 altogether – chiefs, senior civil servants, elected representatives, managers and entrepreneurs – gained a great deal. But it was this core, with a vested interest in the homeland policy, which was able to ensure that it worked. In other homelands the same pattern developed.

Once installed in government, homeland politicians took every opportunity to consolidate their positions through the use of patronage and other official prerogatives. Since in every homeland the government constituted the main employer and the mainstay of the economy, politicians placed in control were able to wield huge influence. Chiefs too were used to reinforce the system. Every homeland legislative assembly was dominated by chiefs and head-men rather than by elected members, all beholden to the government for their positions. To add to their arsenal of powers, homeland governments retained formidable security legislation and used it on appropriate occasions to curb opposition. Just before the 1976 election in Transkei, Chief Matanzima did not hesitate to imprison leading members of the opposition Democratic Party which had shown signs of gaining a large following.

The popularity of homeland leaders varied considerably. In Transkei, Chief Matanzima, after thirteen years of controlling public resources, exercising patronage, using his chiefly connections and finally by locking up his radical opponents, succeeded at his forth election in 1976 in capturing seventy-one of the seventy-five elected seats. An aloof and arrogant personality, he ruled, as he had begun, wielding power in an arbitrary and authoritarian manner, paying scant heed to popular politics. In Bophuthatswana, Chief Lucas Mangope, in his first election in 1972, won a clear majority of assembly seats as well as the support of tribal leaders. In Venda, Chief Patrick Mphephu lost his election in 1977 but clung on to power with the help of nominated members and a nod from the South African authorities. In KwaZulu, Chief Mangosuthu Buthelezi, exploiting his position as leader of the Buthelezi clan and as a member of the Zulu royal family, built up a powerful cultural and political movement, *Inkatha yeNkululeko yeSizwe*, which gained support not only in KwaZulu but in urban areas as well. By 1980 Inkatha claimed to have 350,000 paid-up members, making it the largest black political organization allowed to function in South Africa's history. Buthelezi himself, according to some opinion polls at the time, was regarded by many Africans as a more important national leader than Nelson Mandela.

Whatever the level of their popularity, homeland governments

soon became sufficiently well-established for politicians in Pretoria
to plan for the final act of separate development. There was no
evident enthusiasm among the African population for independence.
Indeed, opinion surveys frequently suggested that the African
population would prefer a single multiracial state to any alternative
system. In the eyes of Pretoria, however, independence was the
ultimate solution to its African population: by bestowing independence on all ten homelands, the government would finally remove all
claim that the African population had to South African citizenship.
Moreover, independence would provide proof to the international
community, so officials in Pretoria believed, that the South African
government had fulfilled its obligation to provide full rights to the
African population just as adequately as Europe's colonial powers
had done when granting independence to their African colonies.
South Africa's plan for independence thus merited international
recognition.

A number of homeland leaders were willing to fall into line with
this strategy, whatever preference their own populations expressed.
Just as Matanzima had led the way to self-government, so now he
took the Transkei into independence, claiming that his victory in the
1976 election constituted a mandate for him to do so. On 26 October
1976 the Transkei was launched as an independent 'state'. Overnight, 1.6 million Xhosas living there and 1.3 million Xhosas living
in 'white' areas lost their South African citizenship. In theory, the
African population of South Africa was reduced at a stroke. After the
independence of Transkei, the Minister of Information, Connie
Mulder, proclaimed that South Africa was henceforth a country of
22 million people, as opposed to 26 million beforehand. On 6
December 1977, Bophuthatswana followed suit even though there
was evident opposition to independence; in all some 1.8 million
Tswana lost their South African citizenship. Impressed by the
success of the strategy, Connie Mulder, now Minister of Bantu
Affairs and Development, declared soon afterwards: 'If our policy is
taken to its full logical conclusion as far as the black people are
concerned, there will not be one black man with South African
citizenship.' Two more homelands joined the list. In 1979 Venda
opted for independence, even though Chief Mphephu had lost an
election on the issue. Then in 1981, the Ciskei's leader, Chief
Lennox Sebe, ignoring the advice of a distinguished panel of experts
and an opinion survey showing that a majority of Ciskei's citizens

both in the homelands and outside rejected independence, decided
to accept Pretoria's offer. In all, between 1976 and 1981, an
estimated 8 million Africans lost their South African citizenship.

In return, homeland governments obtained some concessions.
Matanzima persuaded Pretoria to grant increased financial aid and to
cede to the Transkei the coastal town of Port St Johns. Bophuthatswana received additional land, including the historically important
town of Mafeking, made famous by its siege during the Anglo-Boer
war. Independence brought homeland politicians new status, power
and wealth. But the homelands themselves remained decaying
backwaters, populated by an impoverished peasantry, dependent for
survival on handouts from Pretoria and migrant labour, masquerad-
ing as independent states but ruled in reality by accomplices to
Pretoria's grand design. Foreign governments took the view that
independence for the homelands was nothing more than a device to
perpetuate white supremacy and withheld all recognition.

The independence process began to falter when Chief Buthelezi,
political leader of some 5 million Zulus, the largest ethnic group in
the country, decided to have no truck with it. Buthelezi's role in the
apartheid system was a complex one. In his youth, he had been
marked down by the authorities as a troublemaker. While studying at
Fort Hare he had joined the Youth League of the African National
Congress and in his final year he had been expelled for taking part in a
political protest; among those whom he openly admired were Chief
Lutuli and Nelson Mandela. Buthelezi nevertheless was prepared to
work within the apartheid system. 'If we can get all these human
rights and dignities through separate development,' he said in 1970,
'well, let's get on with it.' Elected as chief executive officer of the
KwaZulu Territorial Authority in 1970 and as Chief Minister in
1976, he developed the art of opposing Pretoria's homelands policy
while at the same time playing a leading part in it. Cooperation was
justified, he argued, on pragmatic grounds. The homeland policy
enabled Zulus to acquire vital administrative experience which they
would be able to use to good effect in a multiracial South Africa in the
future and it provided them too with a platform from which to
oppose apartheid. Buthelezi's public statements were riddled with
ambivalence as he endeavoured to maintain a balancing act between
the authorities in Pretoria, his supporters in KwaZulu, African
nationalist groups abroad, other homeland leaders, urban Africans

and liberal whites who saw him as a star of the future. Sometimes he spoke out in support of majority rule in a united South Africa; at other times he expressed his willingness to consider other constitutional options such as federation or confederation. Sometimes he appeared to favour militant action against apartheid; at other times he condemned confrontation and violence. As the acknowledged leader of the Zulu people, winning the first election in KwaZulu in 1978 with nearly a clean sweep of the seats, he lent the homeland system greater credibility than any other homeland leader; then he delivered it a crippling blow by refusing independence.

Addressing the KwaZulu Assembly, he said:

> We have opted to occupy a pivotal opposition policy. They rammed homeland institutional developments down our throats – and informed us we had no choice in the matter. The Government was soon to find out, and it will find out repeatedly, that you can take a horse to the water but you cannot make it drink. If they think that they can do anything without our approval, they will be shown to be wrong.

The setback for Pretoria was severe. Buthelezi's stand against independence was bound to influence the attitude of other homeland leaders. 'There is no way of forcing a homeland leader to accept independence,' remarked Connie Mulder in 1978. 'Naturally we hope the final stage of their development will be independence. But depending on how many homelands are not independent, the whole situation will have to be reconsidered and a new dispensation worked out.'

It was not only with the homeland policy that the government was facing difficulty. In urban areas, as the Soweto revolt had shown, the black population was growing ever more restive. Industrial discontent was spreading. Old apartheid practices were coming under stress and strain. In the view of many Nationalist politicians in Pretoria, new ones needed to be devised.

CHAPTER SIXTEEN

Pressures for Change

The changes that occurred in the apartheid system that Verwoerd bequeathed to South Africa grew from small beginnings but aroused such fierce dissension at every stage that Afrikanerdom was left permanently divided into rival factions. What was at stake, in the view of some of the protagonists, was nothing less than the very soul of Afrikanerdom, its standards and values which Afrikaners were said to have cherished for centuries. Their opponents argued the need for Afrikanerdom to break out from its hidebound traditions and come to terms with the modern world.

The first battles were fought in the field of literature. A group of young Afrikaner writers known as *Die Sestigers* (School of the Sixties), resenting the moral boundaries fixed by Afrikaner society, began to write novels and poetry with modern ideas and in modern language. The *Sestiger* movement as the writer André Brink saw it at the time was 'a safe revolt', conducted within careful limits. 'It attacks religious and moral taboos because they are not so vital to the Afrikaner mind as political taboos,' he remarked. Yet the movement was to provoke a powerful counter-attack by Afrikaner traditionalists determined to preserve Afrikaner heritage against any intrusion by 'foreign' elements or outlandish ideas, bringing the quarrel from the cultural into the political arena. In 1966 a bitter dispute broke out within the *Akademie vir Wetenskap en Kuns* (Academy for Science and Art) over a literature prize awarded to a prominent *Sestiger* writer, Etienne le Roux. That same year an Afrikaner academic and editor, Willem de Klerk, identified the two rival camps within Afrikanerdom as the *verkrampte*, meaning the narrow-minded, reactionary ones, and the *verligte*, meaning open-minded, enlightened ones. This division within Afrikanerdom, of minor significance in the beginning, was to grow over the years until eventually it engulfed the whole Afrikaner community, provoking splits within the National Party, the Broederbond, the churches, the press and cultural organizations.

In dealing with the conflicting pressures within Afrikanerdom, Vorster, as prime minister, sought to remain above the fray, trying to achieve a balance between its two wings. A dour, unsmiling figure, who as a law student had attended Verwoerd's lectures at Stellenbosch University, he was as committed to apartheid ideology as Verwoerd himself. Indeed, it was during Vorster's term of office that the apartheid system was enforced with ever greater vigour. Yet unlike Verwoerd, Vorster was willing on occasion to adapt apartheid to changing circumstances. It was this degree of flexibility he showed that brought him increasingly into conflict with the *verkrampte* camp.

His main opponent was Albert Hertzog, son of the former prime minister, for whom the purity of Afrikanerdom was a greater cause than any other. While both Verwoerd and Vorster saw an advantage in encouraging cooperation between the Afrikaner and English-speaking communities and promoting the idea of a white 'nation', Hertzog believed such policies amounted to a betrayal of true Afrikaner principles. He despised the English for their 'liberalism'. 'This liberalism is so deeply ingrained in our English-speaking compatriots,' he argued, 'that they themselves find it difficult to take action against those communistic and leftish movements when these movements make an attack upon them.' But for the Afrikaners, he declared, the English would have collapsed before the onslaught of liberalism. It was the Afrikaners, with their Calvinist upbringing, who made 'such ideal fighters and such good soldiers for white civilization'. Anchored to their church and their religion, they had grown strong in isolation and should remain there. Those Afrikaners who cooperated with the English were in danger of infecting themselves with liberalism and would be incapable of defending white civilization against the *swart gevaar*. For much the same reasons, Hertzog was vehemently opposed to the large number of immigrants from Europe that Verwoerd and Vorster had decided to encourage, in particular, as he put it, 'the scum of southern Europe', Greeks, Italians and Portuguese.

To these old controversies over the English and over immigration were added new ones. Hoping to reestablish South Africa's sporting links abroad, Vorster agreed to make minor concessions in sports policy of the kind that Verwoerd had never been willing to tolerate. Whereas Verwoerd had refused to allow Maoris to participate in New Zealand rugby teams visiting South Africa, prompting the New

Zealanders to decline an invitation to play there, Vorster decided in 1967 that Maoris could henceforth be included. Faced with this momentous decision, Hertzog retorted: 'It will lead to social integration, since they will dance with our Afrikaner girls at social functions.' Vorster's approach towards modifying sports segregation was at best hesitant and produced few results. Hoping that South Africa would gain admission to the Olympic Games in Mexico City in 1968, he announced that the government was prepared to allow a racially mixed team to participate there; but to ensure that no racial mixing occurred in South Africa beforehand, he instructed that whites and 'non-whites' should be prevented from competing against each other in the trials for the Olympic team. Vorster's efforts in the end were to no avail. South Africa's invitation to the Olympic Games was withdrawn after protests and threats of boycott by African and Asian states. Vorster complained bitterly: 'If what is happening now is to be the pattern according to which matters will be arranged in the world in future, then . . . it is not necessary for us to hold Olympic Games, then we should arrange for tree-climbing events, for then we are in the jungle.' His *verkrampte* critics meanwhile accused him of yet another betrayal.

Vorster's attempts to forge new diplomatic and trade ties with Africa were more successful but provoked similar controversy. In contrast to Verwoerd's preference for 'isolationist' policies, Vorster believed that an 'outward' foreign policy would not only improve South Africa's international image but open up new markets for its expanding industries. Vorster's efforts at 'detente' were rewarded in 1967 when Malawi became the first black African state to agree to an exchange of diplomats. His *verkrampte* critics, however, feared that the effect of Vorster's outward policy would be to work 'inwards', to change the relationship between white and black in South Africa. They were particularly incensed by the announcement that Malawi's black diplomats would be accorded the same privileges and immunities as white diplomats and allowed to live in the white suburbs of Pretoria.

These issues were trivial enough in themselves, but aroused powerful emotions. For months on end much of Afrikanerdom was caught up in vicious infighting. In 1969 the National Party finally split. Hertzog, dismissed from the cabinet the previous year, broke away to form the *Herstigte Nasionale Party* (Reconstituted National Party), claiming to speak for the true interests of Afrikanerdom. The

HNP, as its name implied, was a throwback to Malan's National Party of the 1930s. It was committed unashamedly to a pro-Afrikaner platform in which the English were relegated to the status of a second-class language group, immigration was severely restricted and apartheid was enforced even more strictly. The HNP also inveighed against the 'materialism' that now affected Afrikaner society, attacking the new 'elite' class of Afrikaner industrialists and bankers for corrupting Afrikaner traditions and portraying itself as the defender of Afrikaner workers. To head off the HNP threat, Vorster in 1970 called an early election and succeeded in inflicting a crushing victory over it: not a single HNP candidate came close to winning a seat. But the HNP, when breaking away from the National Party, had represented only a small part of the *verkrampte* camp willing to follow Hertzog. A far larger part remained within the National Party ready to challenge any 'liberal' tendencies the government showed.

The pressures for change, however, steadily mounted. The economic boom of the 1960s, together with the increasing use of advanced production techniques, had produced such a serious shortage of skilled labour that it was hampering further economic growth. The reservoir of white skills had simply run out. White immigration was not sufficient to fill the gap. White businessmen, for reasons of self-interest, argued that the only solution was to scrap the job reservation system giving whites a monopoly of skilled work and to allow blacks to move upwards in the labour market. The manufacturing sector, a major employer of black labour, took the lead in campaigning for change. Its labour requirements had always been different from other sectors like mining and agriculture. Whereas mining and agricultural enterprises had traditionally needed only cheap, unskilled workers, the manufacturing sector had been keen since the 1940s to promote the growth of a more skilled and more stable black workforce. For two decades, while the ideologues of apartheid were in the ascendant, its interests had tended to be eclipsed. But in the 1960s, as the leading growth sector in the economy contributing more to national output than mining and agriculture combined, its influence was increasingly felt. Moreover, the concern that the manufacturing sector expressed about the shortage of skilled labour was widely shared. The mining industry by 1969 was short of 2000 skilled men, 5 per cent of its white labour force. State-owned corporations like the railways and tele-communications were affected by the same problem. By 1970 the skill shortage amounted to nearly 100,000 jobs. Afrikaners and English-speaking businessmen alike suffered and found common cause in exerting pressure on the government for change in the system.

Wary of antagonizing the white labour unions and providing his *verkrampte* critics with new ammunition, Vorster was anxious to give way as little as possible. His Deputy Minister of Labour remarked in 1970, 'Important as the growth rate may be, it is not the most important factor. It does not weigh up against the position of the White worker. It can be said that such an outlook is contrary to the economic laws but it should be understood that this is the policy of the Nationalist Party.' Rather than allow blacks to be promoted to skilled work, the government devised other methods to try to solve the shortage. It introduced the idea of a 'floating' colour bar under which white jobs were split into two parts: whites were to perform the more skilled part leaving blacks to do the less skilled part, as long as it did not involve 'skilled' work. The government also hoped that white immigration would help ease the shortage. But none of its measures had much effect. In practice, employers resorted increasingly to their own solution by circumventing the job bar or simply disregarding it. White workers were given higher pay, promoted or shifted sideways allowing black workers to fill their previous jobs at lower pay. New job designations were devised. By 1972, for example, the railways began hiring Africans as 'train marshallers', a job virtually identical to that of 'shunters' performed by whites, though the pay was only half as much. By 1973, Vorster was ready to make major concessions. Provided that black advancement to skilled work occurred in 'an orderly fashion and with the concurrence of [white] trade unions', then the government would not oppose it. Because job reservation was so firmly entrenched in South Africa, whether as a matter of common practice or negotiated arrangement, the practical effect of Vorster's concessions was small. Nevertheless, they marked the first significant retreat in the apartheid system since 1948.

In recognizing the need for blacks to move into skilled work, Vorster also conceded that they would have to be provided with better education and training facilities. Discarding Verwoerd's policy of pegging expenditure on African education to the level of

African taxes, he authorized funds for a major expansion of the school system. Improvements were also conceded for the Indian and Coloured populations. Education was made compulsory for Indians in 1973, and for Coloureds in 1976. Industrial training centres for blacks were set up in townships by the government and in white industrial areas by private industry. A growing number of African students were given special licences to attend white university courses.

More attention was also paid to the wages and conditions of black workers, particularly after the wave of strikes which broke out in 1973. Vorster himself concluded that there were lessons to be learned from the strikes. 'Experience tells me this,' he pronounced, 'that employers should not only see in their workers a unit producing for them so many hours of service a day; they should also see them as human beings with souls.' For a government used to treating the African population either as 'productive units' or as 'non-productive units', this was a considerable advance.

As well as accepting the need for higher wages, employers' organizations and the government alike committed themselves publicly to reducing pay differentials between white and black and to moving towards equal pay for the same work. Both had a common motive in wanting to ensure industrial peace and to improve economic efficiency. Employers in particular hoped to gain from higher productivity, lower labour turnover and greater competition in the labour market. As thousands of blacks fought their way up the economic ladder and the black workforce gained higher wages, a marked shift in the pattern of income distribution occurred. In 1970, the white share of total personal income stood at 72 per cent, the African share at 19 per cent; by 1980 the white share had been reduced to 60 per cent, the African share had increased to 29 per cent.

The most dramatic advance took place in the mining industry. In the 1960s the gold mines had been on a declining path. While the price of gold had remained fixed at 35 dollars per ounce since 1933, their costs, particularly for white labour, had steadily increased. By 1970 the mining sector accounted for no more than 10 per cent of national output. Its fortunes were transformed in the years after 1970 when the gold price was set free. From an average price of 40 dollars per ounce in 1971, it moved to 97 dollars in 1973, to 159 dollars in 1974, to 612 dollars in 1980, reaching at one stage a peak of 850 dollars. By 1980 the mining sector's contribution to national output had risen to 23 per cent. The gold bonanza, as well as benefiting the mining corporations and the government's treasury, was used to raise the pitifully low rate of African wages. In the 1970s, African wages on the gold mines increased fourfold, while white wages rose by only 12 per cent, clipping the ratio of white wages to black wages from twenty times higher to six times higher. Mining employers also spent substantial sums improving conditions in labour compounds.

White workers reacted to these changes with varying degrees of resistance. The white Mine Workers Union, a key element in the *verkrampte* camp, fought successfully to keep job reservation largely intact. White building workers, denouncing what they called 'a cold-blooded sell-out', were less successful. For many white workers, the prospects of higher pay, promotion and fringe benefits were a sufficient inducement to win their cooperation. Those with higher skills, at a time when skills were in such shortage, no longer felt threatened by black competition. Those with lower skills were no longer so numerous or so politically influential.

White society in general was moving into a more tolerant era in racial matters. More affluent and broad-minded than before, it no longer saw the need for so many of the racial barriers erected since 1948. The Afrikaner elite – businessmen, academics, professionals and journalists, who formed the backbone of the *verligte* camp – were as prominent in campaigning for an end to 'petty' apartheid as their English-speaking compatriots. Travelling abroad, they were particularly susceptible to foreign opinion about the iniquities of racial discrimination. A growing part of the English-speaking population too was becoming more vociferous in its opposition to apartheid. In the 1974 election, the Progressive Party, which for thirteen years had been represented in parliament by the solitary figure of Helen Suzman, captured six more seats. Three years later, after the moribund United Party had disintegrated, the Progressives, or the Progressive Federal Party as they were now officially known, advocating the removal of racial discrimination and an extension of the franchise to all blacks, won 24 seats and 17 per cent of the white vote.

In fits and starts, partly as a result of government policy, partly through independent action by white municipalities, social apartheid began to fray at the edges. One consequence of Vorster's 'detente' policy towards neighbouring black states was that President Banda of Malawi arrived in South Africa for a state visit and gave a banquet at which whites were placed next to blacks, not only foreign blacks but local blacks. Vorster himself was seated between two Malawian women, an event which led to open derision by his *verkrampte* critics. Sensitive to such exposure, Vorster stoically replied: 'I did it in the interests of South Africa and, if it is necessary for the interests of South Africa, I would even do it again.' Vorster's dealings with homeland politicians also opened the way for greater social contact. In order to cope with 'multinational' occasions of this kind, a select number of white hotels and restaurants were given 'international' status and permitted to open their doors to black guests. As with all government policy on racial matters, the new rules and regulations for hotels were weighed down with absurd conditions often causing more offence than before. *The Survey of Race Relations in South Africa* recorded some of the difficulties confronting hoteliers and their new guests in 1978.

> Only black visitors holding foreign passports could use all hotel facilities. Other blacks could not drink in men's only bars. . . . They could swim if resident at the hotel, and be served liquor at mixed-sex bars if resident or a bona fide guest of a resident. Blacks who were not resident could be served liquor only if they were taking or about to take a meal on the premises, or attending a function, such as a conference.

White municipalities exercised their own powers to abolish racial restrictions on the use of public amenities. The Johannesburg City Council opened its museums, art gallery and municipal library to all races and removed 'White' and 'Non-White' signs from benches in its parks. Similar action was taken in Cape Town, Durban and East London. The rigid separation of races in government buildings was also relaxed; post offices which had operated separate windows for blacks and whites, were desegregated. White officials, accustomed to abusing blacks at will, were now told to handle them with respect. White salesgirls began to treat black customers with ostensible politeness. Under tight government supervision, television was finally introduced in 1976.

In the field of sport, the government, still hoping to gain international favour, made further concessions. In 1971, 'multinational' sports were allowed: this permitted the various white and black 'nations' of South Africa to compete against each other within the country in 'open international' events, but barred them from mixing at club, provincial or national levels. In 1976, the policy was changed to allow sporting contests between teams of different races at club level. In 1977 racial restrictions on club membership and on the use of club amenities were relaxed.

For all the advances that were made, the vast superstructure of apartheid remained firmly intact. Nothing of substance had changed. While recognizing the advantage of having a better trained and better paid black workforce, Vorster had no intention of altering its status as a subservient population based temporarily in white areas but possessing no permanent rights there. This traditional view of apartheid, however, brought him increasingly into conflict with the white business community, both Afrikaner and English. Still acting largely for reasons of self-interest but also because of the more enlightened mood affecting the white community, businessmen sought more sweeping changes in black conditions. Their common objective by the mid-1970s was to establish a stable and content black working class with higher levels of productivity and higher levels of consumption, providing commerce and industry with a larger domestic market for their goods and with a more efficient base from which to compete in international markets. In the view of the industrial magnate, Harry Oppenheimer, chairman of the giant Anglo-American Corporation, what South Africa needed was 'a change-over from a labour-intensive, low-wage, low-productivity economic system . . . to the capital-intensive, high-wage, high-productivity system' that advanced industrialized countries possessed. This meant that black workers would have to be given a secure and permanent status in white areas, allowed to live there with their families in their own housing and provided with better amenities. As well as reforms in these areas, employers wanted an overhaul of the whole system of influx control. They spoke out against state control of the labour market and were particularly critical of the way in which the government's labour bureaux operated, treating millions of workers that passed through them as 'an undifferentiated mass' and providing a service that was inefficient, costly and weighed down with bureaucratic machinery. There was criticism too about the operation of the pass laws which rendered workers liable to police raids and to arrest and prison for pass law offences. Employers accepted the need for some controls on urban entry but wanted a system that would permit a competitive and more mobile labour market. They also favoured legal recognition of black trade unions which would allow them to conduct industrial relations on an orderly basis.

The Soweto riots of 1976 intensified all these arguments and added new ones. Not only did the business sector have to contend with urban unrest and labour strikes at home, but a far more hostile environment abroad. The international outcry over South Africa's racial policies and over events like the death of Steve Biko endangered South Africa's export markets, particularly in areas where anti-apartheid groups were active, drove away foreign investors and damaged South Africa's ability to attract foreign capital and technology. Foreign investment in South Africa was a vital factor in its economic growth. Though by 1976 domestic investments accounted for about 90 per cent of capital formation, South Africa still depended on foreign capital to achieve a high rate of growth. In the ten-year period up to 1976, the average net inflow of capital was equivalent to about 3 per cent of national output. In the aftermath of Soweto, however, foreign capital began to flow out. Multinational companies with subsidiaries in South Africa, like Mobil, General Motors, Ford and Barclays Bank, faced intense criticism from anti-apartheid groups, some demanding their withdrawal. Several prominent American and British banks terminated their South African business. The government itself was only able to obtain foreign loans by paying 2 per cent above the rate available to underdeveloped countries with poor credit ratings.

White businessmen worried too about the political implications of the Soweto revolt, in particular the danger that blacks in their resentment of apartheid might turn as well against the free enterprise system. Oppenheimer took the view that 'racial discrimination and free enterprise are basically incompatible and failure to eradicate the one will ultimately result in the destruction of the other'. The *Afrikaanse Handelinstituut*, representing Afrikaner business interests, warned: 'Unless the black man is given a greater share of South Africa's free enterprise system, he will be driven into the arms of Marxism and socialism, as evidenced by events elsewhere in Africa.' The Transvaal Chamber of Industries sent a memorandum to Vorster urging him to win over the black middle class before it was too late.

The thought most basic to our submission is the need to ensure a stable, contented, urbanized black community in our metropolitan and industrialized areas. . . . The mature family-orientated urban black already places the stability of his household uppermost, and is more interested in ˌhis pay-packet than in politics. Our prime point of departure should be that this 'middle-class' is not weakened by frustration and indignity. Only by having this most responsible section of the urban black to our side can the whites of South Africa be assured of containing on a long-term basis the irresponsible economic and political ambitions of those blacks who are influenced against their own real interest from within and without our borders.

As a contribution towards solving the problem, white employers, led by Oppenheimer and the Afrikaner magnate Anton Rupert, set up an Urban Foundation in 1976, aiming to 'improve the quality of life' for urban blacks by raising funds for better housing and better amenities, stressing the role that free enterprise could play. Employers' organizations also drew up codes of employment practice committing them to eliminate all racial discrimination. Foreign multinational corporations with subsidiaries in South Africa took the same action. Codes of conduct were drawn up for American companies in 1977 by the Reverend Leon Sullivan, a black member of General Motors' board of directors, and for European companies by the European Economic Community. But the main efforts of the business community and others in the *verligte* camp were directed towards persuading the government to act. Business leaders constantly harped on the need for major reform.

Vorster possessed neither the imagination nor the willpower to tackle these larger issues and tended to side with the *verkrampte* camp which wanted to keep reforms to a minimum. His business critics were simply told to stay out of politics. 'Efforts to use business organizations to bring about basic change in government policy will fail and cause unnecessary and harmful friction between the government and the private sector,' he warned. 'You cannot ask me to implement policies rejected by the electorate and in which I do not believe.' In the last few years of his tenure as prime minister, Vorster's administration was paralysed by indecision. On every front, the government's strategy was in disarray. Abroad, Western criticism of apartheid was at a new peak. In Africa, the 'detente' policy had collapsed in the wake of South Africa's ill-fated invasion of Angola. At home, *verkrampte* and *verligte* opponents were locked in deadly combat. The economy, moreover, was in the grip of the worst recession for forty years.

What broke the deadlock was a political scandal of such proportions that it caused the downfall not only of Vorster but his heir apparent, Connie Mulder, a leading *verkrampte* figure, enabling the *verligte* camp to gain control of the National Party and move South Africa into an era of reform. The scandal unfolded over a period of eighteen months starting in February 1978 when the Auditor-General tabled a report criticizing unnamed officials of the Department of Information for undertaking unnecessary and extravagant trips abroad. Given this lead, the English-language press, relishing the opportunity to embarrass the government, began to uncover details of a series of secret projects run by the Department of Information with the use of public funds aimed at improving South Africa's image abroad and influencing opinion at home. Millions of rands had been spent clandestinely on schemes to purchase foreign newspapers, bribe foreign politicians and set up front organizations abroad. Some schemes had succeeded, others failed. In the United States, South African funds were used to buy *The Sacramento Union* in California; an earlier attempt to buy the *Washington Star* fell through. In Britain, front organizations like 'The Club of Ten' and the 'Committee for Fairness in Sport' were used to campaign for South Africa's readmission to international sporting events. Information officials running these schemes were also involved in purchasing property in Miami, Cannes and London, arranging expensive holidays for themselves and for their clients and financing dubious business ventures on the side. In South Africa itself, government funds were spent on setting up an English-language daily newspaper, *The Citizen*, which was given specific instructions to promote the government's viewpoint. The origin of all these schemes was eventually traced to a secret meeting in 1972 between Vorster, the Minister of Information, Connie Mulder, and an Information official, Eschel Rhoodie. What damaged Vorster and Mulder in the scandal was not so much the disclosure of the schemes themselves but the lies they told in an attempt to cover them up.

As the scandal developed, Vorster decided to resign as prime minister, citing reasons of ill health, while letting it be known that he would welcome appointment as president, a ceremonial office to which he was duly elected. Vorster's departure in September 1978 set off a vicious struggle for power between Mulder, the *verkrampte* candidate, and the *verligte* camp which made every effort to use the Information scandal to discredit him. In the normal course of events, Mulder would have had no difficulty in being elected prime minister. As leader of the National Party in the Transvaal, he commanded almost half the votes in the parliamentary caucus. But in the election he obtained only seventy-four votes. His *verligte* opponent, Pieter Willem Botha, leader of the National Party in the Cape, won ninety-eight votes.

The denouement of the scandal came in June 1979. On the day that a judicial commission reported that Vorster had not only known all along about the Department of Information's secret projects but had been actively involved in their cover-up, he resigned as president, a weary and discredited figure. The irony was that he was the ultimate victim of his own endeavours to win a better image for South Africa.

CHAPTER SEVENTEEN

Botha's Solution

Botha brought to South Africa a new style of leadership. Like Verwoerd and Vorster he was an authoritarian figure, single-minded, ruthless and intolerant of opposition. His commitment to the cause of white supremacy was no less tenacious than theirs. But Botha preferred a pragmatic approach to the conduct of government rather than an ideological one. Though at times impetuous and quick-tempered, he possessed a talent for organization and a liking for order and discipline which had made him increasingly impatient with Vorster's lax methods of administration and his inability to provide more effective leadership. In the closing stages of Vorster's regime, the two men clashed repeatedly. Botha later admitted to his biographers: 'I was a bit difficult in the last few years before I became prime minister.'

Botha's outlook was affected by two powerful influences. As leader of the National Party in the Cape he came from a tradition of Afrikaner politics different to that of Transvaal politicians like Verwoerd and Vorster. Whereas in the Transvaal the National Party tended to reflect the interest of Afrikaner workers, farmers and civil servants, in the Cape it was dominated by large Afrikaner business and financial enterprises like Andries Wassenaar's Sanlam and Rupert's Rembrandt Corporation. Botha himself had spent his entire career inside the National Party in the Cape. Starting in 1936 as a full-time organizer at the age of twenty, he first made a name for himself as a roughneck by breaking up meetings of General Smuts' United Party; he went on to gain a seat in parliament in 1948 and rose to become a cabinet minister under Verwoerd. As party leader in the Cape for twelve years he was fully conversant with the growing frustration that Afrikaner businessmen felt about Vorster's conservatism. His sudden leap to office as prime minister, though largely an accident, was brought about with the help of businessmen and others in the *verligte* camp hoping to engineer a change in government strategy. Botha, once in power, was ready to respond.

An equally potent influence on Botha was the military. As defence minister for twelve years, he had come to admire the military's methods of planning and coordination. As well as dealing with its operational requirements, he had immersed himself in the theories of military strategy, using the military as a form of university education. Like the business community, the military command had become increasingly restive during Vorster's last years in office, critical of the lack of urgency shown by the government in tackling the fundamental issues thrown up by the Soweto revolt. In the immediate wake of the Soweto riots, the military began to speak its mind with unusual candour. 'If we lose the socio-economic struggle,' General Gert Boshoff, the army chief of staff, said, 'then we need not even bother to fight the military one.' The commander of the South African air force, Lieutenant-General Rogers, stressed the government had to 'do everything it could to win the hearts and minds of our own indigenous people.' What the military wanted above all were defensible political goals.

The air was soon thick with the promises of reform. Botha began his term of office by emphasizing the need for 'efficient, clean administration' and by preparing the white population for dramatic change. 'We are moving in a changing world,' he said. 'We must adapt otherwise we shall die.' He urged Afrikaners to learn the lessons of their own history: 'The moment you start oppressing people . . . they fight back.' In one speech after another, the same message was conveyed across the country. 'A white monopoly of power is untenable in the Africa of today. . . . A meaningful division of power is needed between all race groups. . . . Apartheid is a recipe for permanent conflict.' Botha declared himself to be in favour of removing 'hurtful unnecessary discrimination' and suggested that even laws like the Land Act, the Mixed Marriage Act and the Immorality Act, which prohibited sexual relations between white and black, catching hundreds of whites in its seamy net each year, should no longer be regarded as 'holy cows'. The campaign for a new image was conducted abroad as well as at home in the hope of winning South Africa foreign support. Touring the United States in 1979, one of Botha's ministers, Pieter Koornhof, told an audience in Washington: 'Apartheid as the world came to know it . . . is dead.'

The signs of change were soon evident. Botha placed his own *verligte* supporters in key ministries, strengthened the powers of the prime minister's office and reorganized the civil service, reducing the number of departments by nearly half. A cabinet secretariat was established for the first time, agendas were circulated, minutes were kept. Botha also brought into government experts and specialists outside the narrow circle on which previous Nationalist prime ministers had preferred to rely. Vorster had been content with the company of a few close colleagues, most notably his old friend General van den Bergh, head of the security apparatus. Botha sought advice from a wider range, including academics and business-men well known for their *verligte* views. In a symbolic gesture of reconciliation with the business community, in November 1979 he took his entire cabinet to attend a conference in the Carlton Hotel in Johannesburg with the country's leading industrialists and bankers, among them Harry Oppenheimer, whom Vorster had never chosen to meet. 'We have our differences,' said Botha, 'but we are creating reciprocal channels to plan national strategy in South Africa as a team.' All there were agreed that economic growth, sustaining whites in power and providing blacks with higher living standards, should become the country's main objective. At the end of the conference, one newspaper remarked: 'The Anglo-Boer war is finally over.'

A conscious effort was made as well to establish better relations with the black population. Much of Verwoerd's nomenclature was dropped. The Department of Bantu Administration was renamed the Department of Plural Relations in 1978 and then the Department of Cooperation and Development in 1979; the Department of Bantu Education became the Department of Education and Training; Bantu homelands were now referred to as 'Black States' or 'national' states. Botha made his own contribution by paying a visit to Soweto, the first prime minister ever to set foot in a black township, proclaiming as he did so: 'We are all South Africans.'

The reform process began, albeit with extreme caution, with government moves to create stable black urban communities with a vested interest in the free enterprise system. Much of the govern-ment's thinking was influenced by two official commissions which recommended in 1979 that the old apartheid policy of depriving blacks of permanent rights in 'white areas' should be dropped altogether. The Wiehahn Commission, set up to investigate labour relations, argued that in view of the rapid growth of unregistered unions since 1973, which now constituted an informal industrial system outside the officially sanctioned one, it was in the best interests of the government to incorporate them into the system.

'Black trade unions are subject neither to the protective and stabilizing elements of the system nor to its essential discipline and control.' By bringing the unions into the system, the government would be able to monitor their activities more closely and encourage 'responsible behaviour'. If left unsupervised, they might fall under foreign influence and be used for political purposes. The commission recommended that all African workers, including migrants and commuters, should be eligible for membership of registered unions, whether African or multiracial, and brought into the collective bargaining process. It urged furthermore that job reservation laws still on the statute book should be abolished and that artisan training programmes should be provided for Africans.

The Riekert Commission, called upon to devise a solution to the problems of African urbanization, took a similar view of the need to incorporate African urban communities into the system. It placed strong emphasis on dividing the African population into 'insiders' who already possessed claims to permanent urban residence and 'outsiders' with no such claims. What was needed, said the Riekert Commission, was a system of orderly urbanization which allowed 'insiders' better facilities and the right to move in a free labour market but which placed greater control over 'outsiders' trying to gain entry. 'Control over the rate of urbanization is, in light of circumstances in South Africa, an absolutely essential social security measure. Even though . . . the abolition of such control would lead to further economic growth, the price to be paid for it in terms of direct and indirect social costs would be too high.' In specific terms, the Riekert Commission proposed that permanent urban residents, who numbered about half of the urban African labour force and about one quarter of the total African labour force, should be allowed to live with their families in towns and to move more freely between jobs and between towns; they should also be given first access to urban employment. The commission further recommended that restrictions on African trading rights should be lifted and that more family housing should be constructed in townships. Meanwhile, the entry of outsiders into urban areas should be more strictly controlled by more extensive use of labour bureaux, by penalizing more heavily white employers who hired illegal, unregistered workers, and by enforcing the law against illegal squatting and lodging more rigorously. What the Riekert Commission was proposing, in effect, was the establishment of a labour elite, involving about 12 per cent of the African population.

The government eventually accepted most of these proposals. After thirty years of harsh legislation designed to prevent the African population from putting down roots in 'white' areas, their rights to live there permanently were finally recognized, just as the Fagan Commission had recommended in 1948. A 99-year leasehold scheme was offered to qualified Africans in townships outside the Western Cape. Residents with Section 10 rights were allowed to bring wives and children from homelands to live with them. New housing programmes were started. An electrification project for Soweto was put underway. African workers were permitted to join registered unions. Except in the mining industry, legal job reservation was abolished. Restrictions on African, Coloured and Indian business-men were eased. A parastatal organization was set up to provide training and aid for small businessmen. The role of the Industrial Development Corporation was extended to cover blacks. In the field of education, the government committed itself to the goal of providing equal, though separate, education for all population groups, while emphasizing that 'the historical backlog cannot be overcome overnight'. By 1983 only seven times as much was spent on white children per capita as on African children, compared to sixteen times as much in 1968.

A more lenient attitude was adopted to two long-standing African 'troublespots'. In 1979 the government decided to reprieve Alexandra, an overcrowded and ramshackle black ghetto north of Johannesburg, surrounded by affluent white suburbs, which Verwoerd had condemned in 1962 as a 'black spot' and which was marked down for destruction to make way for a massive complex of migrant labour hostels. The local community there had put up strong resistance against the government's plans to move them. A similar reprieve was given to the Crossroads squatter settlement on the outskirts of Cape Town, whose inhabitants had achieved international fame by defying the government's forceful efforts to expel them and raze the settlement to the ground, as had happened to other squatter camps in the Cape peninsular. Such actions, as officials made clear, were exceptions to general policy. Nevertheless they marked a significant shift in approach for a government renowned for handling African issues with iron-fisted tactics.

All these concessions to the African population stirred intense anger and resentment among right-wing whites. The Afrikaans-speaking

Confederation of Labour, once a staunch ally of the government, complained that 'never before in the history of the country' had white workers received 'such a slap in the face'. The all-white Mine Workers Union described the labour reforms as 'the greatest treachery against the white employees of South Africa since 1922' and called for strike action in the hope of provoking a major confrontation. Throughout the network of Afrikaner institutions, in the churches, the Broederbond, the cultural organizations, and in the civil service, there were signs of mounting opposition to Botha's new strategy. A series of parliamentary by-elections in 1979 showed a marked upsurge in support for the *Herstigte Nasionale Party* (HNP), hitherto regarded as a group of right-wing cranks.

The full extent of the right-wing backlash was revealed by the general election in 1981. Portraying Botha as a dangerous liberal, the HNP leader, Jaap Marais, warned that the government's 'left-wing' policies meant 'giving up, giving in, giving over and eventually giving away our own country'. Forced on to the defensive, the National Party in its campaign backed away from presenting ideas of reform and reverted to its traditional stand of defending white interests to the last. In the event, the HNP failed to gain a parliamentary seat. But the trend towards extreme right-wing parties was unmistakable. Their share of the total vote increased from 3 per cent in 1977 to 15 per cent; their share of the Afrikaner vote rose from 7 per cent to 33 per cent. White workers, low-ranking civil servants and smallholders, those who felt most threatened by black advancement, deserted the National Party in droves. Whereas in elections in 1970, 1974 and 1977 the National Party had won between 83 and 85 per cent of the Afrikaner vote, in 1981 it collected only 63 per cent. Its share of the total vote fell from 65 per cent in 1977 to 56 per cent. An important proportion of the National Party's support came once again from the English-speaking population – about 28 per cent voted for Botha. Even though the National Party was returned to power with a huge majority – 131 seats out of 165 – its hold over the Afrikaner community had been seriously weakened. 'Afrikaner unity in the political sense of the word,' commented the Afrikaans newspaper, *Rapport*, 'no longer exists.'

Botha regarded the election result as a strong enough mandate for him to continue with further reforms, but he faced strong opposition from inside the National Party from *verkrampte* politicians encouraged all the more to stand firm against him by the rising tide of right-wing opinion. Botha wanted to expand the political base of the white population by incorporating the Coloured and Indian communities into the white political system, providing them with political rights while ensuring that political power remained securely in the hands of the whites. The terminology he used for describing this exercise was 'a healthy form of power sharing'. For *verkrampte* politicians determined to uphold Verwoerd's doctrine of total separation, such proposals amounted to heresy. Botha knew that if he pressed forward with the scheme, he would precipitate a split not only in the National Party but throughout Afrikanerdom.

Botha took the risk and plunged Afrikanerdom into its greatest crisis since the Second World War, leaving wounds that have never healed. In Afrikaans it was known as *volkskeuring* – a rending of the people. In March 1982 a group of seventeen Nationalist MPs, headed by Dr Andries Treurnicht, a cabinet minister and leader of the National Party in the Transvaal, broke away to form the Conservative Party. Among those who gave the new party their support was Vorster.

Treurnicht, a former *predikant*, a newspaper editor, erstwhile chairman of the Broederbond, was the true heir of Verwoerd, a middle-class ideologue wedded to ideas of racial purity and power. What he advocated was absolute apartheid, a geographical separation between the races with separate homelands for Coloureds and Indians as well as Africans. Any tampering, even at the edges of apartheid, he argued, would lead in the end to fundamental change, unravelling the whole fabric of apartheid. Botha's proposals for power sharing, he said, meant 'the abolition of white supremacy' and amounted to a recipe for racial strife. 'Any attempt at multi-racialism, especially in government, must of necessity lead to never-ending conflict between the race groups,' he said.

In the months that followed, the split spread to every institution throughout Afrikanerdom, rending apart the Broederbond, the *Federasie van Afrikaanse Kultuurvereniginge*, the *Afrikaanse Studentebond*, the *Voortrekker* youth movement and the churches, reaching down to town councils, school boards and business associations. New extremist groups sprang up competing for the loyalty of the *volk.* In Pretoria, Afrikaner women formed the *Kappiekommando*, dressed in full-length skirts and bonnets of *Voortrekker* matrons and marched to Union Buildings, the administrative headquarters of the government, carrying a coffin. A former chairman of the Broederbond, Carel Boshoff, ousted for refusing to accept Botha's proposals, headed a new cultural organization, the *Afrikaner Volkswag*, (Sentinel of the People) 'for Afrikaners who refuse to relinquish their Afrikaner aspirations for mere South Africanism'. Right-wing fanatics found a home in the *Afrikaner Weerstandsbeweging*, the Afrikaner Resistance Movement, an overtly fascist organization affecting Nazi-style ritual and insignia with aims of restoring the old nineteenth-century Boer republics. Its most renowned act was to break up a lecture in Pretoria being given by a distinguished historian, Floris van Jaarsveld, about the myths surrounding the Covenant of 1838, and to tar and feather him.

Undeterred by the furore, Botha turned his attention to examining what constitutional formula would best suit his plans for incorporating Coloured and Indian communities into the political system without interfering with the structure of white control. A vast literature on constitutional options for South Africa existed. Over the years white planners and theorists, think-tanks and universities had poured out ideas on partition, federation, confederation, consociational democracy and other more abstruse schemes, all persevering in the belief that some magic formula could be found for South African conditions. Only a limited effort was ever made to consult the 'non-white' population. Change, when it came, was simply imposed from above. The government's reasoning was explained by Botha's minister of transport, Hendrik Schoeman, in parliament in August 1981: 'In this country,' he said, 'four million whites must think and plan for 25 million people. It is a question of the protection of the minority with whom the brain power lies.'

The constitution upon which Botha decided was complex, inevitably so given its purpose. Much emphasis was placed on the importance of 'group rights', a term which, according to the government's explanation, meant that each race group was allowed to govern itself without interference or domination by any other, but which in practice added up to little more than the old system of racial separation run by whites. Parliament was divided into three chambers: a House of Assembly consisting of 178 members for the white population of 4.5 million; a House of Representatives consisting of 85 members for the Coloured population of 2.5 million; and a House of Deputies consisting of 45 members for the Indian population of 800,000. Each chamber possessed a ministers' council and had responsibility for 'own' affairs; these were defined as being matters of concern to only one race group, like education, social welfare, health, housing and local government. The conduct of 'general affairs', matters such as foreign affairs, defence, state security, law and order, commerce, industry, African affairs and budgets, remained in the hands of the government. Legislation for 'general affairs' was discussed in 'joint standing committees' and required the assent of all three chambers. A new office of State President was established, combining the previous posts of prime minister and president, and giving the head of government greatly increased powers. The State President was chosen by an electoral college in which the majority white party had control. In cases where there were disputes between different chambers on 'general' legislation, the President and the President's Council, a body in effect controlled by him, were empowered to resolve the matter. The overall consequence of the new constitution was to diminish further the importance of parliament and to increase the powers of the executive. Apart from the need to seek parliamentary approval of budgets, the government could conduct state business largely without reference to parliament at all. Far from being an exercise in power sharing, in fact, the new constitution concentrated even greater power in the hands of white politicians in control of the government.

Neither the Coloured nor the Indian communities showed much sign of enthusiasm for the new constitutional dispensation. But Botha was successful in finding Coloured and Indian politicians willing to make it work. The Labour Party, a Coloured party which had previously participated in the discredited Coloured Representative Council, agreed to cooperate maintaining that it would be possible to dismantle apartheid 'from within'. Its leader, Allan Hendrickse, a former teacher, described the new constitution as 'a springboard for change'. Indian politicians took much the same view. One remarked: 'We may be travelling second-class, but at least we are on the train.' Despite demands for referenda on the constitution, no test of opinion for the Coloured and Indian communities was permitted. Voters were presented with a *fait accompli* and told that they could express their views at election time. When elections came in 1984, the results were tantamount to a rejection of the new system. Voter participation was officially set at 30 per cent in the Coloured election and 20 per cent in the Indian election. These were low enough figures in themselves. But since only about 60 per cent of eligible Coloured voters had registered, the effective poll was far lower. In the Cape peninsular, where the bulk of the Coloureds lived, the official turnout was 11 per cent; the 'real' turnout was as low as 5 per cent. For eligible Indian voters, the 'real' turnout was 16.6 per cent. Taken together, the results showed that less than one in five Coloureds and Indians thought there was any point in voting.

The white population meanwhile was invited to give its views on the new constitution in a referendum in November 1983. Fearful of the impact that white opponents of the new constitution, from the left as well as the right, might make on white opinion, the government took unprecedented steps through radio, television and newspapers to bombard the public with propaganda about its virtues. Both the Conservative Party led by Treurnicht and the Progressive Federal Party, led by a young Afrikaner intellectual, Frederik van Zyl Slabbert, opposed the new constitution, the Conservative Party on the grounds that it signalled the end of white civilization, the PFP on the grounds that it brought apartheid even further into the heart of public life by partitioning the legislature itself.

The result was a triumph for Botha. Two-thirds of the white population voted in favour of the new constitution. Even though the new dispensation had cost him the price of party unity, a sacrifice no previous Nationalist prime minister would have considered making, he had emerged with a clear mandate in support of his programme of reform, acquired new allies in the Coloured and Indian communities and fashioned the presidency with formidable power. There was, however, one remarkable failure. Botha had not stopped to consider what effect the new constitution might have on an African population excluded from it.

CHAPTER EIGHTEEN

The Security Machine

In tandem with his reform programme, Botha began to develop a national security system designed to overcome any challenge mounted against the government either internally or externally. From Pretoria's perspective, the threats to white rule were gathering pace from every quarter. In the southern African region, each of South Africa's white-ruled neighbours, Angola, Mozambique and Rhodesia had succumbed to guerrilla warfare waged by African nationalist movements with the help of the Soviet Union and adjacent African states. Guerrilla activity was also increasing in South West Africa (Namibia) which South Africa controlled in defiance of United Nations' rulings. The collapse of Portuguese rule in Angola and Mozambique in 1974 left large gaps in the white buffer zone which had once insulated South Africa from black Africa to the north. In the civil war in Angola that followed, an army of Cuban troops and Soviet advisers arrived in Luanda in a Soviet airlift to support the Marxist MPLA's bid for power against pro-Western nationalist movements, providing the Soviet Union with an opportunity to establish a permanent military presence in the region and, to Pretoria's dismay, Western states showed little inclination to intervene. The only Western assistance forthcoming for South Africa's ill-fated military campaign to defeat the MPLA in 1975 was a clandestine venture launched by the CIA which Congress soon cut short once it knew of their involvement. The upshot was that from 1975 South Africa possessed as its neighbours Marxist governments in Angola and Mozambique, friendly to the Soviet Union and willing to provide the exiled African National Congress with sanctuaries and training facilities. Of South Africa's white allies, only Ian Smith's Rhodesia held out, fending off international sanctions and nationalist guerrillas, but from a position which the South Africans believed in the long run was no longer tenable, regardless of how much military and financial support they provided.

At an international level, too, Pretoria faced an increasingly hostile world. The voluntary arms embargo first imposed by the United Nations Security Council in 1963 became mandatory in 1977, cutting South Africa off from its last major arms supplier, France. In 1973, OPEC states announced an oil embargo against South Africa. The South Africans evaded the embargo by turning to Iran, but in 1979 after the fall of the Shah, Iran's oil exports too were stopped, forcing South Africa to rely on clandestine trade. Relations with Britain and the United States were also affected. In 1975 Britain terminated the Simonstown naval agreement, severing its last defence link with South Africa. In 1977 a Democratic president, Jimmy Carter, came to power promising a more aggressive approach on human rights issues in South Africa. In one country after another, anti-apartheid groups campaigned with increasing vigour for boycotts, sanctions and disinvestment.

Botha's explanation for this tide of events was that it was all part of a master plan by the Soviet Union to achieve global domination. He had a fixed and simple view of world politics, believing that they revolved around a struggle between communist and anti-communist forces, in which South Africa, with its vast mineral resources and maritime facilities, was a glittering prize. Whatever ills befell South Africa, whether it was regional instability, international pressure or domestic unrest, were attributed ultimately to Moscow's grand design.

> The ultimate aim of the Soviet Union and its allies is to overthrow the present body politic in the Republic of South Africa and to replace it with a Marxist-oriented form of government to further the objectives of the USSR. Therefore all possible methods and means are used to attain this objective. This includes social and labour unrest, civilian resistance, terrorist attacks against the infrastructure of South Africa, and the intimidation of black leaders and members of the security forces. This onslaught is supported by a worldwide propaganda campaign and the involvement of various front organizations, such as trade unions and even certain church organizations and leaders.

What made matters worse was that Western states no longer possessed the will to stand up to this challenge. 'South Africa is also experiencing double standards on the part of certain Western bodies in their behaviour towards her. They are doing this in an attempt to pay a ransom to the bear whose hunger must be satisfied.'

Botha's answer to this 'total onslaught' was 'total strategy'. The idea had become fashionable in military circles in the mid-1970s during Botha's term of office as defence minister, and, as prime minister, he used it to form a central part of the government's method of operation. Hitherto South Africa had dealt with external threats on an individual basis. As a result of the United Nations arms embargo in 1963, South Africa had begun to develop its own arms industry. The state-owned Armaments Development and Manufacturing Corporation (Armscor), set up in 1968, provided the basis of an industrial and military network which eventually produced not only a vast range of weapons for South Africa's needs, but became one of the world's largest armaments export industries. As a result of the threats to its oil supplies, South Africa developed its own facilities for producing oil from coal. The parastatal South African Coal, Oil and Gas Corporation (Sasol) had been established in 1950. Its first plant, Sasol 1, had been in operation since 1955, producing about 2 per cent of domestic consumption. In 1974, after the OPEC ban came into effect, the government approved construction of a second Sasol plant more than three times the size of Sasol 1. A third plant on the same scale as Sasol 2 was ordered in 1979. The aim was to raise the country's oil production to meet a half of domestic requirements. In addition, large stockpiles of oil were purchased, sufficient to last for at least two years in the event of a comprehensive oil embargo.

What Botha proposed, once he was prime minister, was that henceforth all efforts to combat threats to state security, whether external or internal, should be coordinated and controlled from a central organization drawing upon the expertise of the military, the intelligence community, government administrators, business leaders and any other experts whenever needed. The extent of the challenge facing the government, said Botha in a defence white paper in 1977, was so great that it required 'coordinated action in all fields – military, psychological, economic, political, sociological, technological, diplomatic, ideological and cultural' – and hence the involvement of all sections of society. The head of the South African Defence Force, General Magnus Malan, one of Botha's principal confidantes, put the military's view in even more dramatic fashion in September 1977: 'South Africa is today . . . involved in total war,' he said. 'The war is not only an area for the soldier. Everyone is involved and has a role to play.' Neither Botha nor Malan believed that the government yet faced serious danger. But the long-term outlook seemed ominous. By emphasizing the 'total onslaught' theme, Botha's aim was to mobilize white South Africans against external foes and to arouse Western support for its position as a beleaguered outpost of 'Western civilization'. What Botha was also doing was laying the groundwork for a new era of state control.

The nerve centre of Botha's new national security system was the State Security Council (SSC). It had been established originally under Vorster's auspices in 1972 to advise the government on intelligence and security matters, but like so much else in Vorster's administration, it functioned only on a haphazard basis. It was merely one of twenty different cabinet committees which met infrequently and to which Vorster paid scant attention. When dealing with intelligence and security matters, Vorster had relied almost exclusively on the Bureau for State Security, usually known as BOSS, set up in 1969 by his old colleague from the security police, Colonel Hendrik van den Bergh, who was given a free hand to engage in espionage and 'dirty tricks' both inside South Africa and abroad. Promoted to the rank of general, van den Bergh was allowed to play a key role in the execution of foreign policy, in particular in Vorster's 'detente' initiative with black African states, and gained the reputation for being 'the second most powerful man in the country'. He built BOSS into a formidable organization that was generally feared by the government's critics and much resented by the military establishment led by Botha as minister of defence. Whereas Botha favoured the invasion of Angola in 1975, van den Bergh opposed it. With the downfall of Vorster in 1978, the ground was cut from underneath van den Bergh's feet.

In his reorganization of the government, Botha reduced the number of cabinet committees from twenty to four, giving each one greater status and a permanent staff. Of the four committees – dealing with security, constitutional affairs, economic affairs and social affairs – by far the greatest weight was accorded to the State Security Council. Its role was to establish and then to control a National Security Management System (NSMS) covering all fields of strategic importance. In practice this gave the SSC a decisive influence not just over defence and security policies but over the entire range of government business. To support this undertaking the SSC was provided with a large secretariat and allowed to establish a network of agencies and committees which constituted in effect an alternative system of government. In control of this new apparatus was a select group of senior politicians including the prime minister, the ministers of defence, foreign affairs, law and order and justice, and senior members of the defence forces, the police and intelligence services. Van den Bergh's Bureau for State Security was replaced by a new National Intelligence Service with a greatly reduced role and a single seat on the SSC along with military intelligence and the security police. What the SSC represented in effect was the emergence of a new security establishment, empowered to devise a counter-revolutionary strategy and to execute it. Henceforth, the traditional forums of political power – the cabinet, parliament and the National Party – were of declining significance.

In dealing with the regional threat, as Pretoria perceived it, Botha's approach was two-fold. His priority, as it had been during his days as minister of defence, was to strengthen South Africa's defence capability to ensure it maintained 'a solid military balance' with neighbouring states and was effective in stopping guerrilla infiltration. This process had begun in earnest in 1974 as the Portuguese army's hold on Mozambique and Angola disintegrated, exposing Namibia to the danger of increased infiltration from Angola by Swapo guerrillas. The force levels of each service were steadily increased. Between 1974 and 1980, the permanent force in the army – its professional core – was raised from 7000 to 11,000 men; its national service contingent rose from 27,500 to 60,000. The permanent force in the air force was raised from 8500 to 10,300; its national service contingent rose from 3000 to 4000. The Citizen Force, a part-time army in which all former servicemen were required to serve for set periods each year, expanded from 60,000 to 120,000. Whereas in 1960 only a small proportion of white civilians were caught up in the military net for a brief three-month period of training, by 1980 virtually every white male over the age of eighteen had a defence commitment. In 1977 the duration of national service was extended from twelve months to two years. After that, civilians were required to serve a further two months annually for the next twelve years, followed by another twelve days annually for the next five years as members of the Citizen Force Reserve, after which they joined the Commandos and then the National Reserve. With force levels kept so high, the drain on white manpower from the economy was severe. The cost of the increased defence effort was also substantial. Purchases of military equipment produced locally by Armscor grew thirtyfold during the 1970s. In 1960 less than 7 per cent of government expenditure had been spent on defence; by 1980 it had risen to 16 per cent.

So stretched were the manpower resources of the white community that the government began with extreme caution to use 'non-white' volunteers in the Permanent Force. For the National Party which had repeatedly insisted that it would 'never arm the natives', the move was a traumatic one. By tradition, the only role permitted for Coloureds and Africans was as non-combatants, as drivers, clerks, cooks, orderlies and labourers. But in 1973 Coloured recruits in the South African Coloured Corps were trained for combat in counter-insurgency operations. An officer-training course was started. In 1975 seven Coloured officers were commissioned. The following year a Coloured infantry company was sent for border duty in Namibia. In 1975 it was decided that Africans could join the Permanent Force. A training headquarters was established at Lenz near Johannesburg. In 1979 African regional companies consisting of separate Zulu, Swazi, Venda and Shangaan units were attached to regional commands. Africans were promoted to officer rank. The first two senior officers to emerge were a chaplain with the rank of colonel and a public relations officer with the rank of captain. By 1980 the number of Coloureds, Africans and Indians in the South African Defence Force had risen to 5250, constituting 15 per cent of the army's permanent force and one third of the navy's permanent force. In addition, 'independent' homeland governments were allowed to establish their own national guards. In the police force too 'non-whites' were given faster promotion and greater responsibility for police work in their own areas. By the end of 1980 there were twenty-one Indian, thirty-three Coloured and eighty-five African commissioned officers in the police force. Nearly fifty police stations were under 'non-white' command.

The second part of Botha's regional strategy was to assert South Africa's position as a regional power. Through a network of trade, transport, labour and investment links, South Africa had traditionally played a dominant role throughout southern Africa. Some African states – like Botswana, Lesotho and Swaziland – were inextricably tied to the South African economy. Others – like Zambia and Rhodesia – were heavily dependent on South African services. The region's railway network which South Africa ultimately controlled operated as their umbilical cord. Believing that 'moderate' African states in southern Africa shared his concern about the 'Marxist onslaught', Botha in 1979 proposed the idea of a 'constellation of states' in which neighbouring countries would collaborate with South Africa, both at an economic level and through 'non-aggression pacts' binding them in mutual defence against communist encroachment. One of his principal objectives was to ensure that neighbouring states were not used as springboards for guerrilla attacks against South Africa. A key part of this new regional alliance was to be Rhodesia, which in 1979, with South African encouragement, had passed into the hands of a moderate black government led by Bishop Abel Muzorewa who had been willing to concede the white community there a powerful role in government.

Hardly had it been launched when Botha's proposal for a 'constellation of states' met serious difficulty. As a result of the Lancaster House agreement in 1979 ending Rhodesia's rebellion against Britain, a new election was held in Rhodesia under British auspices which brought to power not a moderate government under Muzorewa's leadership, as South Africa had hoped, but a radical government led by an avowed Marxist, Robert Mugabe, who had headed the guerrilla campaign against white rule and who now adopted an openly hostile stance towards South Africa. Even worse, not a single government in the region showed any interest in participating in Botha's constellation of states. Indeed, in April 1980, all nine African states in the region – Angola, Botswana, Lesotho, Malawi, Mozambique, Swaziland, Tanzania, Zambia and Zimbabwe (as Rhodesia was now named) – formed their own regional economic organization, the Southern African Development Coordination Conference, with the specific aim of reducing their dependence on South African routes and sources of supply. Moreover, several of South Africa's near neighbours, far from being lured into security pacts with South Africa, proved willing to allow the African National Congress use of their territories as infiltration routes into South Africa, opening a new phase in the nationalist struggle for power.

The fortunes of the ANC improved dramatically after 1975. In fifteen years in exile, it had met diplomatic success but failed to make any impact on the ground. At an international level it had received support and recognition from foreign governments in the West as well as the Eastern bloc, from political parties, trade unions, student groups and church organizations. The Soviet Union had provided most support, supplying funds, equipment and training. But assistance had been forthcoming as well from Sweden, Denmark, Norway and Holland. The British Labour Party, European socialists and liberals in Congress were also helpful. At the United Nations, the ANC had been granted observer status since 1974 and allowed access to international agency bodies from which the South African government had been barred. The ANC's leader, Oliver Tambo, Mandela's old law partner, who had taken over as president in 1967 after the death of Chief Lutuli, had travelled the world seeking to build support from as many different quarters as possible, gaining widespread respect for his skill at diplomacy.

But as for its main task of confronting the South African government, the ANC had little to show. At a conference in 1969 at its military headquarters in Morogoro in Tanzania, where guerrilla training camps had been established four years earlier, the ANC formed a Revolutionary Council with responsibility for conducting guerrilla warfare and expressed its strategy for the first time in revolutionary terms. Among the members of the Revolutionary Council were Oliver Tambo, its chairman, Yusuf Dadoo, leader of the South African Indian Congress and a prominent communist, and Joe Slovo, the ANC's principal military strategist, chief of staff of *Umkhonto we Sizwe*, also a leading member of the South African Communist Party. For the first time, too, the ANC opened its membership to whites, Coloureds and Indians, though the national executive remained exclusively African.

Yet for all the enthusiasm shown for revolutionary ideas, the ANC's years in exile were marked more by internal disputes and dissension than by any headway in implementing them. Located a thousand miles away from the borders of South Africa, unable to find a way through the white buffer states which surrounded it, the guerrillas in Tanzania succumbed to boredom, frustration and inactivity. In the leadership, splits developed over the decision to allow whites to join the ANC's ranks and over the role of members of the Communist Party. Attempts made to infiltrate agents into South Africa were often amateurish, detected well in advance by BOSS spies who had penetrated deep inside the organization.

The breakthrough came when Angola and Mozambique were taken over by nationalist guerrilla movements in 1975 and the

Soweto revolt the following year brought an army of eager recruits. In the wake of Soweto, an estimated 4000 youths left South Africa, most of them joining the ANC. Many went to military camps established in northern Angola under the control of ANC instructors. The more promising recruits were sent for training in the Soviet Union and East Germany. The capital of Mozambique, Maputo, less than fifty miles from the South African border, became a key operational centre, to where much of *Umkhonto*'s command structure was transferred. Joe Slovo and his wife Ruth First moved there in 1977. ANC groups were also set up in Botswana, Swaziland and Lesotho – 'forward areas', as they were called – to help establish an internal network and to supervise the flow of recruits.

Choosing targets mainly with a high propaganda value, *Umkhonto* began a low-level sabotage campaign in 1977 intended more to reestablish a political following among the black population and to raise its morale than to threaten the economy or white security. Its targets included police stations in black residential areas, administrative buildings, railway lines and electricity substations. A number of informers, security policemen and state witnesses were assassinated. The tally of ANC incidents officially recorded in 1978 was thirteen; in 1979 it was twenty-two. From 1980 more ambitious targets were selected. In June 1980 guerrillas attacked Sasol plants at Sasolburg and Secunda, destroying fuel storage tanks; in 1981 rockets were fired at Voortrekkerhoogte military base; in 1982 bombs exploded in the Koeberg nuclear power station near Cape Town, damaging one of the reactors and two transformers; in 1983 a car-bomb attack was made outside the South African Air Force headquarters in Pretoria in which sixteen people were killed and more than 200 injured, the most serious sabotage incident in South Africa's history. Between 1980 and 1983, the official record showed 169 ANC attacks.

The government retaliated against neighbouring states with a combination of military might and economic coercion intended to force them into submission and to expel the ANC. Its main target was Mozambique. From bases in the Transvaal, the South African military trained, armed and directed a Mozambique rebel group, *Resistência Nacional Mocambiçana* (MNR), which it had inherited from Rhodesian intelligence in 1980, with instructions to carve a trail of devastation across Mozambique, attacking bridges, railways, road transport, schools and clinics, and to destroy the government's hold on rural areas. Direct military raids were made on ANC targets in

Maputo. In 1982 a parcel bomb sent to the Eduardo Mondlane University in Maputo killed Ruth First. Mozambique was also subjected to economic pressure. South Africa cut its recruitment of Mozambicans for work in the mines, reduced its use of the port of Maputo, interrupted rail traffic and withdrew technical personnel. Similar methods were employed against other neighbouring states. The stranglehold that South Africa possessed over transport routes into the interior was used time and again to exert pressure on African governments. If 'railway diplomacy' failed, the military was ready with other ploys. In 1982 commando units struck at ANC residences in Maseru, the capital of Lesotho, killing forty-two people. The following year an attempt was made to assassinate Prime Minister Leabua Jonathan in a car bomb attack. In Angola, South African forces launched frequent ground and air attacks against suspected Swapo bases, permanently occupied an area some twenty-five miles deep along Angola's southern border, and gave direct support to Jonas Savimbi's rebel movement, Unita.

Unable to withstand the pressure, South Africa's neighbours capitulated to its demands one by one. In February 1982, Swaziland, offered financial inducements, signed a secret security agreement with Pretoria, undertaking to expel ANC personnel from its territory and 'to combat terrorism, insurgency and subversion' in cooperation with South Africa. In 1983, Lesotho, subjected to South African blockade measures, agreed to expel scores of ANC members. Mozambique, too, decided it had no option but to fall into line. Facing ruin from a combination of drought, cyclones, floods and years of economic mismanagement as well as the depredations of MNR rebels, President Samora Machel at first appealed to his Soviet allies for assistance, but when none was forthcoming, he turned to the United States for help in arranging a rapprochement with South Africa. In March 1984, on the banks of the Nkomati river marking the border between Mozambique and South Africa, Machel and Botha signed an 'Agreement on Non-Aggression and Good Neigh-bourliness' known as the Nkomati Accord, in which South Africa promised to withhold support for the MNR and Mozambique for the ANC. In the weeks that followed Mozambique expelled some 800 ANC members allowing only a mission of ten to remain. On the Angolan front, South Africa and Angola signed a cease-fire agreement in Lusaka in February 1984 in which South Africa agreed to withdraw its forces from Angola while the Angolan government undertook to prevent Swapo guerrillas from crossing the border into Namibia.

For Botha, the Nkomati Accord represented a major achievement. It cast him in the role of regional peacemaker, dealing on friendly terms with neighbouring African leaders, just as he had hoped when presenting his plan for a 'constellation of states' five years before. It dealt a severe blow to the ANC which was deprived of its most important forward position and forced to operate from headquarters in Lusaka, Zambia, hundreds of miles away from the front line. It also showed up the Soviet Union's commitment in the region in a poor light. At home, Botha's display of *kragdadigheid* – forcefulness – in handling recalcitrant black neighbours was highly popular with the white electorate. Abroad, his efforts at diplomacy gained him applause from Western governments which had begun to fear that southern Africa was slipping into a cycle of violence. Two months after the Nkomati Accord was signed, Botha reached new heights of respectability. In May 1984 he embarked on an eight-nation tour of Western Europe, pointing to the Nkomati Accord and to his new constitutional deal for Coloureds and Indians as evidence that South Africa was 'on a path of renewal'. Among those who gave him an audience were Britain's prime minister Margaret Thatcher and the Pope. To many whites, it seemed that South Africa's pariah status, its isolation in the world, was finally coming to an end. In the white press, Botha was acclaimed a 'hero', 'pioneer' and 'conqueror'. His triumph, however, was short-lived.

CHAPTER NINETEEN

The Townships Revolt

The momentum of black opposition to apartheid, which the government had tried to snuff out in 1977, faltered only briefly. While the black consciousness movement, after bearing the full brunt of government repression, fell into decline, there was a resurgence of interest in the African National Congress, prompted in part by the activities of ANC guerrillas, many of them former Soweto activists infiltrating back into South Africa from training camps abroad. As opinion surveys testified, a growing number of blacks accepted the belief that fundamental change could only be brought about by revolutionary violence. Robert Mugabe's victory in neighbouring Zimbabwe in 1980, after a guerrilla campaign lasting eight years, provided a potent example. Among many young blacks there was also a growing determination to bring down not only apartheid but the capitalist system which they identified with it. The mood of defiance affected Coloureds as much as Africans. In 1980 Coloured students were at the forefront of a wave of school boycotts, focusing on political demands as well as educational grievances. Scores of community associations sprang up around the country campaigning over issues like housing conditions, rents, bus fares and service charges. Radical newspapers appearing in Cape Town, Pretoria and other towns helped bolster community demands. There was growing interest shown in the Freedom Charter adopted in 1956 by the ANC outlining a programme for a non-racial state based on universal suffrage; though a banned document until 1983, it gained an increasing circulation. Black organizations, unable to express open approval of the ANC, pledged support instead for the Freedom Charter to indicate where their loyalties lay. The 'charterist' movement that developed in South Africa in the early 1980s marked the beginning of a new phase of black resistance to apartheid. It was to lead eventually to the most prolonged and violent challenge the South African government had ever faced.

*

Among the campaigns launched at this time was a petition demanding Nelson Mandela's release from prison. Started in March 1980 by the Soweto newspaper, *The Post*, the campaign attracted support from white university students and liberal politicians as well as from a host of black organizations. Since his imprisonment in 1962 and the Rivonia trial in 1964 in which he was given a life sentence, Mandela's fame had grown into a legend. By banning his speeches and by keeping him under a strict regime on Robben Island, the government had done its best to erase memory of him from the public mind. Virtually no outsiders other than lawyers and members of his immediate family had been allowed to see him or talk to him, and then only under strict supervision. Yet the effect had been to increase his stature not to diminish it. Abroad, he had become one of the most famous prisoners in the world; songs had been written about him; streets named after him; awards showered upon him. In South Africa, he represented a unifying symbol of black opposition to apartheid, revered alike by black radicals and conservative leaders in the homelands. Reports of him which filtered out of Robben Island spoke of a man of immense authority and influence, still resilient after twenty years of prison life. Two outsiders permitted to talk to him at length in 1985 in Pollsmoor maximum security prison on the mainland, where he had been moved in 1982, both testified to his commanding personality. Samuel Dash, an American lawyer, described him as looking far younger than his sixty-six years. 'He appeared vigorous and healthy, with a calm, confident manner and dignified bearing that seemed incongruous in our prison surroundings. Indeed, throughout our meeting I felt that I was in the presence not of a guerrilla fighter or radical ideologue, but of a Head of State.' Lord Nicholas Bethell, a British parliamentarian, emphasized the moderation of his political views. Botha's response to the campaign for Mandela's release in 1980 was to denounce him as an 'arch-Marxist' committed to violent revolution who would have to serve the sentence imposed on him by a court of law. But he was unable to prevent Mandela's presence in prison from reaching mythic proportions.

The opportunity to take national action against apartheid came in 1983 when the government published its proposals for a new constitution. Dismissing the constitutional plan as 'a fraud', a prominent Coloured priest, Dr Allan Boesak, Assessor of the *Sendingkerk* branch of the Dutch Reformed Church and newly-elected president of the World Alliance of Reformed Churches, called for a 'united front' to protest against its implementation. 'There is . . . no reason why the churches, civic associations, trade unions, student organizations and sports bodies should not unite on this issue, pool our resources, inform people of the fraud that is about to be perpetrated in their name and, on the day of the election, expose their plans for what they are.'

The outcome was that in August 1983, at a meeting at Mitchell's Plains, a Coloured township near Cape Town, delegates representing more than 300 organizations launched the United Democratic Front in the broadest display of public opposition to apartheid in nearly thirty years. Among its leaders were veterans from the Congress campaigns of the 1950s: Archie Gumede, a Durban lawyer, who served as chairman of the Release Mandela Committee; Albertina Sisulu, wife of Walter Sisulu, imprisoned along with Mandela in Pollsmoor prison; Helen Joseph, a former member of the banned Congress of Democrats who had endured years of banning orders; and Oscar Mpetha, a Cape trade union leader. Mandela was chosen as one of its patrons. The mood of the meeting was summed up by a remark made by Boesak: 'We want all our rights. We want them here and we want them now.'

The UDF functioned as a popular front rather than as a political organization. It set out only the broadest aims – to create a united democratic South Africa free from homelands and group areas and based on the will of the people – leaving its affiliates to decide their own activities. Its purpose was to draw together as wide a range of opposition forces as possible, cutting across lines of class and colour. White organizations, like the National Union of South African Students and the Johannesburg Democratic Action Committee – were welcomed into its fold. Some 600 organizations eventually formed its membership, more than half of them youth groups and student branches. Most of its support came from the Eastern Cape and the Transvaal; in Natal and the Western Cape it was noticeably weak. Formed ostensibly to promote opposition to the new constitution, the UDF was also a conscious effort to revive the style of nationalist politics adopted by the Congress movement of the 1950s. Only by repudiating the use of violence were its broad aims distinguishable from those of the ANC.

A rival federation was formed from the remnants of the black consciousness movement. The National Forum, launched at a meeting in Hammanskraal, north of Pretoria, in June 1983, also set out to oppose the new constitution but employed a style of rhetoric that placed it on the outer fringes of black politics. Its moving spirit was the Azanian People's Organization (Azapo), established in 1978 as the heir to the black consciousness organizations banned the previous year and to the tradition of the banned Pan-Africanist Congress which in exile had settled on the name 'Azania' as a suitable alternative for South Africa. It was a name derived from an Arabic description for East Africa which early Greek cartographers had put on their own maps of the world and which the writer Evelyn Waugh had later used for an African kingdom in his novel *Black Mischief*. Under the influence of a number of Robben Island prison graduates, Azapo welded on to black consciousness thinking a class analysis of South African society, claiming to take the black consciousness movement beyond the phase of black awareness into class struggle. A *Manifesto of the Azanian People*, adopted at the Hammanskraal meeting in 1983, declared:

> Our struggle for national liberation is directed against the system of racial capitalism which holds the people of Azania in bondage for the benefit of the small minority of white capitalists and their allies, the white workers and the reactionary sections of the black middle class. The struggle against apartheid is no more than the departure for our liberation efforts. Apartheid will be eradicated with the system of racial capitalism. The black working class inspired by revolutionary consciousness is the driving force of our struggle. They alone can end the system as it stands today. . . .

Azapo attacked the UDF for being 'soft' on such issues as capitalism, the role of the working class and the role of white liberals in the liberation struggle. It rejected the Freedom Charter as a bourgeois document, and it was critical of what it called 'ethnic' organizations: the existence of racially defined organizations within the UDF, such as the Natal Indian Congress. It barred whites from membership on the grounds that it was impossible for any white, however well intentioned, to identify with the class interests of the oppressed black masses. Non-racial organization, it asserted, was no more than a ploy 'to smuggle whites into the black national liberation struggle'. Despite its rhetoric, Azapo gave the impression of being led by a small group of intellectuals largely out of touch with mass opinion.

As well as campaigning against the new constitution, the UDF and Azapo were active in opposing a new system of local government for African townships introduced by Pretoria in 1983. In keeping with its decision to concede Africans permanent status in urban areas, the government set up new local authorities with powers, similar to those given to white municipalities, to administer their 'own affairs'. The new councils were authorized to collect taxes and rents, run beerhalls, and take care of public amenities and essential services. This new system allowed the government to disentangle itself from township administration and the problems of local transportation, housing and services, while ostensibly giving African communities greater political power, commensurate, so government ministers argued, with that given to white communities. With its habitual lack of foresight, however, the government permitted the councils no adequate means of financing. At Pretoria's insistence, they were to be self-financing. But lacking an industrial or commercial base to provide taxation revenues, the councils were left to raise most of their finance from rents and service charges, thus bringing them into direct conflict with a local population that was already hard-pressed. Moreover, the new council system was imposed without reference to local African communities. Opposition groups like the UDF and Azapo denounced it as nothing more than an extension of the apartheid system intended to provide a substitute for national political rights. When elections for twenty-nine new councils were held in November and December 1983, the boycott organized by black opposition groups was largely successful. The overall poll was 21 per cent. In Soweto it was as low as 10.7 per cent and in Cape Town, 11.6 per cent. Thus, not only was there a groundswell of anger building up over African exclusion from the new constitution but deep discontent about a new system of local government run by councillors who were widely regarded as 'stooges' and 'collaborators' and who, in some areas, lost no time in voting themselves large salaries, houses, cars and expensive council chambers.

Throughout 1984, while Botha was celebrating his success with the Nkomati Accord and consorting with foreign dignitaries in Europe, a mood of tension spread through black communities. An economic recession, more severe than anything South Africa had known for fifty years, cast thousands into unemployment. The inflation rate climbed to 14 per cent causing a squeeze on black living standards.

Austerity measures introduced by the government raised consumer prices still further. Rural areas were hit by a devastating drought. In every corner of the country the level of poverty and frustration rose in tandem.

Student groups were active once more, initially protesting on educational issues but constantly seeking to link their demands to the wider struggle for black rights. The expansion of black education, started during the 1970s, had continued apace. Between 1980 and 1984 the number of African secondary school pupils had increased from 577,000 to more than 1 million, and the number of African university students from 10,500 to 36,000, some of whom were allowed to enrol in 'white' universities. But the standards of teaching were low and conditions inadequate. Expenditure on African education per head was still only a seventh of that spent on white education. Failure rates in secondary schools were high. Thousands of school leavers, like their predecessors in 1976, faced nothing more than the prospect of unemployment, some for life. 'Gutter' education was the term students used for it. In January 1984 students in Atteridgeville, a black township west of Pretoria, began a boycott of secondary schools in protest over issues like corporal punishment and the lack of student representation. The boycott, organized by the Congress of South African Students (Cosas), a UDF affiliate, soon spread. By June about twenty schools were affected; by August nearly 100.

The elections for Coloured and Indian representation to the new tricameral parliament in August raised the temperature still further. The UDF, Azapo, Cosas and black labour unions all organized voter boycott campaigns. Nearly 80 per cent of Coloured pupils stayed away from school. All eleven of the country's Coloured teacher training colleges came to a halt. A university survey showed that African resentment at a parliamentary system which included Coloureds and Indians as well as whites was far greater than one that consisted solely of whites. The low turnout of voters suggested massive disapproval of the new system.

Outbreaks of violence began in early September. They were sporadic at first, ignited by local grievances, flaring up with great intensity, shifting from one area to the next and gradually drawing in more and more of an urban population that was alienated, deprived and hostile. At the forefront of the revolt were groups of black youths – 'comrades' as they came to be known – determined to destroy 'the system' and ready to defy armed police and soldiers in the dusty and decrepit streets of the townships with stones, catapults and petrol bombs. Many saw themselves as the shock troops of revolution and believed it was within their reach. The townships' revolt, however, was not solely a 'children's war' as it had been in 1976. This time the revolt was part of a popular movement involving entire communities – parents, teachers, workers, churchmen. Nor were the aims of the black activists confined to resolving particular grievances. This time the objective was to overthrow apartheid.

The epicentre of the first cycle of violence was the townships around the industrial centres of the Vaal Triangle in southern Transvaal. On 3 September 1984, the day on which the new constitution came into effect and Botha was sworn in as the new executive President in grand ceremonies in Cape Town, protests over rent and service charge increases imposed by the local council culminated in riots. Roving mobs attacked local authority buildings, police residences and the homes of councillors. The deputy mayor of Sharpeville was hacked to death on his front doorstep. Three other members of town councils were killed. Businesses and shops were looted. In three days of 'unrest' and clashes with police, twenty-six people died and at least 300 were injured. Funerals for the victims were turned into occasions for mass protest. Sporadic violence occurred elsewhere in the Transvaal. In the weeks that followed, numerous attacks were made on the homes of African councillors and policemen.

The government responded with a show of military force intended to demonstrate to the white electorate as well as to the truculent black population that it was fully in command. On 23 October a combined force of 7000 police and troops descended on Sebokeng, a trouble spot in the Vaal Triangle, searching all 19,500 houses there. Other townships in the area were included in the sweep. The purpose of 'Operation Palmiet', according to the authorities, was 'to curb criminal and revolutionary elements'. On that score it was hardly successful. About 350 people were arrested in Sebokeng, but none of them was charged under security laws. Most were found guilty of relatively minor offences ranging from contraventions of the pass laws to possession of pornographic literature. Moreover, the presence of the army in townships, far from intimidating the local populace, raised tension further and provided black activists with another cause for protest. The conduct of police units in the townships, often acting with indiscriminate brutality, aroused even worse antagonisms. A report issued by Catholic bishops in December accused the police of behaving like 'an occupying foreign army controlling enemy territory by force without regard for the civilian population and, it appears, without regard for the law'.

Opposition groups replied with their own show of strength. Barely a week after 'Operation Palmiet' ended, black organizations meeting in Johannesburg drew up a list of demands and called for a two-day stayaway in the Transvaal from 5 November in support of them. The demands included the withdrawal of the army and armed police from the townships; the resignation of all councillors; a freeze on township rents and bus fares; and the unconditional release of political prisoners and detainees. As well as student groups and local UDF affiliates, labour unions undertook to support the stayaway, lending their weight for the first time to a mass protest over political grievances. Hitherto, the unions had tended to refrain from overtly participating in political issues, confining their activities to labour matters, for fear of provoking government retaliation and forfeiting advances made in industrial organization.

The two-day stayaway was the most successful of its kind in nearly thirty-five years. An estimated 500,000 workers went on strike, causing serious disruption in much of the Transvaal. A mass boycott of schools took place simultaneously. In scores of incidents, the homes and offices of councillors, mayors and other local African officials were attacked, causing many to flee for their lives. Black activists talked confidently of launching a new phase of protest: 'We now have the power in our hands and can use it any way we like,' said Thami Mali, chairman of the Transvaal Regional Stayaway Committee. 'Our duty is to create an ungovernable situation and actually force the state to declare some of the area as liberated zones.'

Shaken by the extent of the strike, the government ordered the detention of union and community leaders, convinced that forceful action would curb the 'unrest'. But its strong-arm tactics brought it into direct confrontation with the white business community which had become increasingly frustrated with the government's lack of any clear strategy for dealing with black grievances other than repression. In an unprecedented rebuke of the government, three major business associations issued a joint warning in November that the detention of trade union leaders would endanger industrial peace. An even larger phalanx of business interests – the Federated Chamber of Industries, the Association of South African Chambers of Commerce, the *Afrikaanse Handelsinstituut*, the Chamber of Mines, the National African Federation of Chambers of Commerce and the Steel and Engineering Industries Federation, representing altogether four-fifths of the country's employers – issued a 'manifesto' two months later condemning detention without trial and calling for black political rights, common citizenship, free trade unions, open trading areas, the abolition of influx controls and an end to forced removals. The Johannesburg *Financial Mail* commented: 'Not in modern times in this country have businessmen been so united in their condemnation of government and its social and economic policies.'

Abroad, too, there was mounting anti-apartheid activity. From late 1984 the anti-apartheid movement in the United States developed a new momentum, gathering supporters in Congress and in other institutions across the country. Campaigns aimed at American investors to persuade them to divest their shareholdings in corporations involved in South Africa gained increasing attention. A growing number of state legislatures, municipal authorities, colleges, universities and churches decided to sell their holdings. Public demands for disinvestment from South Africa became more vociferous. In Congress moves were made to institute sanctions against South Africa. On a tour of the United States in 1985, Bishop Desmond Tutu, the first black bishop of Johannesburg and winner of the 1984 Nobel Peace Prize, made a deep impression on American audiences with his strident criticism of apartheid and articulate appeals for help. For US companies and banks with South African interests, the future looked increasingly troublesome. At home, they found themselves constantly on the defensive, obliged to fend off angry protest groups and shareholders and threatened with the loss of valuable contracts. In South Africa, they faced a major recession, labour unrest, an obdurate government and diminishing returns. Whereas the average return on foreign investments in South Africa had stood at 20 per cent in 1980, by 1985 it had slid to 5 per cent. The long-term prospects for economic growth, moreover, looked uncertain. During the 1980s the gross domestic product had grown on average by less than 1 per cent a year, compared with 3.6 per cent in the 1970s and 5.9 per cent in the 1960s. Some corporations decided to scale down their operations or dispose of them. For those wanting to stay, the 'hassle factor' at home assumed increasing importance.

Confronted by a rising clamour for major reform, Botha had only a limited stock of ideas upon which to draw. He was prepared to make modifications to the apartheid system but only where they did not diminish white power and privilege. Thus in a speech in January 1985, he accepted the need to allow Africans in urban areas greater status. He proposed the idea of a non-statutory 'forum' in which Africans could raise their grievances. He talked of possible changes to influx controls, agreed to suspend the forced removals policy, promised to open central business districts to all races and offered Africans freehold rights in urban areas. Laws which barred sex and marriage across the colour line and which prohibited the formation of multiracial political parties were repealed. The Coloured Labour Preference Area policy, designed to restrict African entry into the Western Cape, was abandoned. The white population generally regarded Botha's reform measures as generous concessions. The black population tended to dismiss them as cosmetic moves irrelevant to their main demands.

In a further gesture, Botha offered to release Mandela from prison on condition that he renounced violence, knowing that Mandela would not accept conditional release but hoping that the responsibility for his continued detention could be shifted on to Mandela himself. 'It is not the South African government which now stands in the way of Mr Mandela's freedom,' Botha told parliament. Mandela's defiant response was relayed to a mass rally at a stadium in Soweto in February 1985 by his daughter Zindzi:

I cherish my own freedom dearly but I care even more for your freedom . . . I am not less life-loving than you are. But I cannot sell my birthright, nor am I prepared to sell the birthright of the people, to be free. I am in prison as the representative of the people and of your organization, the African National Congress, which was banned. What freedom am I being offered whilst the organization of the people remains banned? What freedom am I being offered when I may be arrested on a pass offence? . . . What freedom am I being offered when I must ask for permission to live in an urban area? What freedom am I being offered when I need a stamp in my pass to seek work? What freedom am I being offered when my very South African citizenship is not respected?

Only free men can negotiate. Prisoners cannot enter into contracts.

A second cycle of violence, more intense and more prolonged, began in March 1985 centred on the townships of the Eastern Cape, an area long regarded as troublesome by the authorities and now suffering from the worst effects of the recession. Unemployment in the Port Elizabeth-Uitenhage area, where much of the automobile industry was located, was estimated to be as high as 56 per cent. The black slums there were renowned for their extreme poverty. In mid-March, a local UDF community association organized a three-day stayaway in protest against the rising cost of living and mass unemployment. Gangs of youths attacked government offices, police vehicles and the shops and homes of those deemed to be 'collaborators'. In clashes with police twelve youths were killed. On 21 March, in Langa township outside Uitenhage, a procession of Africans on their way to a funeral was fired upon without provocation and without warning by armed police in two armoured vehicles who apparently feared that they might threaten a nearby white township. Twenty Africans were killed, many of them as they tried to flee. The shooting, coming on the twenty-fifth anniversary of the Sharpeville massacre, sent a shockwave through South Africa and around the world.

The townships of the Eastern Cape exploded in violence lasting for weeks on end. Angry mobs attacked the homes of African policemen, set fire to government buildings and turned vengefully on blacks accused of being 'sell-outs'. In KwaNobuhle, the last remaining town councillor, Ben Kinikini, and his two sons were dragged out of a funeral parlour and bludgeoned to death by a mob which then covered the bodies with tyres setting them alight. The 'necklace' method of killing – a tyre filled with petrol, thrown over a victim and set on fire – soon became a trademark of 'comrades' in their war against 'collaborators' and informers. In the wake of the Langa massacre, forty-six councillors in the Eastern Cape resigned. Army units were sent in to the townships to quell the violence but their efforts made little impact. Street battles broke out daily as comrades attempted to destroy government authority in the townships. By June, some 240 councillors had resigned, leaving only five of thirty-eight newly established town councils functioning properly. In a separate struggle for control of the townships, rival gangs of

UDF and Azapo supporters engaged in internecine warfare. In-cidents of protest and violence spread to *platteland* towns in the Cape and the Orange Free State. In June, the focus of unrest shifted to the mining towns of the East Rand. In July, Soweto erupted in disorder. As well as the daily chronicle of violence there was an upsurge of boycotts, stayaways, rent strikes, marches and demon-strations. Funeral services were turned into political rallies where ANC flags and banners were openly flaunted, all adding to the climate of insurrection.

On 21 July Botha declared a state of emergency in thirty-six magisterial districts in the Eastern Cape, the East Rand, the Vaal Triangle and Johannesburg, giving the police and the army virtually unlimited powers to deal with the local population and indemnifying them against all legal claims arising from their actions. The state of emergency was intended to demonstrate to the white electorate as well as the black population the government's determination to stamp out all lawlessness and dissent. In the following week security forces arrested hundreds of community leaders, student activists, church workers and union officials hoping to break the back of local opposition. But the violence did not end. In areas outside the state of emergency it spread even further.

The daily spectacle of violent protest and government repression, shown on television screens around the world, provoked a chorus of international condemnation and calls for action against Botha's government to force him to undertake major reforms and open negotiations with black leaders, including Mandela. In Congress, conservative as well as liberal politicians supported legislation for economic sanctions against South Africa, pressing President Reagan to abandon his policy of quiet diplomacy – 'constructive engage-ment', as it was called – in favour of a harder line. Respectable US corporations with South African connections found themselves denounced for being 'partners in apartheid'. In Europe, foreign ministers recalled their envoys in Pretoria to help formulate a common anti-apartheid policy. The French government, hoping to steal a march on other governments, announced a ban on new investment. Foreign investors, taking fright at the continuing violence and the possibility of international action, began unloading their South African shares. The value of the rand fell sharply.

The most damaging blow came from American bankers who in the past had been only too willing to help South Africa tide over times of crisis but who now had become weary of the 'hassle factor'. On 31 July, Chase Manhattan, an ally during the Sharpeville crisis, decided to stop rolling over loans to South African borrowers. On its own, the Chase Manhattan decision was of minor importance. It meant the repayment of loans over the next year of about 400 million dollars. But, as Chase Manhattan well knew, it was bound to start a chain reaction. Because of heavy borrowing abroad mainly of short-term loans over the previous three years, South Africa was particularly vulnerable to the actions of foreign banks. In all, a sum of 14 billion dollars was due for repayment over the next twelve months, about a third of it to American banks. New financing was essential. In normal circumstances it would have been forthcoming; the South African economy, despite recession, was financially sound. But once Chase Manhattan had decided to stop lending to South Africa, other US banks followed suit. Their action was to precipitate the worst financial crisis South Africa had ever known.

In an attempt to restore foreign confidence, government officials, notably Foreign Minister Pik Botha, hinted that major reforms were imminent and pointed to an address that President Botha was due to make at the opening of a National Party Congress in Durban on 15 August as a likely occasion when they would be unveiled. But such efforts only served to compound the crisis. In a performance that was watched on television around the world, Botha, in a truculent mood, wagging his finger, contemptuously dismissed demands for greater change. 'I am not prepared to lead white South Africa and other minority groups on a road to abdication and suicide,' he said. He offered not a single new reform, blamed violence in the townships on 'communist agitators' and the foreign media, and castigated his critics at home and abroad, warning, 'Don't push us too far.' It was a display of intransigence which worked well with Afrikaner audiences but which in the world of finance made South Africa an international outcast.

Foreign investors deserted South Africa in droves. By 27 August the value of the rand had fallen by a third against the US dollar in the four-week period since the state of emergency had been declared. Unsure of how many more foreign banks would withdraw lending facilities to South Africa, the government suspended trading on the foreign exchange market, closed the Johannesburg stock exchange for five days and then announced a four-month freeze on repayments of principal of foreign debt and the introduction of new exchange control measures. From being high on the list of credit worthy countries, traditionally conscientious in managing its external finances, South Africa had become a leper in the world's financial markets within days. When the governor of the Reserve Bank, Gerhard de Kock, travelled to the United States and Europe in September in search of help, he was shunned at every port of call. With none of the main creditor banks willing to deal directly with South Africa, de Kock was obliged to find an international negotiator who could act as intermediary. Five months of tortuous negotiations followed before a short-term accord was agreed.

Even conservative Western leaders like President Reagan and Prime Minister Thatcher, both adamantly opposed to sanctions as a means of dealing with South Africa, were forced to bend before the tide of international and domestic opinion. To avoid defeat at the hands of Congress which wanted decisive action against South Africa, Reagan in September introduced his own package of sanctions mostly limited to measures already in force, such as a ban on all new US loans to the South African government. Two weeks later, Thatcher, after first refusing to go along with a limited range of sanctions adopted by members of the European Economic Community, felt obliged to fall in line and accept them. The following month, under pressure from members of the Commonwealth at a summit meeting in Nassau, she was obliged once more to modify her opposition to sanctions and accept a Commonwealth package. She also joined other Commonwealth leaders in calling on Pretoria to dismantle apartheid, end the state of emergency, release Mandela and lift the ban on the ANC. Though the action taken in Washington and London was only of token importance – 'a tiny little bit', according to Thatcher – it was a sign of the strength of hostility towards South Africa that it was taken at all. Further sanctions would be forthcoming, Botha was warned, if his government did not improve its record on reform.

Watching in despair the unending cycle of black anger, government ineptitude, disinvestment, financial mayhem, and international sanctions the white business community resolved to take its own initiative. One business association after another lined up to condemn the government's failure to introduce meaningful reform and to demand urgent action. Afrikaner and English business leaders alike joined in the attack. 'Time has run out,' declared Anton Rupert, chairman of the Rembrandt Tobacco Company, 'this is the government's final opportunity to correct past wrongs and introduce the sort of reforms the country is strongly signalling it needs so urgently.' Business demands now included the release of Mandela and 'a new political system of genuine power sharing'. Ten of the largest American companies operating in South Africa, including General Motors, Citicorp and Mobil, formed their own association, the US Corporate Council on South Africa, to act as a lobby for reform. The Federated Chamber of Industries issued a 'Charter of Social, Economic and Political Rights', warning that South Africa was in danger of drifting into 'a repressive siege society'.

The most dramatic initiative was taken by a small group of businessmen and journalists, led by the chairman of the Anglo-American Corporation, Gavin Relly, who flew to Zambia in September for talks with ANC leaders. From its headquarters in Lusaka, the ANC had played only a marginal role in the upheaval in the townships, urging blacks there to make the townships ungovernable, broadcasting inflammatory statements, but possessing few means itself of controlling, directing or even influencing the level of violence. Its own organized network within the country was too small. Yet the government's failure to suppress the townships' revolt had greatly enhanced its stature. In opinion polls and social surveys it constantly registered widespread internal support. While Botha continued to dismiss the ANC as an organization under communist control bent on destroying white civilization, his critics had come to regard it as an indispensable part of any political settlement and were anxious to open channels of communication to see if a way out of the impasse could be found.

The meeting in Zambia was a curious affair, a group of tycoons and revolutionaries sitting down side by side at a presidential lodge in a game park, the blacks dressed impeccably in suits and ties, the whites wearing more casual attire, looking almost unkempt by comparison, everyone in a friendly mood discussing in good humour the rival virtues of capitalism and socialism. 'What we are concerned with,' Relly told Oliver Tambo, 'is not so much whether the following generation will be governed by white or black people, but that it will be a viable country and that it will not be destroyed by violence and strife.' Tambo replied that he personally abhorred violence – 'I even take insects out of the bath' – but warned that the conflict was bound to escalate unless apartheid was dismantled. He warned too of the likelihood of nationalization. 'We cannot leave the large corporations operating as they do. They represent tremendous wealth in the midst of unspeakable poverty.' When the meeting was over, the participants all declared their satisfaction with the outcome. 'It was one of the nicest days I've ever spent,' Relly said. 'A picnic among South Africans talking about their future together.'

But the meeting was memorable not because of any result that it achieved but because so few occasions like it ever occurred. In the wake of Gavin Relly's party, other groups found their way to Lusaka and Harare for meetings with the ANC – opposition politicians like Frederik van Zyl Slabbert, churchmen and students – but set against the gathering momentum of violence inside South Africa they made no impression. Botha meanwhile denounced businessmen for their 'disloyalty' and for showing 'signs of weakness towards the enemies of South Africa' and did his best to obstruct further contacts. A group of respected Dutch Reformed Church clergymen who wanted to talk to the ANC he branded as 'naive' and 'childish' and threatened to confiscate their passports.

Month after month, the townships revolt continued, flaring up in areas hitherto untouched, sustained for days on end by rage and defiance, then dying out, leaving behind a legacy of hatred and suffering that smouldered on ready to be ignited again. Riots broke out in the Cape Peninsula when thousands of demonstrators defied a ban against public rallies and staged a series of marches to demand the release of Mandela. In Durban, as well as clashes with security forces, there was internecine warfare between UDF, Azapo and Inkatha supporters in a struggle for local supremacy which briefly engulfed the Indian community. In the Eastern Cape, community organizations enforced a prolonged boycott of white-owned shops causing severe losses to some and driving others into bankruptcy. Across the country hundreds of thousands of pupils kept up a schools boycott, demanding 'liberation before education' and throwing themselves tirelessly into street activity, many believing that with a few more heaves the whole edifice of white rule would come crashing down. 'We are going to burn this whole country,' a youth leader, Steve Tshwete, told a crowd of 70,000 mourners attending a mass funeral in Duncan Village, a slum on the outskirts of East London. 'We will destroy everything here, and on the ashes of apartheid a new society will emerge.' As the main target of attack of the comrades, black councillors, businessmen and traders began hiring their own groups of vigilantes first for protection, then in retaliation sent them out into the streets with hit lists to wage war against youth organizations and community associations opposing them, adding another dimension to the maelstrom of violence.

As township administration disintegrated, residents started to form their own street committees and area committees in an attempt to reintroduce some form of discipline into township life. The committee system, which emerged during the mid-1980s, bore resemblance to a scheme proposed in 1953 by Mandela – the 'M' plan – to establish 'cells', 'zones' and 'wards' in townships as a way of supporting underground resistance. Street committees first appeared in Eastern Cape townships in 1985, mainly in response to chaotic conditions there, and then spread to other areas. The activities of these radical urban groups and the extent to which they used coercion to enforce their control varied considerably. Some groups concentrated on controlling petty crime, organizing rallies, funerals and protests, promoting consumer and rent boycotts, undertaking garbage collection and running alternative education programmes. Other groups used force to ensure support for boycotts and strikes and set up kangaroo courts to deal with their opponents.

In some townships, the government's authority was reduced to the brief presence of the army and police on patrol in armoured vehicles called Caspirs and Hippos. In wave after wave of arrests, the government attempted to cripple youth groups and community associations which formed the backbone of black resistance, but with no measureable result. When one layer of leadership was removed, another swiftly emerged, often more radical and more reckless than before. When the Congress of South African Students was banned in August 1985, other youth organizations quickly stepped in to fill the gap. In six months of emergency rule, nearly 8000 arrests were made under security legislation, a high proportion of them – about a quarter – children and youths aged between eight and sixteen, reflecting the growing extent to which primary school pupils were being drawn into the fray. In prison, as independent organizations like the Institute of Criminology in Cape Town testified, detainees were subjected to maltreatment and torture as standard practice. Some succumbed to become informers. Others left prison all the more embittered and hostile.

*

A new phase of black resistance emerged towards the end of 1985. Reacting against the tides of random violence that ebbed and flowed through township life, black community leaders sought to reassert their own authority and to direct political activity to more constructive ends. There was deep concern at the constant disruption to children's education caused by school boycotts and student agitation. With the approach of the tenth anniversary of the Soweto student uprising, student activists were demanding a year-long boycott of classes, insistent that all their efforts should be directed towards fighting apartheid. To many parents and teachers it seemed that the student rebellion was getting out of hand. A whole generation of children were in danger of losing education, skills and training. There was also growing resentment among older township residents at the methods of coercion used by young comrades to enforce their will. In an unprecedented manoeuvre, members of the Soweto Parents' Crisis Committee, formed in October to help resolve the crisis in education, travelled to Harare to seek the assistance of the ANC. The ANC's view was that black education should not be used as a weapon in the liberation struggle and it urged students to return to school in the new year: 'The schools are your trenches,' it advised.

The issue was decided at a conference of the National Education Crisis Committee in Durban in March 1986 attended by 1500 representatives of pupils, parents and teachers. The keynote speech, brimming with confidence and expectation, was given by Zwelakhe Sisulu, a prominent journalist and the son of Walter Sisulu, imprisoned with Mandela, and Albertina Sisulu, a UDF leader. The state had lost the initiative to the people, he said. It was no longer in control of events. He recognized that the masses were calling for action. But it was important that the right action was taken at the right time. 'We are not poised for the immediate transfer of power to the people,' he said. 'The belief that this is so could lead to serious errors and defeats.' He went on, 'We are, however, poised to enter a phase which could lead to the transfer of power. What we are seeking to do is to shift the balance of forces in our favour decisively. To do this we have to adopt the appropriate strategies and tactics, we have to understand our strengths and weaknesses, as well as that of our enemy.'

The new strategy, approved by the Durban conference, meant that schools were no longer to be used as the main thrust against government authority. The aim now was to broaden political activity into 'united mass action involving the whole community'. In the townships, people's committees would take the place of government town councils. More use would be made of consumer boycotts, rent strikes and industrial protests. In the schools, greater emphasis would be placed on 'alternative' education – political discussion groups, black history, agitprop theatre, methods of underground organization and street warfare classes. A new slogan was devised: 'People's education for people's power.' In sum, the objective was to make black townships 'self-governing', to turn them, in Sisulu's words into 'semi-liberated' zones.

Episodes of violence still continued though less frequently. The black ghetto of Alexandra erupted in violence in February bringing scenes of death and arson to the very edge of the wealthy white suburbs of northern Johannesburg. Councillors and resident black policemen were forced to evacuate the township with their families leaving comrades to fill the vacuum and claim a 'semi-liberated' zone. In the squatter camps around Crossroads, vigilantes known as *witdoeke*, controlled by a long-established squatter boss, Johnson Ngxobongwana, succeeded in driving out comrades from their strongholds there in ferocious fighting which left seventy dead and 70,000 homeless, an action condoned by the authorities. One commentator described the event as 'the fastest and cheapest forced removal we have seen', accomplishing in days what the authorities had failed to achieve in years.

In Pretoria, meanwhile, Botha, ruing the effects of his ill-tempered outburst in August and anxious to improve South Africa's standing with foreign banks and foreign governments and head off the possibility of another debt crisis or a more punishing round of sanctions, decided to move ahead with further reforms. The air was soon thick with the rhetoric of goodwill. In a speech to parliament in January 1986, monitored with close interest around the world, Botha made free use of phrases about 'liberty', 'democracy', 'equal treatment and opportunities' and 'the sovereignty of the law'. Apartheid, he declared, was 'an outdated concept'. Later, on television, in an unprecedented address to black viewers, he made a direct appeal for black support promising 'far-reaching' reforms. In double-page newspaper advertisements carrying his personal signature, he pledged his commitment to power sharing, insisting that no South Africans would be excluded from full political rights.

'Those who want to seize power shout that apartheid lives,' he said. 'Those who want to share power say that it is dying.' To foreign audiences, he emphasized that South Africa had no wish to isolate itself from the world. As for foreign pressure, he accepted that 'not all the pressure is necessarily malicious'. In keeping with the more open image that Botha now sought to convey to the outside world, he agreed to allow a Commonwealth negotiating team, the Eminent Persons Group, to visit South Africa as part of a mission to promote a dialogue between the government and black political leaders, including Mandela and ANC officials in exile.

The actual content of Botha's new round of reforms was considerably less impressive than his promises. In place of the non-statutory 'forum' for Africans which he had suggested a year before, Botha now proposed a national statutory council with advisory functions, an idea similar to the Native Representative Council which the Nationalist government had abolished forty years before. He also agreed to restore South African citizenship to Africans living in 'white' areas who had lost it when the tribal homelands of the Transkei, Bophuthatswana, Venda and Ciskei, to which they supposedly belonged, were declared 'independent'.

But one reform was of major importance. Finally conceding the inevitability of African urbanization, Botha agreed to scrap pass laws and influx controls, once considered to be a vital protection for the white population and which for much of the century had constituted a crippling burden for the African population. Since 1916 more than 18 million Africans had been arrested under pass laws. More than any other measure they had represented, as Africans described them, 'a badge of inferiority'.

In view of the years of government propaganda about the danger of Africans swamping urban areas, a concerted effort was made through the state-controlled media to reassure the white electorate that the old system had been largely ineffective anyway in slowing down the rate of African urbanization and that through the use of controls over land, housing and squatters, the government would be able to ensure that urbanization proceeded at an 'orderly' pace. According to the South African Broadcasting Corporation, the attempt to effect a 'mass physical separation of the peoples . . . became futile, and increasingly destructive of economic growth, social stability and viable political solutions'. The homelands, originally intended 'to accommodate virtually all the original members of their nations', could provide 'work and living space' for no more 'than a fraction of the Black people in the national states', thus rendering 'the original partition aims obsolete'. Trying to make the old system effective by applying it even more rigorously could be done 'only by courting disaster: ruthless repression, economic depression, mass famine in the rural areas and unmanageable social unrest'. In Botha's own words in January 1986, the influx control system had become 'costly and obsolete' and needed to be dismantled. But this did not mean, said the government, that the cities and towns were heading for a period of chaotic growth, inundated with millions of Africans. Strict controls over urbanization would still be enforced. 'People in our rural areas,' said Chris Heunis, the Minister of Constitutional Development and Planning, 'will be ill advised to flock to the metropoles *en masse* because, as in the past, squatting, unhygienic conditions, overcrowding and the associated conditions which create squalor and misery cannot be allowed in the public interest.' In the government's calculation, the rate of urbanization would increase between 17 and 32 per cent by the year 2000 over and above what it would have been with influx controls. 'I think the country will be able to handle that,' said Heunis. Thus, after forty years of punitive measures against the African population, the Nationalist government had come to accept the position on urbanization that others had recommended in the 1940s, and to describe its previous policy as 'futile' and 'destructive'.

In a final gesture intended to impress foreign audiences that South Africa was now returning to peace and stability, Botha in March 1986 decided to lift the partial state of emergency he had imposed eight months before. Because of the vast security powers at the government's disposal, the end of the state of emergency made no difference to its handling of black unrest. Nor did it indicate that the level of unrest and violence was subsiding. But foreign bankers and foreign governments had made clear their dislike of emergency rule and Botha saw tactical advantage in announcing its end.

However magnanimous his concessions over influx controls, pass laws and citizenship seemed to Botha, the black population gave him little credit for them. Not a single reputable African politician stepped forward to join Botha's proposed national statutory council. Even conservative leaders like KwaZulu's Chief Buthelezi demanded far more from Botha, including the release of Mandela and the lifting of the ban on the ANC, before they were willing to enter negotiations. To many blacks, it seemed that white resolve, under the combined weight of internal resistance and external pressure, was weakening and that finally they had the government on the run. The mood of expectation was kept high by black leaders predicting the government's downfall. The ANC declared 1986 to be the Year of *Umkhonto we Sizwe* and talked of 'turning every corner of our country into a battlefield'. Mandela's wife, Winnie, released after nine years' restriction to a small township in the Orange Free State, declared that liberation would come by the end of the year and paid tribute to the efforts of the comrades: 'Together, hand-in-hand with our boxes of matches and our necklaces, we shall liberate this country,' she said. In scores of townships across the country, the tide of black militancy was thought to be unstoppable. On May Day workers and students in a nationwide strike staged the largest anti-apartheid protest in South Africa's history. An even larger three-day general strike was planned for 16 June to commemorate the tenth anniversary of the Soweto uprising.

The fervour within the black community was matched by growing signs of a white backlash. Opinion polls and parliamentary by-elections showed a clear resurgence of support for extreme right-wing parties which accused the government of dealing leniently with township unrest for fear of offending foreign opinion. In the industrial constituency of Sasolburg, the *Herstigte Nasionale Party* gained its first parliamentary seat in seventeen years. Crowds flocked to meetings of the overtly fascist *Afrikaner Weerstandsbeweging* (AWB) to hear its leader, Eugene Terre' Blanche, a former policeman with a flare for right-wing oratory, preach messages of white power and racial hosility.

> If the blacks start a revolution, if our government capitulates and hands over our land, if the blacks start a revolution to destroy our property, rape our women, even our children, there will be a white force under the leadership of the Afrikaner Resistance Movement that will fight back in a kind of counterrevolution. And we will take back our lands which are rightfully ours. We will implement a white people's state.

In February, before a wildly cheering throng of Afrikaners, Terre' Blanche announced the formation of a paramilitary wing, *Brand-wag* (Sentry), to defend whites in the chaos he predicted could result from Botha's reform programme. Government ministers addressing National Party rallies in the northern Transvaal found themselves shouted down by AWB activists, denounced as traitors to the Afrikaner *volk*.

The white backlash was not confined to Afrikaners. Right-wing parties gained support too from the English community and from immigrants from Angola, Mozambique and Rhodesia, embittered by the loss of white rule there. Added to fears about black unrest and the government's failure to deal with it effectively there was a deep alarm about how far the government was prepared to go with its reform programme. A chance remark by the *verligte* foreign minister, Pik Botha, that he could foresee circumstances in which South Africa might one day have a black president, sent a shockwave through the white community. Botha repudiated any such notion, but the damage was done. National Party officials in the Transvaal reported mass defections to right-wing parties.

By May, Botha had reached a watershed. Black activists, convinced that they were on the road to victory, were becoming ever more defiant. The mood of the white electorate, meanwhile, was moving strongly in favour of government repression. By hesitating to take action, Botha risked losing further support to his right-wing opponents. By ordering repression, though, he would almost certainly precipitate a new round of sanctions by South Africa's main trading partners and the further withdrawal of foreign companies. He had already been warned of the possibility of new sanctions if he refused to meet demands over the release of Mandela and to make other concessions on apartheid laws. Under pressure from every quarter, Botha reacted impetuously with a display of belligerence and ill-temper that brought upon him universal condemnation and ensured that punitive action would be taken.

His immediate target was the team of Commonwealth negotiators, the Eminent Persons Group, which had been shuttling around southern Africa endeavouring to find a common basis for negotiation between the South African government and the African National Congress. The formula they had devised went far beyond anything that Botha was willing to concede. In exchange for a commitment from the ANC to suspend violence and enter into negotiation, the South African government would have to release Mandela and other political prisoners and detainees, withdraw the military from the townships, lift the ban on the ANC and PAC, suspend detention without trial and permit normal political activity. For two months, while Botha sought to stave off the threat of sanctions, this 'negotiating concept' had lain with the South African government unanswered. Botha now gave his answer in a crude and petulant fashion. In a speech broadcast on national television on 15 May, he accused outsiders of 'meddling in South Africa's affairs', warning that he would not tolerate 'unsolicited interference'. Then, four days later, in what was intended to be a demonstration of South African *kragdadigheid*, he ordered air strikes against targets in three neighbouring capital cities, Lusaka, Harare and Gaberone, claiming they were ANC bases. In parliament subsequently he bragged that the raids were just a 'first instalment' and that they showed that 'South Africa has the capacity and the will to break the ANC'.

Botha next turned his attention to the black opposition and ordered outright repression. Under a new nationwide state of emergency declared on 12 June, four days before the Soweto anniversary, the security forces set out to decapitate all black resistance through mass arrests and tight control of township activity. The army surrounded whole townships and moved into schools. Prisons were soon filled with community leaders, trade unionists, church workers, students and other anti-apartheid activists. Strict censorship was imposed on the media prohibiting all but official information on security force activities and black resistance. Defending his proclamation of a state of emergency, Botha claimed he faced a choice akin to that 'between war and a dishonourable, fearful peace'. He acknowledged that there would be a price to pay in terms of sanctions. But he declared that South Africa would not 'crawl before anyone' to avert the threat of sanctions and was quite prepared to 'go it alone'.

In Europe and in the United States the sanctions debate raged on for much of the summer. No major Western government showed any enthusiasm for sanctions. President Reagan and Prime Minister Thatcher once again took the lead in resisting sanctions, arguing that they would make white South Africans more obdurate while harming the black population and increasing the risk of South African retaliation against neighbouring African states. But the momentum for sanctions was unstoppable. The Commonwealth Eminent Persons Group, after cutting short its mission to southern Africa as a result of the May bombing raids, produced a report the following month damning in its verdict on Botha's policies. 'The government is not prepared to negotiate fundamental change, nor to countenance the creation of genuine democratic structures, nor to face the prospect of the end of white domination and white power in the foreseeable future.' The group went on to recommend economic reprisals.

We are convinced that the South African government is concerned about the adoption of effective economic measures against it. If it comes to the conclusion that it would always remain protected from such measures, the process of change in South Africa is unlikely to increase in momentum and the descent into violence would be accelerated. In these circumstances the cost of lives may have to be counted in millions.

The tide of opinion swept Thatcher and Reagan along with it. In August, Thatcher, put under severe pressure at a special Commonwealth summit meeting in London, conceded further measures including a ban on the import of coal, iron, steel and gold coins from South Africa. In September, the European Economic Community agreed on a similar batch of measures. In October, the United States Congress overrode President Reagan's veto to set a new international level of sanctions including bans on imports of South African coal, uranium, agricultural produce and textiles and bans on new investment, loans and other extensions of credit to the South African public and private sectors. Further sanctions were threatened if South Africa failed to take significant steps to dismantle apartheid. The impact of all these measures on the South African economy in the short term was of minor importance. The long-term significance, however, was that they marked the beginning of a permanent withdrawal of foreign economic support and investment which hitherto had been crucial in providing South Africa with a high growth rate. An exodus of major international corporations followed.

The state of emergency, meanwhile, made its mark. Crippled by mass detentions, numbering eventually more than 20,000, opposition groups fell into disarray. Youth organizations, once at the forefront of the township revolt, lost all vigour. Black leaders who managed to escape the dragnet were forced into an underground existence, often unable to keep in touch with their supporters. The UDF, though allowed to continue in existence, was reduced to a mere shadow of its former strength. By 1987 the schools had returned to normal activity.

At the end of one of the most turbulent periods in South African history, the black opposition movement had taken significant strides forward. Its campaign of protest was more sustained and more widespread than any previous challenge the government had faced. It had achieved a new level of mass organization, taking the initiative in schools, factories and on the streets of black townships. The scale of black protest had prompted the white business community to demand fundamental reform and had brought about an unprecedented degree of foreign pressure on the South African government. Even conservative Western governments had been obliged to take a more rigorous position on South Africa. Yet for all the courage and endurance that had been shown, black activists still lacked a coherent strategy. As a means of forcing change, random violence in the townships had strict limitations: whatever impression it made on foreign audiences, it was never likely to move the government. Attempts at 'self-government' in the townships, while an exhilarating exercise for young radicals to conduct, simply presented targets for government retaliation. Meanwhile, the white areas of South Africa had emerged virtually unscathed. Barely a ripple from the daily violence of township strife had disturbed the placid surface of white society. The harsh reality, after two years of bitter conflict which left more than 2000 dead and thousands more injured, was that the black opposition movement was still no match for a government bent on a policy of repression.

CHAPTER TWENTY

Digging in for Posterity

Forty years of Nationalist government had left the white community still prosperous and powerful, but plagued by doubt, uncertainty and fear. The government's principal objective in 1988 was the same as it had been in 1948: it was to entrench white rule and Afrikaner leadership permanently. But President Botha, after ten years in office, had found no viable political settlement to support that objective. His reform programme had reached its outer limits without ever coming close to finding a political role for the black majority of which they might approve. Many of the props of the old apartheid system had meanwhile fallen away. The ideological certainties of the Verwoerd era were now dismissed as impractical theories. No one, except right-wing extremists, placed much faith any more in blueprints for the future. Nor did apartheid have the continued blessing of the church. In 1986, the *Nederduitse Gereformeerde Kerk*, largest of the Dutch Reformed Churches, which had been such a constant source of support for the Nationalist government since it came to power, announced after much heart-searching that apartheid was morally and scripturally unjustifiable. 'The forced segregation and separation of groups is not biblical and an attempt to justify this from the Bible should be recognized as a fault,' a church synod decided. 'Apartheid is contrary to the principle of family life and justice.' It urged members to 'confess their participation in apartheid with humility and sorrow'.

What was left as the centrepiece of the government's strategy was an overriding emphasis on security. In the aftermath of the township revolt of 1984–6, both sides recognized that, in the absence of a political settlement, it was but a dress rehearsal for a greater conflict ahead. With the same thoroughness that the Nationalists had once pursued apartheid doctrine, they now devoted their energies to developing the National Security Management System (NSMS) into a comprehensive network covering the entire country, reaching down to every level of society and capable of meeting any contingency. A complex web of committees was constructed to give the State Security Council direct control over a vast range of government activity. Specialist teams were set to work on every subject from manpower and transport to cultural affairs and community services. At a regional level the State Security Council was linked to Joint Management Centres (JMCs) in the main cities, placed under the command of senior military or police officials, and below them, to a network of sixty sub-JMCs covering metropolitan areas and some 450 mini-JMCs covering local authority areas. The aim was to alert the State Security Council to potential trouble spots and grievances and to ensure that corrective action was taken. Everything from the provision of adequate water supplies to rent and consumer boycotts came within the purview of the JMC system. Under JMC control, large sums were allocated for the upgrading of black townships, like Alexandra, in the hope that better housing, sewerage, roads and welfare programmes would eliminate sources of black discontent. The overall effect was to place the administration of large parts of South Africa into the hands of security managers answerable to an elite group within the State Security Council.

Internal security was further strengthened by the recruitment of thousands of black 'special constables' – *kitskonstabels* – to augment police riot squads. Local councils were instructed to raise their own municipal police forces to enable them to reassert control over the townships and to protect the lives and property of councillors. Many of the recruits for these auxiliary forces came from the ranks of vigilante groups. Plans were also set in motion to increase the size of the regular police force from 48,000 in 1986 to 86,000 by 1994. In the 1987 budget, expenditure on the police rose by more than 50 per cent and on defence by 30 per cent.

The guiding principle behind the government's policy for urban Africans, once it had accepted the inevitability of African urbanization, was to shift the burden of township control on to its allies in the black community – councillors, policemen, businessmen, traders, vigilante groups – in much the same way as it had established local government for the homelands two decades before, providing them with all the means necessary to defend their position against radical forces. At the same time it hoped to defuse the impetus towards revolution by concentrating on black welfare programmes and by creating a solid, property-owning core of middle-class blacks with a stake in the system and opportunities for political advancement at a local level.

> We must provide for urban blacks own political institutions, own political power bases, own legislatures, own executives, so that they can get the same degree of self-determination as the 'homeland' blacks, as the whites have within the House of Assembly and as the Coloureds have in their Chamber [a leading Nationalist minister, F. W. de Klerk explained in 1987]. When that is attained every South African will elect leaders with important and visible powers.

As an example of what the government had in mind, it suggested the possibility of establishing black city states administered as independent ventures alongside white metropolitan areas. The only opening offered to blacks at a national level was Botha's advisory National Statutory Council on which he hoped that 'decent-minded, well-balanced, peaceful black leaders' would be willing to serve. In essence, the government's plan for the black population was simply a more sophisticated version of apartheid that left the whites comfortably in control of national government.

Botha's refusal to countenance any real change in the apartheid system, his insistence on adhering to 'group' politics as the basis for all government policy and his increasingly domineering style of leadership caused deep dissension on the left wing of the National Party. A group of dissidents known as 'New Nationalists', together with prominent Afrikaner academics and journalists, agitated for a clear break with the old methods of white supremacy. They urged the abolition of basic apartheid laws like the Group Areas Act, advocated a non-racial system of government, and spoke out in favour of negotiations with the ANC. They also challenged official thinking on security. In a magazine article in January 1987, a prominent *verligte* MP, Albert Nothnagel, declared it was a myth to believe that 'military or semi-military management or rule could substitute for full participation by blacks in government'.

Botha had no patience for such views. Preoccupied with the threat he faced from extreme right-wing groups, he called an election in May 1987, adopting a tough, aggressive posture on security and pushing aside all talk of reform, in the hope of crushing his right-wing opponents. In a campaign which played heavily on white fears of black unrest and foreign interference, he condemned his liberal critics for being soft on 'terrorism' and constantly evoked the menace of 'total onslaught'. One commentator, Professor John Barratt, later noted, 'The *swart gevaar*, the *rooi gevaar*, the *buitelandse gevaar* [the black danger, the red danger, the foreign danger] were combined into one really big *gevaar*.' When the Reverend Allan Hendrickse, the sole Coloured member of the cabinet, dared to take a swim from a whites-only beach in Port Elizabeth as a protest against apartheid legislation, Botha went on television to subject him to a public humiliation lasting twenty minutes. Appalled by such tactics, twenty-seven senior academics at Stellenbosch University, the cradle of Afrikaner nationalism, resigned from the National Party and issued a manifesto demanding the abolition of all 'residuals of apartheid'. Three hundred other Afrikaner academics signed the manifesto. An 'independent' movement was started by three former prominent Nationalist supporters standing as independent candidates against the National Party.

The election result showed how much the white electorate could be swayed by the politics of fear. A massive lurch to the right occurred. While Botha succeeded in holding on to his two-thirds majority in parliament, the extreme right wing made dramatic gains, picking up nearly 30 per cent of the vote. For the first time since the 1940s at least half of the Afrikaner vote went against the National Party. Botha survived by attracting as much as half of the English-speaking vote as the English community rushed *en masse* for the protection of the Afrikaner laager. In all, 82 per cent of the white electorate voted for right-wing or extreme right-wing parties which rejected all notion of fundamental change to the apartheid system. Liberal opposition parties – the Progressive Federal Party and the New Republic Party – fared badly, losing twelve of their thirty-two seats. The Progressive Federal Party, whose charismatic leader, Frederik van Zyl Slabbert had resigned the previous year dismissing parliamentary politics as 'a grotesque ritual of irrelevance', now forfeited its position as the official opposition to Treurnicht's Conservative Party and began to break up. Henceforth political debate was to be conducted more in terms of right-wing demands to curb reform than liberal demands to increase it.

For the foreseeable future, therefore, the pattern of white rule seemed destined to remain unchanged. In the forty years since the Nationalists first began to construct apartheid, it had undergone many modifications, growing from a crude formula for white domination into an elaborate and complex system of racial rule. It had taken on new appearances and acquired new terminology. It had shed much of its ideological and religious coating. But the heart of apartheid beat as firmly as before. The core elements of white control remained deeply entrenched. While Botha was not averse to making further modifications to apartheid, he had no intention of altering its basic structure. The group basis of politics, the homeland system, segregated housing, education and health, all remained inviolable. Though there were critics within the white community who argued that such a system could have no long-term future, the bulk of the white electorate clearly placed their faith in Botha's strategy.

The government's ability to defend the apartheid system was still formidable. Its powers of repression had hardly been tested. It possessed the means for totalitarian control and frequently used them. Laws like the Internal Security Act enabled the government to detain anyone indefinitely without trial and without any interference from the courts. Banning orders were used to cripple anti-apartheid organizations endeavouring to survive. Censorship regulations were enforced to suppress information on a whole range of opposition activity. Dissent in any form became an increasingly risky venture. To make the system work, the government could also depend on a significant number of allies within the black community – homelands leaders, urban politicians, vigilante groups – and it constantly sought to extend the list of those willing to be coopted. At a regional level, through military and economic leverage, its hegemony over southern Africa remained unchallenged. At an international level, despite the worldwide opprobrium that South Africa aroused, it faced no serious threat. Yet ultimately the survival of apartheid depended on the use of force. By insisting on permanent white control of the government, the Nationalists precluded any possibility of a political settlement which might last. The fate to which South Africa was condemned, therefore, was to live perpetually in the shadow of conflict and revolution.

CHAPTER TWENTY-ONE

The Long Haul

In forty years of Nationalist rule, in their quest for political rights, the black opposition had tried public protest, petitions, passive resistance, boycotts, sabotage, guerrilla warfare and urban insurrection. At each stage, the confrontation had become more widespread and more violent. There had been times of crisis when it had seemed to black activists that victory was imminent; but not once in that forty-year period had they ever come close to attaining their objective. In the aftermath of the townships revolt from 1984–6, when the sheer strength of white power became evident, a more sombre assessment of the task facing the black opposition prevailed. Activists still at liberty spoke of 'a long and hard struggle' ahead. Shortly before his arrest in 1987, a prominent UDF official, Murphy Morobe, gave this appraisal:

> Clearly, we aren't looking at freedom tomorrow or next week. Looking at the present scenario here, one could easily come to the mistaken belief that there is no prospect that the democratic forces will come to power. The struggle could take another ten to fifteen years – for the pessimistic, twenty. But the events of the past five years show a clear development in a positive direction.

A transformation of black opinion had indeed occurred in the 1980s. Many of the old fears and complexes about white rule had been shed during the townships revolt. No longer was white power thought to be invincible. No longer was the possibility of revolutionary upheaval seen as such a remote and awful prospect. 'Blacks finally broke through the psychological barrier of thinking that the whites were all-powerful and could not be challenged,' a black clinical psychologist, Professor Chabani Manganyi, observed about the events of 1984–6. Moreover, there was a widespread understanding that the central issue at stake was no longer reform of the kind the Nationalists were prepared to hand down, but the matter of political power. The significance of the townships revolt was that much of the black population had caught a glimpse of the possibility of gaining power and, despite the repression that followed, had held on to it.

As the main standard-bearer of resistance against apartheid, the African National Congress had benefited immeasurably from the resurgence of black militancy. Both inside South Africa and outside it acquired a greater prominence and greater credibility during the 1980s than at any time in its history. It also succeeded in reestablishing itself at the centre of gravity in black politics. Opinion surveys indicated a vast potential following which cut across tribal and ethnic groups, regional differences, classes, age and education. ANC flags, colours, slogans and songs testified to its everyday presence in township life. As the internal representative of ANC interests, the United Democratic Front, before falling victim to government repression, had proved itself capable of rallying mass opinion. Despite the difficulties of life in exile, the ANC managed to hold itself together as an omnibus movement in which every shade of opinion from liberal democrat to hardline communist was represented, thus enhancing its credentials as a broad anti-government coalition. Its diplomatic efforts had won it worldwide recognition. Even the United States and British governments, under President Reagan and Prime Minister Thatcher, while disapproving of its commitment to overthrow the South African regime by force and distrusting its links with the South African Communist Party and the Soviet Union, eventually saw fit to allow the ANC contact at a high level, accepting that it had become an indispensable factor in any attempt to achieve a negotiated settlement in South Africa. Celebrating its seventy-fifth anniversary in 1987, the ANC noted confidently how many countries and governments looked on the movement 'virtually as a government in waiting'.

Yet in terms of gaining real ground against the South African government, the ANC had far less to show. Neither internally nor externally had it managed to take significant advantage of the opportunities created by two years of turmoil in South Africa. Its own military strategy was largely ineffective. Though the number of its guerrilla attacks steadily increased, none resulted in lasting damage. Nor did they pose anything but a minor threat to the authorities. Operating from headquarters in Zambia, its lines of communications and logistics were stretched and prone to disruption. It encountered severe difficulties in smuggling quantities of weapons into South Africa and keeping in touch with operatives there, to such an extent that activists in the townships complained volubly about the ANC's failure to provide them with arms. No neighbouring African state was willing to risk anything but minimum support for the ANC for fear of provoking South African reprisal. The fate of Mozambique, which continued to suffer from the depredations of South African-supported rebels despite signing the Nkomati Accord, served as a potent warning to the whole region. Indeed, the ANC appeared to base its overall strategy on the assumption that it could never count on having reliable forward bases in neighbouring countries. Meanwhile, an army of some 8000 guerrillas, stationed in different parts of black Africa, was left lying largely inactive.

In an attempt to overcome these handicaps, ANC delegates at a Second Consultative Conference held in the Zambian town of Kabwe in 1985 approved a new strategy for a 'People's War'. This envisaged the recruitment of 'part-time' guerrillas inside South Africa for operations in their normal home areas. Under *Umkhonto*'s auspices, recruits were to be given basic training courses in the use of weapons and explosives. In this way, the ANC would reduce its dependence on men and munitions crossing South Africa's frontiers from neighbouring states; it would broaden the base of its disciplined following in South Africa; it would present a greater threat to the South African authorities; and it would place itself in the vanguard of popular insurrection. But the plan was fraught with practical difficulties and made little headway.

Divisions among the black population presented further obstacles. The ideological fault-line between Africanists and African nationalists, which had first appeared in the 1940s, surfaced again and again, setting the Pan-Africanist Congress against the African National Congress, the black consciousness movement against the charterist movement, Azapo against the UDF, in perpetual rivalry which showed no sign of abating in the 1980s. The labour unions, emerging as a potentially powerful source of opposition to the government, were afflicted by the same split. In 1985 one group of unions formed a multiracial federation, the Congress of South African Trade Unions (Cosatu), supporting the charterist position. The following year, another group of unions formed a rival federation, the Council of Unions of South Africa and the Azanian Confederation of Trade Unions, insisting on 'black working-class leadership'.

Another formidable complication in the black political spectrum was the position of Chief Buthelezi. As the only homeland leader with a strong political base and with ambitions to play a national role in South African politics, Buthelezi represented a major challenge to the wider nationalist movement. His Inkatha party, claiming a membership of more than 1 million, was the best organized black political movement in the country. As head of the KwaZulu government, he possessed considerable powers of patronage and control and used them ruthlessly. In many respects he resembled a tribal potentate and seemed ideally suited as an ally in Botha's new dispensation. Buthelezi vociferously opposed violence, sanctions and disinvestment and showed willingness to compromise on the central issue of one person one vote in a unitary state. Yet, from Botha's standpoint, he was certainly no moderate. His demands for the release of Mandela and other political prisoners, for the lifting of the ban on the ANC and the Pan-Africanist Congress, for the abolition of all apartheid measures and for negotiations on a new constitution, were no different from those made by radical groups. There were high risks in the independent third course that Buthelezi chose to take. Though he continued to distance himself from Botha, his own support showed signs of slipping away, particularly among urban blacks in Natal. The ANC and the UDF dismissed him as a traitor to the nationalist cause. Buthelezi, for his part, resented any challenge to his authority. In a letter to Oliver Tambo in 1984 he wrote: 'In this part of South Africa, we come from warrior stock and there is a resilient determination in KwaZulu and in Inkatha which even the full might of the State will never be able to flatten. Do your colleagues really think they can flatten us on the way to their envisaged victory?'

For all the obstacles that lay in the way, the potential for black resistance against apartheid remained high. The lack of political rights, discriminatory laws, inferior education, police harassment, poverty, urban overcrowding, unemployment, inflation, all were sources of deep anger and frustration. They affected the small black middle class whom the government hoped would underpin the system as much as any other section of the black community. Indeed, middle-class blacks tended to resent even more strongly the barriers to black advancement that denied them positions in government, the civil service, business and other sectors. The government believed that by continuing to suppress black organizations it could effectively cripple anti-apartheid activity. In February 1988 it prohibited seventeen prominent anti-apartheid organizations, including the UDF and Azapo, from engaging in any political activity; similar restrictions were imposed on the labour federation Cosatu. But the effect of such measures was only to drive political activity underground.

The pressures of population growth meanwhile compounded the areas of discontent. In 1946 the African population stood at 7.8 million. Forty years later it had reached nearly 25 million. By the year 2000 it was expected to grow to 35 million, nearly seven times more than the white population. The ranks of the unemployed were growing ever larger. Merely to keep pace with new entrants to the labour market required the creation of 300,000 jobs a year, a target South Africa had little hope of achieving. Unemployment estimated at about 3 million in 1988 was expected to rise by the year 2000 to 5 million. The combination of political and economic discontent had proved explosive in the past. With each passing year, the dimensions of the crisis were increasing. Even without apartheid, the economic and social difficulties facing South Africa were daunting enough. In the circumstances that the Nationalist government had created, the prospect of revolution seemed to draw inexorably closer.

Select Bibliography

In the writing of this book, as well as drawing upon my own experiences and research in South Africa over a twenty-year period, I have relied on the work of many other authors. The select bibliography contains a general list of books and articles I found to be helpful. It includes several works of particular interest and value which deserve special mention: on the Anglo-Boer war, Pakenham; on the rise of Afrikaner nationalism, Adam and Giliomee, de Klerk, du Toit, Moodie, O'Meara, Thompson, van Jaarsveld; on the rise of African nationalism and black politics, Benson, Biko, Karis and Carter, Lodge, Mandela, Walshe; on Verwoerd, Hepple, Kenney; on forced removals, Desmond, Platzky and Walker, Surplus People Project; on economic change, Lipton. A number of personal accounts also stand out. They include Bernstein, Carson, Finnegan, First, Joseph, Lelyveld, Winnie Mandela, Modisane, Mphahlele, Woods.

Adam, Heribert, *Modernizing Racial Domination: South Africa's Political Dynamics*, University of California Press 1971
—(ed.), *South Africa: Sociological Perspectives*, Oxford University Press 1971
Adam, Heribert and Giliomee, Hermann, *Ethnic Power Mobilized: Can South Africa Change?* Yale University Press 1979
Adam, Heribert and Moodley, Kogila, *South Africa Without Apartheid: Dismantling Racial Domination*, University of California Press 1986
Archer, Robert and Bouillon, Antoine, *The South African Game: Sport and Racism*, Zed Press, London 1982
Arnold, Millard (ed.), *The Testimony of Steve Biko*, Maurice Temple Smith, London 1978
Attwell, Michael, *South Africa: Background to the Crisis*, Sidgwick and Jackson, London 1986
Austin, Dennis, *Britain and South Africa*, Oxford University Press for the Royal Institute of International Affairs 1966
Barber, James, *South Africa's Foreign Policy, 1945–1970*, Oxford University Press 1973

—*The Uneasy Relationship: Britain and South Africa*, Heinemann, London 1983

Barnard, Fred, *Thirteen Years with Dr H. F. Verwoerd*, Voortrekkerpers, Johannesburg 1967

Benson, Mary, *The African Patriots: The Story of the African National Congress of South Africa*, Faber, London 1963, republished as, *South Africa: The Struggle for a Birthright*, Penguin, London 1966

—*Chief Albert Lutuli of South Africa*, Oxford University Press 1963

—*Nelson Mandela*, Penguin, London 1986

Bernstein, Hilda, *The World That Was Ours*, Heinemann, London 1967

Bethell, Nicholas, 'An Interview with Nelson Mandela', in Uhlig (ed.) *Apartheid in Crisis*, Penguin, London 1986

Biko, Steve, *I Write What I Like*, Bowerdean Press, London 1986

Blumenfeld, Jesmond (ed.), *South Africa in Crisis*, Croom Helm for the Royal Institute of International Affairs, London 1987

Bozzoli, Belinda, *The Political Nature of a Ruling Class: Capital and Ideology in South Africa, 1890–1933*, Routledge and Kegan Paul, London 1981

Bozzoli, Belinda (ed.), *Labour, Townships and Protest*, Ravan Press, Johannesburg 1979

—*Class Community and Conflict: South African Perspectives*, Ravan Press, Johannesburg 1987

Brandel-Syrier, Mia, *Reeftown Elite: A Study of social mobility in a modern African community on the Reef*, Routledge and Kegan Paul, London 1971

Brewer, John D., *After Soweto: An Unfinished Journey*, Clarendon Press, Oxford 1986

Breytenbach, Breyten, *The True Confessions of an Albino Terrorist*, Faber, London 1985

Brokensha, Miles and Knowles, Robert, *The Fourth of July Raids*, Simondium, Cape Town 1965

Bromberger, Norman, 'Economic Growth and Political Change in South Africa', in Leftwich (ed.) *South Africa: Economic Growth and Political Change*, Allison and Busby, London 1974

Brooks, Alan and Brickhill, Jeremy, *Whirlwind Before The Storm*, International Defence and Aid Fund for Southern Africa, London 1980

Brown, Douglas, *Against the World: A Study of White South African Attitudes*, Collins, London 1966

Bundy, Colin, *The Rise and Fall of the South African Peasantry*, University of California Press 1979

Bunting, Brian, *The Rise of the South African Reich*, Penguin, London 1964

—*Moses Kotane, South African Revolutionary*, Inkululeko Publications, London 1975

Butler, Jeffrey, Elphick, Richard and Welsh, David (eds.), *Democratic Liberalism in South Africa: Its History and Prospects*, David Philip, Cape Town 1987

Butler, Jeffrey, Rotberg, Robert I., and Adams, John, *The Black Homelands of South Africa: The Political and Economic Development of*

Bophuthatswana and KwaZulu, University of California Press 1977

Callinicos, Alex and Rogers, John, *Southern Africa after Soweto*, Pluto Press, London 1977

Calvocoressi, Peter, *South Africa and World Opinion*, Oxford University Press for the Institute of Race Relations 1961

Campbell, Kurt M., *Soviet Policy Towards South Africa*, Macmillan, London 1986

Carson, Joel, *No Neutral Ground*, Davis-Poynter, London 1973

Carnegie Corporation Commission, *The Poor White Problem in South Africa*, 5 vols, Pro-Ecclesia, Stellenbosch 1932

Carter, Gwendolen M., *The Politics of Inequality: South Africa since 1948* (rev.ed), Thames and Hudson, London 1962

Carter, Gwendolen M., Karis, Thomas and Stultz, Newell M., *South Africa's Transkei: The Politics of Domestic Colonialism*, Northwestern University Press 1967

Charney, Craig, 'Towards rupture or stasis? An analysis of the 1981 South African general election', *African Affairs*, 81, 1982

Cock, Jacklyn, *Maids and Madams*, Ravan Press, Johannesburg 1981

Cockram, Gail, *Vorster's Foreign Policy*, Academica, Pretoria 1970

Cohen, Robin, *Endgame in South Africa? The Changing Structures and Ideology of Apartheid*, James Currey, London 1986

Coker, Christopher, *The United States and South Africa, 1968–1985: Constructive Engagement and Its Critics*, Duke University Press 1986

Cole, Josette, *Crossroads: The Politics of Reform and Repression, 1976–1986*, Ravan Press, Johannesburg 1987

Commonwealth Group of Eminent Persons, *Mission to South Africa*, Penguin, London 1986

Crapanzo, Vincent, *Waiting: The Whites of South Africa*, Granada, London 1985

Cronjé G., *'n Tuiste vir die Nageslag*, Publicité, Cape Town 1945

Davenport, T. R. H., *South Africa: A Modern History*, third edition, Macmillan, London 1987

Davies, Robert, *Capital, State and White Labour in South Africa, 1900–1960*, Harvester Press, Brighton 1979

Davies, Robert and O'Meara, Dan, 'Total Strategy in Southern Africa: An Analysis of South African Regional Policy since 1978', *Journal of Southern African Studies*, Vol II, No 2, 1985

Davis, Stephen M., *Apartheid's Rebels: Inside South Africa's Hidden War*, Yale University Press, 1987

de Gruchy, John W., *The Church Struggle in South Africa*, David Philip, Cape Town 1979

de Kiewiet, C. W., *A History of South Africa: Social and Economic*, Oxford University Press 1941

—*The Anatomy of South African Misery*, Oxford University Press 1956

de Klerk, W. A., *The Puritans in Africa: The Story of Afrikanerdom*, Rex Collings, London 1975

de Ridder, J. C., *The Personality of the Urban African in South Africa*,

Routledge and Kegan Paul, London 1961

Desmond, Cosmas, *The Discarded People: An Account of African Resettlement in South Africa*, Penguin, London 1971

de Villiers, Dirk and de Villiers, Johanna, *PW*, Tafelberg, Cape Town 1984

de Villiers, H. H. W., *Rivonia: Operation Mayibuye*, Afrikaanse Pers-Boekhandel, Johannesburg 1964

de Villiers, Les, *South Africa Drawn in Colour: The Smuts Years, 1945–6*, Gordon Publishing, Johannesburg 1980

d'Oliveira, John, *Vorster – the Man*, Stanton, Johannesburg 1977

Dreyer, Peter, *Martyrs and Fanatics: South Africa and Human Destiny*, Simon and Schuster, New York 1980

Driver, C. J., *Patrick Duncan: South Africa and Pan-African*, Heinemann, London 1980

Dugard, John, *Human Rights and the South African Legal Order*, Princeton University Press 1978

du Toit, André, 'No Chosen People: The Myth of the Calvinist Origins of Afrikaner Nationalism and Racial Ideology', *American Historical Review*, 88, October, 1983

Elphick, Richard and Giliomee, Hermann (eds.), *The Shaping of South African Society, 1652–1820*, Longmans, London 1979

Feit, Edward, *African Opposition in South Africa: The Failure of Passive Resistance*, Hoover Institution, Stanford 1967

—*Urban Revolt in South Africa, 1960–1964*, Northwestern University Press 1971

Finnegan, William, *Crossing the Line: A Year in the Land of Apartheid*, Harper and Row, New York 1986, Hamish Hamilton, London 1987

First, Ruth, *One Hundred and Seventeen Days: An account of confinement and interrogation under the South African Ninety-Day Detention Law*, Penguin, London 1965

First, Ruth, Steele, Jonathan and Gurney, Christabel, *The South African Connection*, Maurice Temple Smith, London 1972

Foreign Policy Study Foundation, *South Africa: Time Running Out*, University of California Press 1981

Forman, Lionel and Sachs, E. S., *The South African Treason Trial*, Calder, London 1957

Foster, Don, Davis, Dennis and Sandler, Diane, *Detention and Torture in South Africa: Psychological, Legal and Historical Studies*, David Philip, Cape Town 1987

Frankel, Philip H., *Pretoria's Praetorians: Civil–military Relations in South Africa*, Cambridge University Press 1984

Frankel, Philip, Pines, Noam, and Swilling, Mark (eds.), *State, Resistance and Change in South Africa*, Croom Helm, London 1988

Friedlander, Zelda (ed.), *Jan Smuts Remembered: A Centennial Tribute*, Allan Wingate, London 1970

Friedman, Bernard, *Smuts: A Reappraisal*, St Martin's Press, New York 1976

Friedman, Steven, *Building Tomorrow Today: African Workers in Trade*

Unions, 1970–1984, Ravan Press, Johannesburg 1987

Gann, L. H. and Duignan, Peter, *Why South Africa Will Survive*, Croom Helm, London 1981

Gastrow, Shelagh, *Who's Who in South African Politics*, Ravan Press, Johannesburg 1985

Geldenhuys, Deon, *Some Strategic Implications of Regional Economic Relationships for the Republic of South Africa*, Institute of Strategic Studies, University of Pretoria 1981

—*The Diplomacy of Isolation: South African Foreign Policy Making*, Macmillan for the South African Institute of International Affairs, Johannesburg 1984

Geldenhuys, Deon and Kotzé, Hennie, 'Aspects of Political Decision-Making in South Africa', *South African Journal of Political Science*, 10, 1, 1983

Gerhart, Gail M., *Black Power in South Africa: The Evolution of an Ideology*, University of California Press 1978

Giliomee, Hermann, *The Parting of the Ways: South African Politics 1976–82*, David Philip, Cape Town 1982

Giliomee, Hermann and Schlemmer, Lawrence, *Up Against the Fences: Poverty, Passes and Privilege in South Africa*, David Philip, Cape Town 1985

Greenberg, Stanley B., *Race and State in Capitalist Development*, Yale University Press 1980

—*Legitimating the Illegitimate: State, Markets and Resistance in South Africa*, University of California Press 1987

Grundy, Kenneth W., *Soldiers Without Politics: Blacks in the South African Armed Forces*, University of California Press 1983

—*The Militarization of South African Politics*, I. B. Tauris, London 1986

Hachten, William A. and Giffard, Anthony, *The Press and Apartheid: Repression and Propaganda in South Africa*, Macmillan, London 1984

Hancock, W. K., *Smuts: The Sanguine Years, 1870–1919*, Cambridge University Press, 1962

—*Smuts: The Fields of Force, 1919–1950*, Cambridge University Press 1968

Hanlon, Joseph, *Beggar Your Neighbours: Apartheid Power in Southern Africa*, Catholic Institute for International Relations/Indiana University Press 1986

Harrison, David, *The White Tribe of Africa: South Africa in Perspective*, Ariel Books, London 1985

Harrison, Nancy, *Winnie Mandela: Mother of a Nation*, Grafton, London 1986

Hart, Gillian P., *African Entrepreneurship*, Institute of Social and Economic Research, Rhodes University, Grahamstown 1972

Haysom, Nicholas, *Mabangalala: The Rise of Right-Wing Vigilantes in South Africa*, Centre for Applied Legal Studies, University of the Witwatersrand, Johannesburg 1986

Heard, Kenneth A., *General Elections in South Africa, 1943–1970*, Oxford University Press 1974

Hellmann, Ellen and Lever, Henry (eds.), *Race Relations in South Africa*,

1929–1979, Macmillan, London 1980

Hepple, Alexander, *Verwoerd*, Penguin, London 1967

Hill, Christopher, *Bantustans: the Fragmentation of South Africa*, Oxford University Press, for the Institute of Race Relations 1964

—*Change in South Africa: Blind Alleys or New Directions?* Rex Collings, London 1983

Hindson, Doug, *Pass Controls and the Urban African Proletariat*, Ravan Press, Johannesburg 1987

Hirson, Baruch, *Year of Fire, Year of Ash: The Soweto Revolt, Roots of a Revolution?* Zed Press, London 1979

Hoagland, Jim, *South Africa: Civilizations in Conflict*, Allen and Unwin, London 1973

Hooper, Charles, *Brief Authority*, Collins, London 1960

Hope, Christopher, *White Boy Running*, Secker and Warburg, London 1988

Hope, Marjorie and Young, James, *The South African Churches in a Revolutionary Situation*, Orbis Books, New York 1981

Hopkinson, Tom, *In the Fiery Continent*, Gollancz, London 1962

Horwitz, Ralph, *The Political Economy of South Africa*, Weidenfeld and Nicolson, London 1967

Houghton, Hobart D., *The South African Economy*, fourth edition, Oxford University Press 1976

Huddleston, Father Trevor, C. R., *Naught for Your Comfort*, Collins, London 1956

Ingham, Kenneth, *Jan Christian Smuts: The Conscience of a South African*, Weidenfeld and Nicolson, London 1986

Innes, Duncan, *Anglo American and the Rise of Modern South Africa*, Heinemann, London 1984

Jackson, John D., *Justice in South Africa*, Secker and Warburg, London 1980

James, Wilmot G., *The State of Apartheid*, Lynne Rienner, Boulder, Colorado 1987

Jaster, Robert S., 'South Africa and its Neighbours: The Dynamics of Regional Conflict', Adelphi Papers no. 209, International Institute of Strategic Studies, London 1986

—'South Africa's Narrowing Security Options', Adelphi Papers no. 159, International Institute for Strategic Studies, London 1980

Johnson, R. W., *How Long Will South Africa Survive?* Macmillan, London 1977

Johnson, Phyllis and Martin, David (eds.), *Destructive Engagement: Southern Africa At War*, Zimbabwe Publishing House, Harare 1986

Johnstone, Frederick, 'White Prosperity and White Supremacy in South Africa Today', *African Affairs*, 69, 275, April 1970

—*Class, Race and Gold*, Routledge and Kegan Paul, London 1976

Joseph, Helen, *If This Be Treason*, Deutsch, London 1963

—*Tomorrow's Sun*, Hutchinson, London 1966

—*Side by Side: The Autobiography of Helen Joseph*, Zed Books, London 1986

Kallaway, Peter, *Apartheid and Education: The Education of Black South Africans*, Ravan Press, Johannesburg 1984

Kalley, Jacqueline A., *Jan Christian Smuts: a Bibliophile?* University of the Witwatersrand Library 1985

—*South Africa Under Apartheid*, Shuter and Shooter/Institute of Social and Economic Research, Rhodes University, Grahamstown 1987

Kane-Berman, John, *Soweto: Black Revolt, White Reaction*, Ravan Press, Johannesburg 1978

Karis, Thomas and Carter Gwendolen (eds.), *From Protest to Challenge: A Documentary History of African Politics in South Africa*, 4 vols, Hoover Institution Press, Stanford 1972–7

Kenney, Henry, *Architect of Apartheid: H. F. Verwoerd – an Appraisal*, Jonathan Ball, Johannesburg 1980

Kitson, Norma, *Where Sixpence Lives*, Chatto and Windus, London 1986

Kotzé, D. A., *African Politics in South Africa, 1964–1974*, Hurst, London 1975

Kuper, Leo, *Passive Resistance in South Africa*, Cape, London 1956.

—*An African Bourgeoisie: Race, Class and Politics in South Africa*, Yale University Press 1965

Kuzwayo, Ellen, *Call Me Woman*, The Women's Press, London 1985

Lacey, Marion, *Working for Boroko: The Origins of a Coercive Labour System in South Africa*, Ravan Press, Johannesburg 1981

Lambley, Peter, *The Psychology of Apartheid*, Secker and Warburg, London 1980

Lapping, Brian, *Apartheid: A History*, Grafton, London 1986

Laurence, John, *Race, Propaganda and South Africa*, Gollancz, London 1979

Laurence, Patrick, *The Transkei: South Africa's Politics of Partition*, Ravan Press, Johannesburg 1976

Leach, Graham, *South Africa*, Century Hutchinson, London 1986

Leftwich, Adrian, *South Africa: Economic Growth and Political Change*, Allison and Busby, London 1974

Legassick, Martin, 'Legislation, Ideology and Economy in Post-1948 South Africa', *Journal of Southern African Studies*, 1, 1, 1974

—'South Africa: Capital Accumulation and Violence', *Economy and Society*, III, 3, 1974

—'South Africa: Forced Labour, Industrialization and Racial Discrimination' in R. Harris (ed.) *The Political Economy of Africa*, Schenkman, Boston, Mass. 1974

Lelyveld, Joseph, *Move Your Shadow, South Africa, Black and White*, Michael Joseph, London 1986

Le May, G. H. L., *British Supremacy in South Africa, 1899–1907*, Clarendon Press, Oxford 1965

Lemon, Anthony, *Apartheid in Transition*, Gower, Aldershot 1987

Leonard, Richard, *South Africa At War: White Power and Crisis in Southern Africa*, Lawrence Hill, Westport 1983

Lerumo, A., *Fifty Fighting Years: The Communist Party of South Africa, 1921–71*, Inkululeko Publications, London 1971

Lewin, Hugh, *Bandiet: Seven Years in a South African Prison*, Barrie and Jenkins, London 1974

Lewin, Julius, *Politics and Law in South Africa*, Merlin Press, London 1963

Lewis, Stephen R., 'Economic Realities in South Africa', Institute of Development Studies, University of Sussex, Discussion Paper 232, 1987

Lipton, Merle, *Capitalism and Apartheid: South Africa, 1910–1984*, Gower/Maurice Temple Smith, Aldershot 1985

Lodge, Tom, *Black Politics in South Africa Since 1945*, Longman, London 1983

—'Insurrectionism in South Africa: The Pan-Africanist Congress and the Poqo Movement, 1959–1965', Ph.D. Thesis, University of York 1984

—'The African National Congress in South Africa, 1976–1983: Guerrilla War and Armed Propaganda', *Journal of Contemporary African Studies*, Pretoria, Vol 3, No 1/2, 1984

—'State of Exile: the African National Congress of South Africa, 1976–86', *Third World Quarterly*, 9, 1, London 1987

Luthuli, Albert, *Let My People Go*, Fount, London 1982

Macmillan, Harold, *Pointing the Way, 1959–61*, Macmillan, London 1972

Magubane, Bernard Makhosezwe, *The Political Economy of Race and Class in South Africa*, Monthly Review Press, New York 1979

Malherbe, Ernst G., *Education and the Poor White*, Juta, Cape Town 1932

—*Education in South Africa*, 2 vols, Juta, Cape Town 1925, 1977

Mandela, Nelson, *No Easy Walk to Freedom*, Heinemann, London 1965

Mandela, Winnie, *Part of My Soul*, Penguin, London 1985

Mansergh, Nicholas, *South Africa, 1906–1961: The Price of Magnanimity*, Allen and Unwin, London 1962

Marcum, John A., *Education, Race and Social Change in South Africa*, University of California Press 1982

Maré, Gerhard and Hamilton, Georgina, *An Appetite for Power: Buthelezi's Inkatha and the Politics of Legal Resistance*, Ravan Press, Johannesburg, 1987

Marks, Shula and Rathbone, Richard (eds.), *Industrialization and Social Change in South Africa: African class formation, culture and consciousness, 1870–1930*, Longman, London 1982

Marks, Shula and Trapido, Stanley (eds.), *The Politics of Race, Class and Nationalism in Twentieth Century South Africa*, Longman, London 1987

Marquard, Leo, *The Peoples and Policies of South Africa*, fourth edition, Oxford University Press 1969

Mathews, Anthony S., *Law, Order and Liberty in South Africa*, University of California Press 1972

—*Freedom, State Security and the Rule of Law: Dilemmas of the Apartheid Society*, Juta, Johannesburg 1986

Mayer, Philip, *Townsmen or Tribesmen: Urbanization in a Divided Society*, Oxford University Press 1961

Mbeki, Govan, *South Africa: The Peasants' Revolt*, Penguin, London 1964

Meiring, Piet, *Smuts the Patriot*, Tafelberg, Cape Town 1975

Mitchison, Naomi, *A Life for Africa: the Story of Bram Fischer*, Simondium, Cape Town 1965

Modisane, Bloke, *Blame Me on History*, Thames and Hudson, London 1963

Mokgatle, Naboth, *The Autobiography of an Unknown South African*, C. Hurst, London 1971

Moodie, T. Dunbar, *The Rise of Afrikanerdom: Power, Apartheid and the Afrikaner Civil Religion*, University of California Press 1975

Mphahlele, Ezekiel, *Down Second Avenue*, Faber, London 1959

Mtolo, Bruno, *Umkonto we Sizwe: The Road to the Left*, Drakensberg Press, Durban 1966

Munger, Edwin S. (ed.), *The Afrikaners*, Tafelberg, Cape Town 1979

Murray, Martin, *South African Capitalism and Black Political Opposition*, Schenkman, Cambridge, Mass. 1982

—*South Africa: Time of Agony, Time of Destiny, The Upsurge of Popular Protest*, Verso, London 1987

Nattrass, Jill, *The South African Economy: Its Growth and Change*, Oxford University Press 1981

Neame, L. E., *The History of Apartheid*, Pall Mall Press with Barrie and Rockliff, London 1962

Ngubane, Jordan, *An African Explains Apartheid*, Pall Mall Press, London 1963

Nkosi, Lewis, *Home and Exile*, Longman, London 1983

Nolutshungu, Sam C., *Changing South Africa*, Manchester University Press 1982

Odendaal, André, *Vukani Bantu! The Beginnings of Black Protest Politics in South Africa to 1912*, David Philip, Cape Town 1984

O'Dowd, Michael, 'South Africa in the Light of the Stages of Economic Growth', in Leftwich (ed.), *South Africa: Economic Growth and Political Change*, Allison and Busby, London 1974

O'Meara, Dan, 'The 1946 African Mine Workers' Strike', *Journal of Commonwealth and Comparative Politics*, xiii, 2, 1975

—*Volkskapitalisme: Class, capital and ideology in the development of Afrikaner nationalism, 1934–1948*, Cambridge University Press 1983

Omond, Roger, *The Apartheid Handbook*, Penguin, London 1985

Orkin, Mark, *Disinvestment, the Struggle and the Future: What Black South Africans Really Think*, Ravan Press, Johannesburg 1986

Pakenham, Thomas, *The Boer War*, Weidenfeld and Nicolson, London 1979

Pallister, David, Stewart, Sarah and Lepper, Ian, *South Africa Inc.*, Simon and Schuster, London 1987

Paton, Alan, *Cry, the Beloved Country*, Cape, London 1948

—*The Life and Times of Jan Hofmeyr*, Oxford University Press 1964

—*The Long View*, Pall Mall Press, London 1968

Patterson, Sheila, *The Last Trek*, Routledge and Kegan Paul, London 1957

Pauw, B. A., *The Second Generation: A Study of the Family among Urbanized Bantu in East London*, Oxford University Press 1963

Pelzer, A. N. (ed.), *Verwoerd Speaks*, APB Publishers, Johannesburg 1966

Pelzer, A. N., *Die Afrikaner Broederbond: Eerste 50 Jaar*, Tafelberg, Cape Town 1979

Pheto, Molefe, *And Night Fell: Memoirs of a Political Prisoner in South Africa*, Allison and Busby, London 1983

Phillips, Norman, *The Tragedy of Apartheid*, Allen and Unwin, London 1961

Plaatje Sol. T., *Native Life in South Africa*, P. S. King, London 1916; Ravan Press, Johannesburg 1982

Platzky, Laurine and Walker, Cherryl, *The Surplus People: Forced Removals in South Africa*, Ravan Press, Johannesburg 1985

Pollak, Richard, *Up Against Apartheid: The Role and the Plight of the Press in South Africa*, Southern Illinois University Press 1981

Potter, Elaine, *The Press as Opposition: The Political Role of South African Newspapers*, Chatto and Windus, London 1975

Price, Robert M. and Rosberg, Carl G. (eds.), *The Apartheid Regime: Political Power and Racial Domination*, Institute of International Studies, University of California 1980

Reader, D. H., *The Black Man's Portion*, Oxford University Press 1961

Rees, Mervyn and Day, Chris, *Muldergate: The Story of the Info Scandal*, Macmillan, Johannesburg 1980

Reeves, Ambrose, *Shooting at Sharpeville*, Gollancz, London 1960

—*South Africa: Yesterday and Tomorrow*, Gollancz, London 1962

Rich, Paul B., *White power and the liberal conscience: Racial segregation and South African liberalism, 1921–1960*, Manchester University Press 1984

Roberts, Michael and Trollip, A. E. G., *The South African Opposition, 1939–1945*, Longmans, Green, Cape Town 1947

Robertson, Janet, *Liberalism in South Africa, 1948–1963*, Clarendon Press, Oxford 1971

Roux, Edward, *Time Longer than Rope*, second edition, University of Wisconsin Press 1964

Roux, Eddie and Win, *Rebel Pity: The Life of Eddie Roux*, Rex Collings, London 1970

Sachs, Bernard, *The Road from Sharpeville*, Dobson, London 1961

Sachs, E. S., *Rebel's Daughters*, MacGibbon and Kee, London 1957

Salomon, Laurence, 'The Economic Background to the Revival of Afrikaner Nationalism', in Butler (ed.) *Boston University Papers in African History*, Vol 1, Boston University Press 1964

Sampson, Anthony, *Drum: a Venture into the New Africa*, Collins, London 1956

—*The Treason Cage: The Opposition on Trial in South Africa*, Heinemann, London 1958

—*Black and Gold: Tycoons, Revolutionaries and Apartheid*, Hodder and Stoughton, London 1987

Saul, John S. and Gelb, Stephen, *The Crisis in South Africa: Class Defence, Class Revolution*, Monthly Review Press, New York 1981

Scott, Michael, *A Time to Speak*, Faber, London 1958

Sergeant, Harriet, *Between the Lines: Conversations in South Africa*, Cape, London 1984

Seegers, Annette, 'Apartheid's Military', in James (ed.), *The State of Apartheid*, Lynne Rienner, Boulder, Colorado 1987

Segal, Ronald, *Into Exile*, Cape, London 1963

Segal, Ronald (ed.), *Sanctions against South Africa*, Penguin, London 1964

Serfontein, J. H. P., *Brotherhood of Power: An exposé of the secret Afrikaner Broederbond*, Rex Collings, London 1979

Simons, H. J. and R. E., *Class and Colour in South Africa, 1850–1950*, Penguin, London 1969

Sizwe, No, *One Azania, One Nation*, Zed Press, London 1979

Slovo, Joe, 'South Africa: No Middle Road', in Davidson, Slovo and Wilkinson, *Southern Africa: The New Politics of Revolution*, Penguin, London 1976

Smuts, J. C., *Jan Christian Smuts*, Cassell, Cape Town 1952

Southall, Roger, *South Africa's Transkei: The Political Economy of an 'Independent' Bantustan*, Heinemann, London 1982

Spence, J. E., *Republic Under Pressure: A Study of South Africa's Foreign Policy*, Oxford University Press for the Royal Institute of International Affairs 1965

Stadler, Alfred, 'Birds in the cornfield: squatter movements in Johannesburg, 1944–1947', *Journal of Southern African Studies*, vi, 1, 1979

—'A long way to walk', University of the Witwatersrand African Studies Institute seminar paper, 1979

—*The Political Economy of Modern South Africa*, David Philip, Cape Town 1987

Stanton, Hannah, *Go Well, Stay Well*, Hodder, London 1961

St Jorre, John de, *A House Divided: South Africa's Uncertain Future*, Carnegie Endowment for International Peace, Washington 1977

Strangwayes-Booth, Joanna, *A Cricket in the Thorn Tree: Helen Suzman and the Progressive Party of South Africa*, Hutchinson, London 1976

Streek, Barry and Wicksteed, Richard, *Render Unto Kaiser: A Transkei Dossier*, Ravan Press, Johannesburg 1981

Stultz, Newell M., *Afrikaner Politics in South Africa, 1934–1948*, University of California Press 1974

—*Transkei's Half Loaf: Race Separation in South Africa*, Yale University Press 1979

Surplus People Project, *Forced Removals in South Africa*, 5 vols, Surplus People Project, Cape Town 1983

Tatz, C. M., *Shadow and Substance in South Africa: A Study in Land and Franchise Policies Affecting Africans*, University of Natal Press 1962

Temkin, Ben, *Gatsha Buthelezi: Zulu Statesman*, Purnell, Cape Town 1976

Thompson, Leonard M., *The Unification of South Africa, 1902–1910*, Clarendon Press, Oxford 1960

—*The Political Mythology of Apartheid*, Yale University Press 1985

Thompson, Leonard and Butler, Jeffery (eds.), *Change in Contemporary*

South Africa, University of California Press 1975

Thompson, Leonard and Prior, Andrew, *South African Politics*, Yale University Press 1982

Turok, Ben, *Strategic Problems in South Africa's Liberation Struggle*, LSM Press, Richmond, Canada 1974

Trapido, Stanley, 'South Africa in a Comparative Study of Industrialization', *Journal of Development Studies*, vii, 3, 1971

Uhlig, Mark A., *Apartheid in Crisis*, Penguin, London 1986

Unterhalter, *Forced Removal: The Division, Segregation and Control of South Africa*, International Defence and Aid Fund for Southern Africa, London 1987

van den Berghe, Pierre L., *South Africa: A Study in Conflict*, Wesleyan University Press 1965

Vandenbosch, A., *South Africa and the World: The Foreign Policy of Apartheid*, University of Kentucky Press 1970

van der Horst, Sheila T., *Native Labour in South Africa*, Oxford University Press 1942; Frank Cass, London 1971

van der Merwe, Hendrik W. and Welsh, David (eds.), *Student Perspectives on South Africa*, David Philip, Cape Town 1972

van Jaarsveld, F. A., *The Awakening of Afrikaner Nationalism, 1868–1881*, Human and Rousseau, Cape Town 1961

—*The Afrikaner's Interpretation of South African History*, Simondium Publishers, Cape Town 1964

van Onselen, Charles, *Studies in the Social and Economic History of the Witwatersrand, 1886–1914*; vol 1 *New Babylon*; vol 2, *New Ninevah*, Longman, Harlow 1982

van Zyl Slabbert, Frederik, *The Last White Parliament*, Hans Strydom, Johannesburg 1985

Vatcher, William Henry, Jr, *White Laager: The Rise of Afrikaner Nationalism*, Pall Mall Press, London 1965

Walshe, Peter, *The Rise of African Nationalism in South Africa: The African National Congress, 1912–1952*, C. Hurst, London 1970

—*Church versus State in South Africa: The Case of the Christian Institute*, C. Hurst, London 1983

Webster, Eddie (ed.), *Essays in Southern African Labour History*, Ravan Press, Johannesburg 1979

Welsh, David, *The Roots of Segregation: Native Policy in Colonial Natal, 1845–1910*, Oxford University Press 1971

—'The Growth of Towns', in Wilson and Thompson (eds.), *The Oxford History of South Africa*, vol 2, Oxford University Press 1971

—'The Political Economy of Afrikaner Nationalism', in Leftwich (ed.) *South Africa: Economic Growth and Political Change*, Allison and Busby, London 1974

Wilkins, Ivor and Strydom, Hans, *The Broederbond*, Paddington Press, New York 1979

Willan, Brian, *Sol Plaatje: South African Nationalist*, Heinemann, London 1984

Wilson, Francis, *Labour in the South African Gold Mines, 1911–1969*,

Cambridge University Press 1972

—*Migrant Labour in South Africa*, The South African Council of Churches and SPRO–CAS, Johannesburg 1972

Wilson, Francis, Kooy, Alide and Hendrie, Delia (eds.), *Farm Labour in South Africa*, David Philip, Cape Town 1977

Wilson, Monica and Thompson, Leonard (eds.), *The Oxford History of South Africa*, 2 vols, Oxford University Press 1969, 1971

Winter, Gordon, *Inside BOSS: South Africa's Secret Police*, Penguin, London 1981

Wolpe, Harold, 'Industrialism and Race in South Africa', in Zubaida (ed.) *Race and Racialism*, Tavistock, London 1970

—'Capitalism and Cheap Labour-Power in South Africa: From Segregation to Apartheid', *Economy and Society*, 1, 4, 1972

Woods, Donald, *Biko*, Paddington Press, London 1978

—*Asking for Trouble: The Autobiography of a Banned Journalist*, Penguin, London 1985

Wright, Harrison, *The Burden of the Present: Liberal-Radical Controversy over Southern African History*, David Philip, Cape Town 1977

Yudelman, David, *The Emergence of Modern South Africa*, Greenwood Press, Westport 1983

Index